Tai Chi Theory
&
Martial Power

Advanced Yang Style Tai Chi Chuan

Tai Chi Theory
&
Martial Power

Advanced Yang Style Tai Chi

Dr. Yang, Jwing-Ming

YMAA Publication Center
Jamaica Plain, Mass. USA

YMAA Publication Center
Main Office:
 4354 Washington Street
 Boston, Massachusetts, 02131
 617-323-7215 • ymaa@aol.com • www.ymaa.com

10 9 8 7 6 5 4 3

Publisher's Cataloging in Publication
(Prepared by Quality Books Inc.)

Yang, Jwing-Ming, 1946-
 Tai chi theory and martial power : advanced Yang style tai chi
chuan / Yang Jwing-Ming. – 2nd ed., rev.
 p. cm. –(Chinese martial arts, internal)
 ISBN: 1-886969-43-4

 1. T'ai ch'i ch'uan. 2. Martial arts–China. I. Title.

GV504.Y364 1996   796.8'155
                         QBI96-20388

Disclaimer:
The authors and publisher of this material are NOT RESPONSIBLE in any manner
whatsoever for any injury which may occur through reading or following the instructions
in this manual.
The activities, physical or otherwise, described in this material may be too strenuous or
dangerous for some people, and the reader(s) should consult a physician before engaging
in them.

Printed in Canada

Acknowledgements

Thanks to Eng-Lok Lim for the photography, Eric Hoffman for proofing the manuscript and for contributing many valuable suggestions and discussions, and John Casagrande Jr. for his drawings. Special thanks to Alan Dougall for his editing, and a very special thanks to the artist Nian-Fu Zong for his beautiful calligraphy on the front pages of both volumes.

Acknowledgements — New Edition

In this new edition, I would like to express many thanks to Tim Comrie, Kathy K. Yang, and Nicholas C. Yang for general help, to Kain M. Sanderson and Jeff Grace for proofing, and to Andrew Murray for his editing. Thanks also to Deborah Clark for her new cover design.

A Note on English Spellings of Chinese Words

YMAA Publication Center uses the Pinyin romanization system of Chinese to English. Pinyin is standard in the People's Republic of China, and in several world organizations, including the United Nations. Pinyin, which was introduced in China in the 1950's, replaces the Wade-Giles and Yale systems.

Some common conversions:

Pinyin	Also Spelled As	Pronunciation
Qi	Chi	Chee
Qigong	Chi Kung	Chee Kung
Qin Na	Chin Na	Chin Na
Jin	Jing	Jin
Gongfu	Kung Fu	Gong Foo
Taijiquan	Tai Chi Chuan	Tai Jee Chuen

For more complete conversion tables, please refer to the *People's Republic of China: Administrative Atlas, The Reform of the Chinese Written Language,* or a contemporary manual of style.

Please Note: The romanized Chinese words on the front and back covers were written in the Kwoyeu Romatzyh style to avoid confusion as to the subject matter of the book.

About The Author

Yang, Jwing-Ming, Ph.D.

楊俊敏博士

Dr. Yang, Jwing-Ming was born on August 11th, 1946, in Xinzhu Xian (新竹縣), Taiwan (台灣), Republic of China (中華民國). He started his *Wushu* (武術)(*Gongfu* or *Kung Fu,* 功夫) training at the age of fifteen under the *Shaolin* White Crane (*Bai He,* 少林白鶴) Master Cheng, Gin-Gsao (曾金灶). Master Cheng originally learned *Taizuquan* (太祖拳) from his grandfather when he was a child. When Master Cheng was fifteen years old, he started learning White Crane from Master Jin, Shao-Feng (金紹峰), and followed him for twenty-three years until Master Jin's death.

In thirteen years of study (1961-1974 A.D.) under Master Cheng, Dr. Yang became an expert in the White Crane Style of Chinese martial arts, which includes both the use of barehands and of various weapons such as saber, staff, spear, trident, two short rods, and many other weapons. With the same master he also studied White Crane *Qigong* (氣功), *Qin Na* (or *Chin Na,* 擒拿), *Tui Na* (推拿) and *Dian Xue* massages (點穴按摩), and herbal treatment.

At the age of sixteen, Dr. Yang began the study of *Yang* Style *Taijiquan* (楊氏太極拳) under Master Kao Tao (高濤). After learning from Master Kao, Dr. Yang continued his study and research of *Taijiquan* with several masters and senior practitioners such as Master Li, Mao-Ching (李茂清) and Mr. Wilson Chen (陳威伸) in Taipei (台北). Master Li learned his *Taijiquan* from the well-known Master Han, Ching-Tang (韓慶堂), and Mr. Chen learned his *Taijiquan* from Master Chang, Xiang-San (張祥三). Dr. Yang has mastered the *Taiji* barehand sequence, pushing hands, the two-man fighting sequence, *Taiji* sword, *Taiji* saber, and *Taiji Qigong*.

When Dr. Yang was eighteen years old he entered Tamkang College (淡江學院) in Taipei Xian to study Physics. In college he began the study of traditional *Shaolin* Long Fist (*Changquan* or *Chang Chuan,* 少林長拳) with Master Li, Mao-Ching at the Tamkang College *Guoshu* Club (淡江國術社)(1964-1968 A.D.), and eventually became an assistant instructor under Master Li. In 1971 he completed his M.S. degree in Physics at the National Taiwan University (台灣大學), and then served in the Chinese Air Force from 1971 to 1972. In the service, Dr. Yang taught Physics at the Junior Academy of the Chinese Air Force (空軍幼校) while also teaching *Wushu*. After being honorably discharged in 1972, he returned to Tamkang College to teach Physics and resumed study under

Master Li, Mao-Ching. From Master Li, Dr. Yang learned Northern Style *Wushu*, which includes both barehand (especially kicking) techniques and numerous weapons.

In 1974, Dr. Yang came to the United States to study Mechanical Engineering at Purdue University. At the request of a few students, Dr. Yang began to teach *Gongfu (Kung Fu)*, which resulted in the foundation of the Purdue University Chinese *Kung Fu* Research Club in the spring of 1975. While at Purdue, Dr. Yang also taught college-credited courses in *Taijiquan*. In May of 1978 he was awarded a Ph.D. in Mechanical Engineering by Purdue.

In 1980, Dr. Yang moved to Houston to work for Texas Instruments. While in Houston he founded Yang's *Shaolin Kung Fu* Academy, which was eventually taken over by his disciple Mr. Jeffery Bolt after he moved to Boston in 1982. Dr. Yang founded Yang's Martial Arts Academy (YMAA) in Boston on October 1, 1982.

In January of 1984 he gave up his engineering career to devote more time to research, writing, and teaching. In March of 1986 he purchased property in the Jamaica Plain area of Boston to be used as the head-quarters of the new organization, Yang's Martial Arts Association. The organization has continued to expand, and, as of July 1st 1989, YMAA has become just one division of Yang's Oriental Arts Association, Inc. (YOAA, Inc).

In summary, Dr. Yang has been involved in Chinese *Wushu* since 1961. During this time, he has spent thirteen years learning *Shaolin* White Crane (*Bai He*), *Shaolin* Long Fist (*Changquan*), and *Taijiquan*. Dr. Yang has more than twenty-seven years of instructional experience: seven years in Taiwan, five years at Purdue University, two years in Houston, Texas, and thirteen years in Boston, Massachusetts.

In addition, Dr. Yang has also been invited to offer seminars around the world to share his knowledge of Chinese martial arts and *Qigong*. The countries he has visited include Canada, Mexico, France, Italy, Poland, England, Ireland, Portugal, Switzerland, Germany, Hungary, Spain, Holland, Latvia, and Saudi Arabia.

Since 1986, YMAA has become an international organization, which currently includes 31 schools located in Poland, Portugal, France, Latvia, Italy, Holland, Hungary, South Africa, Saudi Arabia, Canada, Ireland, and the United States. Many of Dr. Yang's books and videotapes have been translated into French, Italian, Spanish, Polish, Czech, Bulgarian, and Hungarian.

Dr. Yang has published twenty other volumes on the martial arts and *Qigong*:

1. ***Shaolin Chin Na;*** Unique Publications, Inc., 1980.
2. ***Shaolin Long Fist Kung Fu***; Unique Publications, Inc., 1981.
3. ***Yang Style Tai Chi Chuan***; Unique Publications, Inc., 1981.
4. ***Introduction to Ancient Chinese Weapons***;
   Unique Publications, Inc., 1985.

5. *Chi Kung – Health and Martial Arts*; YMAA Publication Center, 1985.

6. *Northern Shaolin Sword*; YMAA Publication Center, 1985.

7. *Tai Chi Theory and Martial Power*, formerly titled *Advanced Yang Style Tai Chi Chuan, Vol.1, Tai Chi Theory and Tai Chi Jing*; YMAA Publication Center, 1986.

8. *Tai Chi Chuan Martial Applications,* formerly titled *Advanced Yang Style Tai Chi Chuan, Vol.2, Martial Applications*; YMAA Publication Center, 1986.

9. *Analysis of Shaolin Chin Na*; YMAA Publication Center, 1987.

10. *The Eight Pieces of Brocade*; YMAA Publication Center, 1988.

11. *The Root of Chinese Chi Kung – The Secrets of Chi Kung Training*; YMAA Publication Center, 1989.

12. *Muscle/Tendon Changing and Marrow/Brain Washing Chi Kung – The Secret of Youth*; YMAA Publication Center, 1989.

13. *Hsing Yi Chuan – Theory and Applications*; YMAA Publication Center, 1990.

14. *The Essence of Tai Chi Chi Kung - Health and Martial Arts*; YMAA Publication Center, 1990.

15. *Qigong for Arthritis*; YMAA Publication Center, 1991.

16. *Chinese Qigong Massage – General Massage*; YMAA Publication Center, 1992.

17. *How to Defend Yourself*; YMAA Publication Center, 1992.

18. *Baguazhang – Emei Baguazhang*; YMAA Publication Center, 1994.

19. *Comprehensive Applications of Shaolin Chin Na – The Practical Defense of Chinese Seizing Arts*; YMAA Publication Center, 1995.

20. *Taiji Chin Na – The Seizing Art of Taijiquan*; YMAA Publication Center, 1995.

21. *The Essence of Shaolin White Crane*; YMAA Publication Center, 1996.

Dr. Yang has also published the following videotapes:

1. *Yang Style Tai Chi Chuan and Its Applications*; YMAA Publication Center, 1984.

2. *Shaolin Long Fist Kung Fu – Lien Bu Chuan and Its Applications*; YMAA Publication Center, 1985.

3. *Shaolin Long Fist Kung Fu – Gung Li Chuan and Its Applications*; YMAA Publication Center, 1986.

4. *Shaolin Chin Na*; YMAA Publication Center, 1987.

5. *Wai Dan Chi Kung, Vol. 1 – The Eight Pieces of Brocade*; YMAA Publication Center, 1987.

6. *Chi Kung for Tai Chi Chuan*; YMAA Publication Center, 1990.

7. *Qigong for Arthritis*; YMAA Publication Center, 1991.

8. *Qigong Massage – Self Massage*; YMAA Publication Center, 1992.

9. *Qigong Massage – With a Partner*; YMAA Publication Center, 1992.

10. *Defend Yourself 1 – Unarmed Attack*; YMAA Publication Center, 1992.

11. *Defend Yourself 2 – Knife Attack*; YMAA Publication Center, 1992.

12. *Comprehensive Applications of Shaolin Chin Na 1*; YMAA Publication Center, 1995.

13. *Comprehensive Applications of Shaolin Chin Na 2*; YMAA Publication Center, 1995.

14. *Shaolin Long Fist Kung Fu – Yi Lu Mai Fu & Er Lu Mai Fu*; YMAA Publication Center, 1995.

15. *Shaolin Long Fist Kung Fu – Shi Zi Tang*; YMAA Publication Center, 1995.

16. *Taiji Chin Na*; YMAA Publication Center, 1995.

17. *Emei Baguazhang – 1; Basic Training, Qigong, Eight Palms, and Applications*; YMAA Publication Center, 1995.

18. *Emei Baguazhang – 2; Swimming Body Baguazhang and Its Applications*; YMAA Publication Center, 1995.

19. *Emei Baguazhang – 3; Bagua Deer Hook Sword and Its Applications*; YMAA Publication Center, 1995.

20. *Xingyiquan – 12 Animal Patterns and Their Applications*; YMAA Publication Center, 1995.

21. *24 and 48 Simplified Taijiquan*; YMAA Publication Center, 1995.

22. *24 Forms Simplified Taijiquan with Applications, 48 Forms Taijiquan*; YMAA Publication Center, 1996.

23. *Wu Style Taijiquan with Applications*; YMAA Publication Center, 1996.

24. *Sun Style Taijiquan with Applications*; YMAA Publication Center, 1996.

FOREWORD

By Grandmaster Jou, Tsung-Hwa

周宗樺

It is with great pleasure that I introduce the reader to Dr. Yang, Jwing-Ming's new book on *Taijiquan*. In truth, I had come to know Dr. Yang first through his excellent books on the Chinese Martial Arts. Although we had corresponded, it was not until June of 1985 that I first met with Dr. Yang in person. I first met him at the National Chang, San Feng Festival held at the *Taiji* Foundation's training grounds in Warwick, New York. Dr. Yang had graciously accepted my invitation to teach a workshop for the numerous *Taiji* practitioners who had gathered together for the festival. It was at that time that I had the opportunity to see for myself that Dr. Yang's ability was of the same high caliber as his written treatises.

Many practitioners today are satisfied to merely run through the choreography of their particular *Taiji* form without putting any content or effort into their practice. While a routine run-through of *Taiji* may be enjoyable, it will not lead to progress. A hollow form will produce neither health nor martial benefits.

The practitioner who wishes to achieve progress in *Taiji* must be willing to put forth great efforts to master the necessary principles, and to practice diligently and with a sense of purpose, in order to get results. *Taiji* must be a blend of both *Yin* (陰) and *Yang* (陽). Empty form alone will produce nothing. In Dr. Yang's first book the external, martial aspects of *Taijiquan* were clearly presented. In Dr. Yang's present work, he has made a clear and detailed presentation of the more "inner" mechanics of *Taijiquan*.

If the *Taiji* practitioner is willing to invest effort into developing his internal power and awareness, his *Taiji* form and applications will improve. Not everyone today has personal access to accomplished masters of *Taijiquan*. Furthermore, available written materials related to the development of internal energy and force have often been difficult to understand.

For these reasons I urge the reader to pay careful attention to this book. However, as Dr. Yang points out, reading alone will accomplish little. It is up to the individual practitioner to put these concepts into practice. In this regard, the reader is very fortunate to have Dr. Yang for a guide.

Jou, Tsung-Hwa
Warwick, New York, June 9, 1985

Preface — First Edition

Taijiquan has become a popular exercise, not only in China but even in many other countries around the world. Throughout most of its history the art was kept secret, and only taught to family members and trusted students. Since the beginning of this century, when the art was first opened up to the public, many people have taken advantage of *Taiji's* ability to improve health and cure a number of illnesses. In our present hectic society, people are looking for a way to release daily pressures, calm down their minds, and relax their bodies. *Taiji* has been shown to be an excellent way to achieve this.

In spite of the popularity of *Taijiquan*, whether in China, Taiwan, or other parts of the world, the art is gradually becoming incomplete. Because most *Taiji* practitioners are more interested in health than in self-defense, the deeper aspects of the art have been gradually ignored. Many people who have practiced *Taijiquan* for quite a few years still do not understand its theories and principles. They may not know how to coordinate their breathing with the forms, and many do not understand the relationship of *Taiji* and *Qigong*. Some even do not know what *Qi* is, or how to generate it through *Taiji* practice and still meditation. Because of this their art remains superficial. Furthermore, the original, major part of *Taijiquan* - the martial application - is dying out. The reader should understand that *Taiji* was created as a martial *Qigong* art. The self-defense applications remain a necessary part of the wholeness of *Taijiquan*. Its principles and techniques are unique in martial society.

The author hopes through this volume on theory and a subsequent volume on applications to fill in some of the gaps in the general knowledge, and to encourage *Taiji* practitioners to research the deeper aspects of the art. Because *Taiji* is so profound and covers so much, it is not possible for one book, or for that matter one person, to cover the art fully. The author hopes that more *Taiji* masters will share their research experience and knowledge with the public through publications, seminars, and classes. Only in this way can *Taiji* again become a living, vital, complete art.

In these two volumes, the author will discuss the deeper aspects of barehand *Taijiquan* based upon his personal experience and understanding, and the teachings of his masters. The theory and techniques of *Taiji* weapons will be published later. Also, these volumes will not discuss fundamental pushing hands, or the matching set, since they have already been covered in the author's first *Taiji* book: **Yang Style Tai Chi Chuan,** Unique Publications, Inc., 1982. The Taiji beginner should also study the author's book **Chi Kung – Health and Martial Arts,** YMAA, 1985, which explains general *Qigong* theory, methods of training, and the relationship of *Qigong* to health and the martial arts.

This first volume will discuss theory and principles. Chapter 1 will introduce the history of *Yang* Style *Taijiquan*, the definition of *Taiji*, its contents and training procedures. Chapter 2 will discuss the deeper aspects of *Taiji* principles and theory. This chapter will be very important to both beginners and advanced students, and will help to build a comprehensive foundation for later discussion. The third chapter will discuss *Taiji* power - known by the Chinese word *Jin* (勁). *Jin* theory and training methods have been kept secret since the beginning of the art. To the author's knowledge, there is no extensive discussion published in English on this subject, and very little is available even in Chinese. The first volume will conclude with fifteen ancient *Taiji* poems and songs written by famous masters. Translations will be given as well as commentary by the author.

After the reader has studied and built up a foundation of knowledge from this book, the second chapter of **Tai Chi Chuan Martial Applications** will analyze the martial applications of each form in the solo sequence. All the postures in the sequence have a martial purpose - they are not done just for relaxation and the beauty of the exercise. Every posture has multiple levels of martial application. *Taijiquan* specializes in the techniques of Downing the Enemy (*Shuai Jiao*, 摔跤), *Chin Na* Control (*Qin Na*, 擒拿), and Cavity Press (*Dian Xue*, 點穴). After the reader understands the applications of the *Taiji* forms, the third chapter will guide him through pushing hands training theory, methods, and applications. Only after extensive pushing hands practice should the reader learn the *Taiji* fighting set in Chapter 4. This set was created to resemble real fighting, and will gradually lead the *Taiji* practitioner to an understanding of the techniques and the ability to use them in a real fight. Chapter 5 will discuss *Taiji* fighting strategy, which is very different from that of most of the external martial styles. Chapter 6 will conclude with some guidelines to help the reader select a qualified instructor.

Throughout these two books are quotations from various Chinese sources. The author has chosen not to make the translations polished English, but rather to make them as accurate as possible. Wherever feasible the Chinese idioms, and even the Chinese sentence structures, have been used. It is hoped that this contributes enough in flavor and clarity to compensate for the distraction that this approach can cause.

Dr. Yang, Jwing-Ming
1987

Preface — New Edition

Since this book was first published in 1987, more than thirty thousand copies have been sold. That implies two important things. First, *Taijiquan* has become more and more popular in the last ten years. When I came to U.S.A. in 1974, the concept of *Qi* was almost unknown, and very few people practiced *Taijiquan*. Today, *Taijiquan* has become quite popular and is recognized as one of the most effective meditative exercises for relaxation, and for maintaining physical and mental health.

Second, the general understanding of *Taijiquan's* essence has reached a deeper level. More and more *Taiji* practitioners have realized that *Taijiquan* practice goes beyond the forms. They have discovered that the philosophy and theory behind the practice may take a lifetime to master. This is because *Taijiquan* is the product of thousands of years of Chinese culture. *Taijiquan* was developed in Daoist monasteries where the goal of practice was spiritual enlightenment. Once a practitioner enters the deeper places in *Taijiquan*, he or she will be amazed by the abundance of spiritual cultivation training. This book was written to help Western *Taijiquan* practitioners enter these deep places.

Unfortunately, when this book was written, the Chinese romanization system called Pinyin was not yet popular, therefore, an older system was used. However, Pinyin is now widely used in the West in both scholastic and lay societies. YMAA is updating our romanization system, and taking the opportunity to correct some of the translations that may have misled past readers. For example, *Kao* (one of the "four corners" of the eight basic *Taijiquan* fighting techniques) should be translated as "Bump" instead of "Shoulder-Stroke." In addition, new typesetting has been done to make this book easier to read. Finally, the glossary and translation of Chinese terms have been combined, and an index has been added.

Since this book was first published, I have written thirteen more books about *Qigong* and Chinese martial arts. Among them, a few titles are highly recommended to those readers who are interested in learning more about Chinese *Taijiquan* and *Qigong*. These titles are:

1. ***Tai Chi Chuan Martial Applications***. In fact, this book can be considered as a companion book for the one you are now reading. The book you are reading now presents theories and practicing principles. ***Tai Chi Chuan Martial Applications*** demonstrates how *Taijiquan* can be used for martial arts.

2. ***The Root of Chinese Chi Kung***. A clear, in-depth study of Chinese *Qigong* practice. From this book, you can develop a clear understanding of your *Taijiquan* and *Qigong* practice.

3. ***The Essence of Tai Chi Chi Kung***. This book was written to help interested *Taijiquan* practitioners understand the inner side of *Taijiquan* practice. From this book, you will be able to grasp the essence of *Taiji Qigong* practice.

4. ***Taiji Chin Na.*** Never before revealed to Western society, the grabbing and seizing techniques (i.e. *Chin Na*) of *Taijiquan* are presented. This book is for those *Taiji* practitioners who want to know more about the martial applications of *Taijiquan*.

5. ***The Essence of Shaolin White Crane***. Though the title of this book does not appear to be related to *Taijiquan*, in fact, this book contains the most complete theory of Chinese martial *Qigong* training - from the hard styles to the very soft styles, such as *Taijiquan*. This book is highly recommended.

I hope this new edition brings you a better understanding of the essence of *Taijiquan*. In order to promote this art to its highest level, we need all of the talented and experienced *Taiji* masters to open their minds and share their knowledge through publications and instruction. Only then will this profound art continue to grow, and be assured a bright future.

Dr. Yang, Jwing-Ming
July 22, 1996

Contents

Chapter 1
General Introduction

一般介紹

1-1. Introduction

Qigong is a training system which helps to generate a strong flow of *Qi* (Internal Energy) inside the body and then circulate it through the entire body. Many martial and non-martial styles of *Qigong* training have been created in the last four thousand years. The most famous martial styles are *Taijiquan* (太極拳), *Bagua* (八卦掌), *Xingyi* (形意拳), and *Liu He Ba Fa* (六合八法). These are considered "internal" styles (*Nei Gong*, 內功 or *Nei Jar*, 內家 in Chinese), as opposed to "external" styles like *Shaolin*, because they emphasize working with *Qi*. The best known non-martial styles, which emphasize the enhancement of *Qi* circulation to improve health, are *Wu Qin Xi* (Five Animal Sport, 五禽戲), *Ba Duan Jin* (Eight Pieces of Brocade, 八段錦), Da Mo's *Yi Jin Jing* (Muscle Change Classic, 易筋經), and *Shi Er Zhuang* (Twelve Postures, 十二庄).

Taijiquan, which is said to have been created by Chang, San-Feng (張三豐) in the twelfth century, is now the most popular *Qigong* style in the world, even though it was shrouded in secrecy until the beginning of this century. At present it is widely practiced not only in China and the East but also in the Western world.

There are several reasons for the rapid spread of this art. The most important, perhaps, is that the practice of *Taiji* can help to calm down the mind and relax the body, which are becoming survival skills in today's hectic and stress-filled world. Secondly, since guns are so effective and easy to acquire, *Taiji* has been considered less vital for personal self-defense than it used to be. For this reason, more *Taiji* masters are willing to share their knowledge with the public. Thirdly, ever since *Taiji* was created, it has been proven not only effective for defense, but also useful for improving health and curing a number of illnesses.

Unfortunately, because of this healthful aspect the deeper theory and practice of *Taijiquan*, especially the martial applications, are being widely ignored. Most people today think that *Taiji* is not practical for self-defense. To approach the deeper aspects requires much time and patience, and there are very few people willing to make the necessary sacrifices. In addition, some *Taiji* experts are still withholding the secrets of the deeper aspects of the training, and not passing down the complete art.

Anyone who practices this art correctly for a number of years will soon realize that *Taiji* is not just an exercise for calmness and relaxation - it is a complex and highly developed art. It gives the practitioner a feeling of enjoyment and satisfaction which seems to go beyond that of any other art. This is because *Taiji* is smooth, refined, and elegant internally as well as externally. The practitioner can sense the *Qi* (energy) circulating within his body, and can achieve the peaceful mind of meditation. *Qi* circulation can bring good health and may even help you to reach enlightenment. Furthermore, when a *Taiji* practitioner has achieved Grand Circulation, he can use this *Qi* in self-defense. The principles that *Taiji* uses for fighting are quite different from most other martial styles, which rely on muscular force. *Taiji* uses the soft to defend against the hard, and weakness to defeat strength. The more you practice, the better you will become, and this defensive capability will grow with age instead of weaken. However, because the martial theory of *Taijiquan* is much deeper and more profound than that of most other systems, it is much harder to learn and takes a longer time to approach a high level of martial capability. A knowledgeable instructor is very important, for guidance from an experienced master can save many years of wandering and useless practice.

Today, there are still a number of interested practitioners who are researching and practicing the deeper aspects of *Taijiquan* with the help of the very few qualified experts and/or the limited number of in-depth publications. Many questions have arisen: Which is a good style of *Taijiquan*? How can I tell who is a qualified *Taiji* instructor? What is the historical background of the different styles? Which styles can be applied effectively? How do I generate *Qi*? How do I coordinate my breathing with the *Qi* circulation? How do I use *Qi* in self-defense? What is *Jin* (power) and is there more than one kind? How do I train my *Jin* correctly? How does the fighting strategy of *Taiji* differ from other styles? All these questions puzzle people even in China.

This book will describe the deeper aspects of *Taiji* training and is written mainly for the reader who has practiced *Taiji* for a few years. The beginning *Taiji* practitioner should also refer to the author's books: **Yang Style Tai Chi Chuan** and **Chi Kung-Health and Martial Arts**.

1-2. General History of Taijiquan

Many people have learned *Yang* style *Taijiquan*, but few really understand the history, background, and variations of the style. Often a person who has learned *Yang* style *Taijiquan* will see forms which claim to be *Yang* style, but which look different from what he has learned. This sometimes causes consternation and doubt about which form, if any, is the correct '*Yang* style.' A knowledge of the history can help to explain this discrepancy.

It is said that *Taijiquan* was created by Chang, San-Feng in the Song Hui Zong era (宋徽宗)(c. 1101 A.D.). It is also said that techniques and forms with the same basic principles as *Taiji* were already in existence during the Liang Dynasty (梁代, 502-557 A.D.), and were being taught by Han, Gong-Yue (韓拱月), Cheng, Ling-Xi (程靈洗), and Cheng, Bi (程珌). Later, in the Tang Dynasty (唐代, 713-905), it was found that Xu, Xuan-Oing (許宣平), Li, Dao-Zi (李道子), and Yin, Li-Peng (殷利亨) were teaching similar martial techniques. They were called Thirty-Seven Postures (*San Shi Qi Shi*, 三十七勢), Post-Heaven Techniques (*Hou Tian Fa*, 後天法), or Small Nine Heaven (*Xiao Jiu Tian*, 小九天) which had seventeen postures. The accuracy of these accounts is sometimes questionable, so it is not really known when and by whom *Taijiquan* was created. Because there is more formal history recorded about Chang, San-Feng he has received most of the credit.

According to the historical record ***Nan Lei Ji Wang Zheng Nan Mu Zhi Ming*** (南雷集王征南墓誌銘): "Chang, San-Feng, in the Song Dynasty, was a Wudang Daoist. Hui Zong (a Song Emperor, 宋徽宗) summoned him, but the road was blocked and he couldn't come. At night, (Hui Zong) dreamed Emperor Yuan (the first Jin emperor, 元帝) taught him martial techniques. At dawn, he killed a hundred enemies by himself." Also recorded in the Ming history ***Ming Shi Fang Ji Zhuan*** (明史方技傳): "Chang, San-Feng, from Liao Dong Yi county (遼東懿州). Named Quan-Yi (全一). Also named Jun-Bao (君寶). San-Feng was his nickname. Because he did not keep himself neat and clean, also called Chang, La-Ta (Sloppy Chang, 張邋遢). He was tall and big, shaped like a turtle, and had a crane's back. Large ears and round eyes. Beard long like a spear tassel. Wears only a priest's robe winter or summer. Will eat a bushel of food, or won't eat for several days or a few months. Can travel a thousand miles. Likes to have fun with people. Behaves as if nobody is around. Used to travel to Wudang (mountain) with his disciples. Built a simple cottage and lived inside. In the 24th year of Hong Wu (around 1392, 洪武), Ming Tai Zu (the first Ming emperor, 明太祖) heard of his name, and sent a messenger to look for him but he couldn't be found." It was also recorded in the Ming Dynasty in ***Ming Lang Ying Qi Xiu Lei Gao*** (明郎瑛七修類稿): "Chang the Immortal, named Jun-Bao, also named Quan-Yi, nicknamed Xuan-Xuan (玄玄), also called Chang, La-Ta. In the third year of Tian Shun (1460 A.D., 天順) he visited Emperor Ming Ying Zong (明英宗). A picture was drawn. The beard and mustache were straight, the back of the head had a tuft. Purple face and big stomach, with a bamboo hat in his hand. On the top of the picture was an inscription from the emperor honoring Chang as '*Tong Wei Xian Hua Zhen Ren*' (通微顯化真人)(a genuine Daoist who finely discriminates and clearly understands much" (Figure 1-1). This record is suspect, because if it were true, Chang, San-Feng would have been at least 500 years old at that time. Other records state that Chang, San-Feng's techniques were learned from the Daoist Feng, Yi-Yuan (馮一元). Another story tells that Chang, San-Feng was an ancient hermit meditator. He saw a magpie fighting against a snake, had a sudden understanding, and created *Taijiquan*.

Figure 1-1 Chang, San-Feng.

After Chang, San-Feng, there were Wang, Zong (王宗) in Shanxi province (陝西), Chen, Tong-Zhou (陳同州) in Wen County (溫州), Zhang, Song-Xi (張松溪) in Hai Yan (海鹽), Ye, Ji-Mei (葉繼美) in Si Ming (四明), Wang, Zong-Yue (王宗岳) in Shan You (山右), and Jiang, Fa (蔣發) in Hebei (河北). The *Taiji* techniques were passed down and divided into two major styles, southern and northern. Later, Jiang, Fa passed his art to the Chen family at Chen Jia Gou (陳家溝) in Huai Qing County, Henan (河南懷慶府). *Taiji* was then passed down for fourteen generations and divided into Old and New Styles. The Old Style was carried on by Chen, Chang-Xing (陳長興) and the New Style was created by Chen, You-Ben (陳有本).

The Old Style successor Chen, Chang-Xing then passed the art down to his son, Geng-Yun (耕雲), and his Chen relatives, Chen, Huai-Yuan (陳懷遠) and Chen, Hua-Mei (陳華梅). He also passed his *Taiji* outside of his family to Yang, Lu-Chan (楊露禪) and Li, Bo-Kui (李伯魁), both of Hebei province (河北). This Old Style is called Thirteen Postures Old Form (*Shi San Shi Lao Jia*, 十三勢老架). Later, Yang, Lu-Chan passed it down to his two sons, Yang, Ban-Hou (楊班侯) and Yang, Jian-Hou (楊健侯). Then, Jian-Hou passed the art to his two sons, Yang, Shao-Hou (楊少侯) and Yang,

Cheng-Fu (楊澄甫). This branch of *Taijiquan* is popularly called *Yang* Style. Also, Wu, Quan-You (吳全佑) learned from Yang, Ban-Hou and started a well known *Wu* style.

Also, Chen, You-Ben passed his New Style to Chen, Qing-Ping (陳清萍) who created *Zhao Bao* (趙堡) Style *Taijiquan*. Wuu, Yu-Rang (李伯魁) learned the Old Style from Yang, Lu-Chan and New Style from Chen, Qing-Ping, and created *Wuu* Style *Taijiquan*. Li, Yi-Yu (李亦畬) learned the Wuu Style and created *Li* Style *Taijiquan*. He, Wei-Zhen (郝爲楨) obtained his art from *Li* Style and created *He* Style *Taijiquan*. Sun, Lu-Tang (孫祿堂) learned from *He* Style and created *Sun* Style.

All the above mentioned styles are popular in China and Southeast Asia. Among them, *Yang* style has become the most popular. In the next section we will discuss the history of the *Yang* style.

1-3. History of Yang Style Taijiquan

Yang Style history starts with Yang, Lu-Chan (1799-1872, 楊露禪), also known as Fu-Kuai (福魁) or Lu-Chan (祿纏). He was born at Yong Nian Xian, Guang Ping County, Hebei Province (河北，廣平府永年縣). When he was young he went to Chen Jia Gou in Henan province to learn *Taijiquan* from Chen, Chang-Xing. When Chen, Chang-Xing stood he was centered and upright with no leaning or tilting, like a wooden signpost, and so people called him Mr. Tablet. At that time, there were very few students outside of the Chen family who learned from Chen, Chang-Xing. Because Yang was an outside student, he was treated unfairly, but he still stayed and persevered in his practice.

One night, he was awakened by the sounds of "Hen" (哼) and "Ha" (哈) in the distance. He got up and traced the sound to an old building. Peeking through the broken wall, he saw his master Chen, Chang-Xing teaching the techniques of grasp, control, and emitting *Jin* in coordination with the sounds Hen and Ha. He was amazed by the techniques and from that time on, unknown to master Chen, he continued to watch this secret practice session every night. He would then return to his room to ponder and study. Because of this, his martial ability advanced rapidly. One day, Chen ordered him to spar with the other disciples. To his surprise, none of the other students could defeat him. Chen realized that Yang had great potential and after that taught him the secrets sincerely.

After Yang, Lu-Chan finished his study, he returned to his home town and taught *Taijiquan* for a while. People called his style *Yang* Quan (*Yang* Style, 楊拳), *Mian Quan* (Soft Style, 綿拳), or *Fa Chuan* (Neutralizing Style, 化拳), because his motions were soft and able to neutralize the opponent's power. He later went to Beijing and taught a number of Qing officers. He used to carry a spear and a small bag and travel around the country challenging well known martial artists. Although he had many fights he never hurt anybody. Because his art was so high, nobody could defeat him. Therefore, he was called "Yang Wu Di" (楊無敵) which means "Unbeatable Yang." He had three sons, Yang, Qi (楊錡), Yang, Yu (楊鈺)(Ban-Hou, 班侯), and Yang, Jian (楊鑑)(Jian-Hou, 健侯). Yang, Qi died when he was young. Therefore, only the last two sons succeeded their father in the art.

There are a few stories about Yang, Lu-Chan:

1. One time, when Yang was at Guang Ping, he was fighting a martial artist on the city wall. The opponent was not able to defeat him and kept retreating to the edge of the wall. Suddenly he lost his balance and was about to fall. At that moment, Yang suddenly approached him from several yards distance, grasped his foot and saved his life.

2. Yang was good at using the spear. He could pick up light objects by using his spear to adhere to the object, then tossing it up into his hand. He was also good at throwing arrows with his bare hand - he could hit the target accurately while on horse back without using a bow.

3. One rainy day, while Yang was sitting in his living room, his daughter entered from outside holding a basin of water. When she opened the screen, she suddenly slipped on the wet step. Yang saw this and jumped up, held the screen with one hand, and caught his daughter's arm with the other. Not a drop of water splashed from the basin. From this anecdote one can see how quick his reactions were.

4. One day, Yang was fishing at a lake. Two other martial artists were passing by and saw him. They had heard of Yang's reputation and were afraid to challenge him, so they decided to take the opportunity to push Yang into the lake and make him lose face. To their surprise, when their hands touched his back, Yang arched his back and bounced both of them into the lake.

5. When Yang was in Bejing, a famous martial artist was jealous of Yang's reputation and challenged him. Yang politely refused. However, the man insisted. Yang said, "if you want to fight me, you can hit me three times first." The man was delighted and hit Yang's stomach. Yang suddenly uttered the "Ha" sound with a laugh. Before the laugh was finished, the challenger was already on the ground, bounced many yards away.

Yang's second son was Yang, Yu (1837-1890), also named Ban-Hou. People used to call him "Mr. The Second." He studied *Taijiquan* with his father since he was small. Even though he practiced very hard and continuously, he was still scolded and whipped by his father. He was good at free fighting. One day he was challenged by a strong martial artist. When the challenger grasped his wrist and would not let him escape, Yang, Ban-Hou suddenly used his *Jin* to bounce the challenger away and defeat him. He was so proud he went home and told his father. Instead of praise, his father laughed at him, because his sleeve was torn. After that, he trained harder and harder and finally became a superlative *Taiji* artist. Unfortunately, he didn't like to teach very much and had few students, so his art did not spread far after he died. One of his students called Wu, Quan-You later taught his son Wu, Jian-Quan (鑑泉), whose art became the Wu Style *Taijiquan*. Yang, Ban-Hou also had a son, called Zhao-Peng (兆鵬), who passed on the art.

The third son of Yang, Lu-Chan was Yang, Jian (1842-1917), also named Jian-Hou and nicknamed Jing-Hu (鏡湖). People used to call him "Mr. The Third." He also learned *Taiji* from his father since he was young. His personality was softer and more gentle than his brother's and he had many followers. He taught three postures - large, medium, and small - although he specialized in the medium posture. He was also expert in using and coordinating both hard and soft power. He used to spar with his disciples who were good at sword and saber while using only a dust brush. Every time his brush touched the student's wrist, the student could not do anything but bounce out. He was also good at using the staff and spear. When his long weapon touched an opponent's weapon, the opponent could not approach him, but instead bounced away. When he emitted *Jin* it happened at the instant of laughing the "Ha" sound. He could also throw the small metal balls called "bullets." When he had a few balls in his hand, he could shoot three or four birds at the same time. The most impressive demonstration he performed was to put a sparrow on his hand. The bird could not fly away because when a bird takes off, it must push down first and use the reaction force to lift itself. Yang, Jian-Hou could sense the bird's power and neutralize this slight push, leaving the bird unable to take off. From this demonstration, one can understand that his Listening *Jin* and Neutralizing *Jin* (see Chapter 3) must have been superb. He had three sons, Zhao-Xiong (兆熊), Zhao-Yuan (兆元), and Zhao-Qing (兆清). The second son, Zhao-Yuan died at an early age.

Yang, Jian-Hou's first son, Yang, Zhao-Xiong (1862-1929), also named Meng-Xiang (夢祥) and later called Shao-Hou (少侯). People used to call him "Mr. Oldest." He practiced *Taijiquan* since he was six years old. He had a strong and persevering personality. He was expert in free fighting and very good at using various *Jins* like his uncle Yang, Ban-Hou. He reached the highest level of *Taiji Gongfu*. Specializing in small postures, his movements were fast and sunken. Because of his personality, he didn't have too many followers. He had a son called Yang, Zhen-Sheng (振聲).

Yang, Jian-Hou's second son, Zhao-Yuan, died at a young age. The third son was Yang, Zhao-Qing (1883-1935), also named Cheng-Fu. People called him "Mr. The Third." His personality was mild and gentle. When he was young, he did not care for martial arts. It was not until his teens that he started studying *Taiji* with his father. While his father was still alive Yang, Cheng-Fu did not really understand the key secrets of *Taijiquan*. It was not until his father died (1917) that he started to practice hard. His father had helped him to build a good foundation, and after several years of practice and research he was finally able to approach the level of his father and grandfather. Because of his experiences, he modified his father's *Taijiquan* and specialized in large postures. This emphasis was just completely reversed from that of his father and brother. He was the first *Taiji* master willing to share the family secrets with the public, and because of his gentle nature he had countless students. When Nanking Central *Guoshu* Institute (南京中央國術館) was founded in 1926 he was invited to be the head *Taiji* teacher, and his name became known throughout the country. He had four sons, Zhen-Ming (振銘), Zhen-Ji (振基), Zhen-Duo (振鐸), and Zhen-Guo (振國).

Yang Style *Taijiquan* can be classified into three major postures: large, medium, and small. It is also divided into three stances: high, medium, and low. Large postures were emphasized by Yang, Cheng-Fu. He taught that the stances can be either high, medium, or low, but the postures are extended, opened, and relaxed. Large postures are especially suitable for improving health. The medium posture style requires that all the forms be neither too extended nor too restricted, and the internal *Jin* neither totally emitted nor too conserved. Therefore, the form and *Jin* are smoother and more continuous than the other two styles. The medium posture style was taught by Yang, Jian-Hou. The small posture style, in which the forms are more compact and the movements light, agile, and quick, was passed down by Yang, Shao-Hou. This style specializes in the martial application of the art. In conclusion, for martial application the small postures are generally the best, although they are the most difficult, and the large posture style is best for health purposes.

To summarize:

1. *Chen* Style *Taijiquan* was derived from *Jiang* Style. Before *Jiang*, the history is vague and unclear.

2. *Chen* Style was divided into two styles: Old and New. Chen, Chang-Xing learned Old Style and later passed it down to Yang, Lu-Chan. New Style was created by Chen, You-Ben.

3. *Yang* Style was derived from *Chen* Style fourteen generations after the Chen family learned from Jiang.

4. Chen, You-Ben passed his art to Chen, Qing-Ping who created *Zhao Bao* Style.

5. Wuu, Yu-Rang obtained the New style from Chen, Qing-Ping and the Old Style from Yang, Lu-Chan and created *Wuu* Style *Taijiquan*.

6. Li, Yi-Yu learned *Wuu* Style and created *Li* Style.

7. Hao, Wei-Zhen obtained his art from *Li* Style and started *Hao* Style *Taijiquan*.

8. Sun, Lu-Tang learned from *Hao* Style and began *Sun* Style.

9. *Wu* Style was started by Wu, Quan-You who learned from Yang, Lu-Chan's second son Yang, Ban-Hou.

10. *Yang* Style *Taijiquan* has been famous since its creation by Yang, Lu-Chan in the early part of the 20th century.

11. Yang, Cheng-Fu's *Taijiquan* is not the same as his father's, uncle's, or brother's. He modified it and emphasized large postures and improving the health.

The reader should now understand why there are so many variations within the art, even within a style such as the *Yang* style. After so many years and so many generations, countless students have learned the art. Many went on to modify the style in light of their own experiences and research. It is understandable that a student nowadays might learn *Taijiquan* and find that his style is different from another claiming to be from the same source. No one can really tell which is the original style or which is more effective than the others.

1-4. What is Taijiquan?

In Wang, Zong-Yue's *Taiji Classic* he states "What is *Taiji*? It is generated from *Wuji*. It is the mother of *Yin* and *Yang*. When it moves, it divides. At rest it reunites" (see Appendix A-2). According to Chinese Daoist scripture, the universe was initially without life. The world had just cooled down from its fiery creation and all was foggy and blurry, without differentiation or separation, with no extremities or ends. This state was called *Wuji* (無極)(literally "no extremity"). Later, the existing natural energy divided into two extremities, known as *Yin* and *Yang*. This polarity, or tendency to divide, is called *Taiji*, which means "Grand Ultimate" or "Grand Extremity," and also means "Very Ultimate" or "Very Extreme." It is this initial separation which allows and causes all other separations and changes.

When you are standing still before you start the sequence, you are in a state of *Wuji*. Your body is relaxed, with no intentions; your weight is evenly distributed on both legs. When you generate the intention to start the sequence, you are in a state of *Taiji* - you shift from side to side, foot to foot, and each part of your body becomes alternately substantial and insubstantial.

Once you start a motion it is possible to modify or redirect it, but this modification is only possible after the motion has been started. If one change is made, others can be made, and each change opens up other possibilities for variation. Each factor in the situation introduces other factors as possible influences. The initial motion made all other motions possible, and in a sense "created" the other motions. The Chinese express this by saying that *Taiji* is the mother of *Yin* and *Yang*. "*Taiji* begets two poles, two poles produce four phases, four phases generate eight trigrams (gates), and eight trigrams initiate sixty-four hexagrams" (Figure 1-2).

The *Yin* and *Yang* theory is used to classify everything, whether ideas, spirit, strategy, or force. For example, female is *Yin* and male is *Yang*, night is *Yin* and day is *Yang*, weak is *Yin* and strong is *Yang*. It is

Figure 1-2 The Eight Trigrams are derived from Taiji.

from the interaction of all the *Yin* and *Yang* that life was created and grew. *Taijiquan* is based on this theory and applies it to form, motion, force, and fighting strategy. In the thousands of years since the *Taiji* theory was first stated, many *Taiji* symbols have been designed. The best one for both theory and application is a circle which contains *Yin* and *Yang* (Figure 1-3). In this figure, the circle and the curved dividing line between *Yin* and *Yang* imply that both *Yin* and *Yang* are generated and contained in roundness. The smooth dividing line between *Yin* and *Yang* means that they interact smoothly and efficiently. Extreme *Yang* weakens and evolves into *Yin*, first weak and then extreme *Yin*. Extreme *Yin*, in turn, evolves into *Yang*. One evolves into the other and back again, continuously and without stopping. The diagram also shows a small dot of *Yin* in the center of the greatest concentration of *Yang*, and a little bit of *Yang* inside the greatest concentration of *Yin*. This means that there is no absolute *Yin* or *Yang*. *Yang* always reserves some *Yin* and vise versa. This also implies that there is a seed or source of *Yin* in *Yang* and of *Yang* in *Yin*.

    Taijiquan is based on this theory, and therefore it is smooth, continuous, and round. When it is necessary to be soft, the art is soft, and when it is necessary to be hard, the art can be hard enough to defeat any opponent. *Yin-Yang* theory also determines *Taiji* fighting strategy and has led to thirteen concepts which guide practice and fighting. Thus, *Taijiquan* is also called "Thirteen Postures." Chang, San-Feng's **Taijiquan Treatise** states, "What are the thirteen postures? *Peng* (Wardoff, 掤), *Lu* (Rollback, 搌), *Ji* (Press or Squeeze, 擠), *An* (Press Down, Forward, Upward, 按), *Cai* (Pluck or Grab, 採), *Lie* (Split or Rend, 挒), *Zhou* (Elbow, 肘), *Kao* (Bump, 靠), these are the eight trigrams. *Jin*

Pure Yang
純陽

Some Yang in Yin
陰中帶陽

Yang Grows
Yin Weakens
陽長陰消

Yin Grows
Yang Weakens
陰盛陽微

Some Yin in Yang
陽中帶陰

Pure Yin
純陰

Figure 1-3 The Taiji diagram.

Bu (Step Forward, 進步), *Tui Bu* (Step Backward, 退步), *Zuo Gu* (Beware of the Left, 左顧), *You Pan* (Look to the Right, 右盼), *Zhong Ding* (Central Equilibrium, 中定), these are the five elements. Wardoff, Rollback, Press, and Push are *Qian* (Heaven, 乾), *Kun* (Earth, 坤), *Kan* (Water, 坎), and *Li* (Fire, 離), the four main sides. Pluck, Split, Elbow, and Bump are *Xun* (Wind, 巽), *Zhen* (Thunder, 震), *Dui* (Lake, 兌), and *Gen* (Mountain, 艮), the four diagonal corners. Step Forward, Step Backward, Beware of the Left, Look to the Right, and Central Equilibrium are *Jin* (Metal, 金), *Mu* (Wood, 木), *Shui* (Water, 水), *Huo* (Fire, 火), and *Tu* (Earth, 土). All together they are the thirteen postures" (see Appendix A-l). The explanation of the thirteen postures can also be found in the **Taijiquan Classic** written in the Qing Dynasty (Appendix A-13).

The eight postures are the eight basic fighting moves of the art, and can be assigned directions according to where the opponent's force is moved. Wardoff rebounds the opponent back in the direction he came from. Rollback leads him further than he intended to go in the direction he was attacking. Split and Bump lead him forward and deflect him slightly sideward. Pluck and Elbow can be done so as to catch the opponent just as he is starting forward, and strike or unbalance him diagonally to his rear. Push and Press deflect the opponent and attack at right angles to his motion. The five directions refer to stance, footwork, and fighting strategy. They concern the way one moves around in response to the opponent's attack, and how one sets up one's own attacks.

Since ancient times, many *Taiji* masters have tried to explain the deeper aspect of these thirteen postures by using the eight trigrams and the five elements. In order to find a satisfactory explanation, various correspondences between the eight basic techniques and the eight tri-

Figure 1-4 The directions of the eight basic techniques according to Chang San-Feng.

grams, and also between the five directions and the five elements, have been devised. Unfortunately, none of the explanations are completely reasonable and without discrepancy. The author will not attempt to find another explanation which might be just as unsatisfactory. However, in order to help the interested reader in pondering this mystery, we will include some of the available diagrams and an explanation considered the most accurate. We hope that someday someone who is a master of *Yi Jing* and *Bagua* theory and also an experienced *Taiji* researcher can untie this knot of mystery.

First, the relationship of the eight basic techniques (Wardoff, Rollback, Press, Push, Pluck, Split, Elbow, and Bump) with the eight trigrams and the *Taiji* symbol is shown in Figure 1-4. This diagram is drawn following Chang, San-Feng's *Taijiquan* classic. Two alternatives are found in some of the available *Taiji* books and are shown in Figures 1-5 and 1-6. None of the above three diagrams give a satisfactory explanation of the connection between the *Bagua* eight "gates" and the eight techniques. However, from the viewpoint of *Yin* and *Yang* one can obtain a more or less satisfactory explanation. Here, we will discuss the diagram as described in Chang, San-Feng's classic. In a trigram, a straight line expresses *Yang* and a broken line implies *Yin*. Therefore, when two straight lines are put together it means strong *Yang*, and when three straight lines are put together it means very strong *Yang*. The same can be applied to *Yin*. The Chinese have used the trigrams to analyze the

Figure 1-5 The directions of the eight basic techniques according to "Tai Chi Touchstones" (See Bibliography).

Figure 1-6 The directions of the eight basic techniques according to J. J. Soong (See Bibliography).

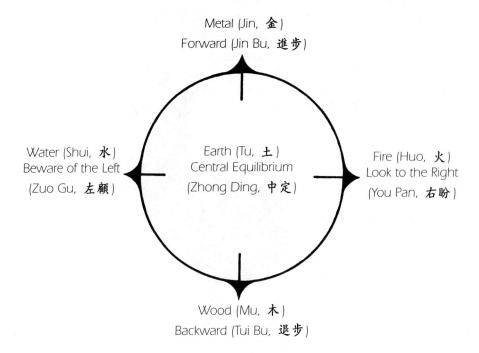

Metal (Jin, 金)
Forward (Jin Bu, 進步)

Water (Shui, 水)
Beware of the Left
(Zuo Gu, 左顧)

Earth (Tu, 土)
Central Equilibrium
(Zhong Ding, 中定)

Fire (Huo, 火)
Look to the Right
(You Pan, 右盼)

Wood (Mu, 木)
Backward (Tui Bu, 退步)

Figure 1-7. The directions of the Five Elements according to Chang, San-Feng.

seasons, the weather, and even the destiny of a person or a country. Initially three lines were used, but when understanding of the relationships grew, trigrams were used in pairs, allowing things to be divided and analyzed in 64 different ways. These 64 hexagrams are the basis of the **Yi Jing (Book of Changes),** which has exerted an enormous influence on Chinese culture.

From Figure 1-4, one can see several things. Wardoff is expressed by three straight lines, which means very strong *Yang*. This means power, aggression and offense. The opponent's attack is bounced back in the direction it came from. Rollback is expressed by three broken lines, which implies defense, withdrawal, or retreat. The opponent's attack is diffused by taking away its target. Pluck, Elbow, and Push are constructed of one *Yin* and two *Yang* lines, which shows that there is offense with some defense. Split, Bump, and Press are characterized by two *Yin* lines and one *Yang* line, which shows that defense is more important than offense in their fighting strategy.

As is the case with the eight trigrams and the eight techniques, the various documents show different ways of matching the five elements with the five directions (Forward, Backward, Beware of the Left, Look to the Right, and Central Equilibrium). Similarly, none of the explanations are completely satisfactory. Figure 1-7 shows the correspondence according to Chang, San-Feng's classic. Figures 1-8 and 1-9 show two other published interpretations.

Figure 1-8. The directions of the Five Elements according to "Tai Chi Touchstones" (See Bibliography).

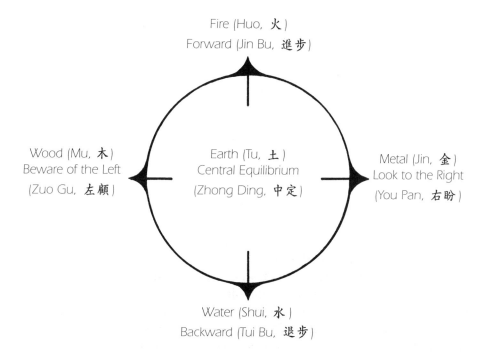

Figure 1-9. The directions of the Five Elements according to J. J. Soong (See Bibliography).

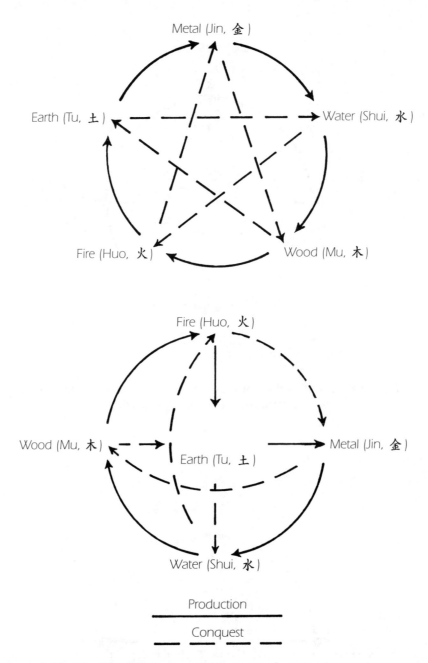

Production

Conquest

Figure 1-10. The Five Elements and the cycles of production and conquest.

Before going further, the reader should first know the general rules and relationships of the five elements. This is shown in Figure 1-10. There are two main cycles of relationships - production and destruction. One can see from the figures that Metal generates Water, Water produces Wood, Wood produces Fire, Fire leads to Earth, and the Earth gives Metal. In the **Yi Jing,** Metal belongs to Heaven and generates Water and rain, Rain will make wood grow, Wood can generate Fire, Fire generates ashes (Earth), and Earth includes and produces Metal. It can also be seen from the figure that Water conquers Fire, Fire conquers

Metal, Metal subdues Wood, Wood defeats Earth, and finally Earth defeats Water. In the real world water can extinguish fire, fire can melt metal, metal can cut wood, wood (roots) can break up earth (rock), and finally dirt can dam the flow of water.

As with the eight trigrams and techniques, we will only discuss the five elements and directions as they are delineated in the Classic of Chang, San-Feng. This is shown in Figure 1-7. Water conquering Fire corresponds to Beware of the Left defeating Look to the Right. This means that if the opponent attacks from your right, you go to the left to avoid his attack and at the same time you can attack his right from your left. Fire conquering Metal matches Look to the Right defending against an attack from the front. That means if your opponent attacks from your front, you can defend against him by sticking to his hand and pulling to the right to immobilize him. Metal conquering Wood matches Forward defeating Backward. This means that when your opponent withdraws, you want to move forward and use Adhere-Connect and Stick-Follow to follow his retreat and immobilize him aggressively. Wood subduing Earth corresponds to using Backward to defeat Central Equilibrium. This refers to using backward pulling power to destroy the opponent's stability and root. Finally, Earth conquering Water matches Central Equilibrium defeating Beware of the Left. This means that in order to defend against force from the left, you have to find your center and stability.

As one can see, trying to fit the five directions into the pattern of the five elements can be even more frustrating and unsatisfactory than is the case with the eight trigrams. It may very well be that the masters of old did not ever intend these philosophical explanations to be taken literally. If you train yourself to always respond a certain way to a certain attack, you are depriving yourself of flexibility and perhaps setting yourself up to be countered. The key point which this philosophy teaches is probably that one must always remain mobile and flexible in both hands and footwork. There are many ways to respond to each and every attack, and the more thinking and research you do, the better off you are. The various interpretations of the philosophy reflect different points of view and give the practitioner different ways to train. The philosophy may give you ideas, but all ideas must be tested out. In the final analysis, it is not the philosophy but the practical experiences which are the foundation of *Taijiquan*.

In addition to the Thirteen Postures, *Taijiquan* is also commonly called *Mian Quan* (Soft Sequence, 綿拳). This is because when *Taiji* is practiced, the forms are soft and smooth, the mind is calm, the *Qi* is round, and *Jin* is fluid. *Taijiquan* is also called *Chang Quan* (Long Sequence). Chang, San-Feng's **Taiji Treatise** states "What is the long sequence? It is like a long river and a large ocean, rolling ceaselessly" (see Appendix A-1). That means, when *Taiji* is practiced, the forms flow smoothly and continuously. The *Qi* flow is also smooth and continuous, and the *Jin* is unbroken. There is another martial style also called *Chang Quan*. However, this *Shaolin* style should be translated as "Long Fist" because it specializes in long range fighting.

1-5. What does Taiji Training Include?

Taiji has been evolving for more than seven hundred years, and it is very difficult to state just exactly what makes up the art. The content of the art has varied from one generation to the next. For example, one generation might specialize in the *Taiji* spear, and gradually come to ignore other aspects of the art such as the sword or saber. The contents of the system can also vary from one teacher to another. One might have learned only the sword from his master, and so naturally the sword would be the only weapon he could teach. Some masters will emphasize a particular principle or training method because of their experience, temperament or research, or perhaps create a new training style for a new weapon.

Since the beginning of this century, *Taiji* weapons practice has been increasingly ignored. Frequently only the barehand solo sequence is taught. In some cases the solo sequence has been modified to make it simpler and shorter, and therefore more accessible to a greater number of people. Although a number of techniques have been eliminated, the sequence still serves the purpose of improving health. However, a simplified sequence may not be enough if one is interested in deeper research and practice. Additionally, the coordination of breath and *Qi* circulation is often ignored. Most people these days learn *Taiji* without ever being exposed to the martial applications of the postures, the concept of *Jin*, barehand fighting sets, or *Taiji* sparring.

Taiji sword and saber sequences, because of their beauty, are practiced in the United States, although the applications of the techniques are seldom taught. *Qi* enhancement and extension training seems almost to have disappeared. *Taiji* spear, staff, and ruler can hardly be found in this country.

The reason for this is nothing new. The practitioners today are usually looking for a relatively quick and easy way to improve and maintain their health. Very few are willing to sacrifice their time for the long, hard training required to develop the other aspects of the art. Because of this, both in China and the rest of the world, even if a master is qualified to teach the whole art, he may be reluctant to pass it down to an unappreciative, if not actually doubting, generation. It seems very possible that the deeper aspects of *Taijiquan* will die out in the near future.

The various aspects of *Taijiquan* that are still available are listed below for reference:

1. Barehand:

 a. *Taiji* Solo Sequence
 b. Applications from the Solo Sequence
 c. Fast *Taiji* Training
 d. Still Meditation
 e. *Qi* Circulation Training
 f. *Jin* Training
 g. Pushing Hands and its Applications
 h. *Taiji* Fighting Set and Deeper Martial Applications
 i. *Taiji* Free Pushing Hands and Sparring

2. Taiji Sword:

a *Taiji* Sword Solo Sequence
b. *Qi* Enhancement and Extension Training
c. Martial Applications
d. *Taiji* Sword Matching Forms
e. *Taiji* Sword Sparring

3. Taiji Saber:

a. *Taiji* Saber Solo Sequence
b. Martial Applications
c. *Taiji* Saber Matching Forms
d. *Taiji* Saber Sparring

4. Taiji Spear and Staff:

a. Individual Spear and Staff Martial Techniques
b. Spear and Staff Sticking-Matching Practice
c. Long Weapons Sparring

5. Taiji Ball:

a. Listening and Understanding *Jin* Training
b. Adhere-Stick *Jin* Training
c. Two-person *Taiji* Ball Training

6. Taiji Ruler:

Unknown to author

It can be seen that some of the training areas are already incomplete. For example, there is no longer a complete traditional staff or spear sequence, although a few individual techniques are still taught by some masters. In mainland China, complete sequences are being practiced for a number of weapons, but these sequences have been developed only in the last few years. There are very few masters anywhere who still know and train with the *Taiji* ruler or ball. However, even with the abridged list of *Taiji* activities available today, it would still take about twenty years to learn the art.

1-6. The Proper Approach and the Sequence of Learning Taiji

The Proper Approach to Learning Taiji:

Whether or not a person learns something depends upon his attitude and seriousness. First he must make a firm decision to learn it, and then he must have a strong will to fulfill his intention. He needs perseverance and patience to last to the end. Even if a person has all these virtues, his achievement might still be different from that of another person who has the same qualities and personality. The difference is due to their manner of learning. If a person practices and then ponders every new thing he has learned, and keeps going back to research and master it, he will naturally be better than the person who never explores what he has learned. Both students may learn a method for changing rocks into gold, but only the first one will know why the method works. The former's knowledge will continue to grow and he will soon become a master, the latter will always be only a practitioner.

Taiji theory is deep and profound. It takes many years of learning, research, pondering, and practice to gradually grasp the key to the art and "enter into the temple." However, the more you learn, the less you are likely to feel you understand. It is just like a bottomless well or a ceaselessly flowing river. In Appendix A-6, the reader can find an ancient list of five mental keys the student of *Taiji* needs in order to reach the higher levels of the art. It is said: 1. Study wide and deep; 2. Investigate, ask; 3. Ponder carefully; 4. Clearly discriminate; and 5. Work perseveringly. If you follow this procedure you can learn anything, even how to become a wise and knowledgeable person.

In addition to the above learning attitude, a good master is also an important key to learning the high art of *Taijiquan*. In China, there is a saying: "A disciple inquires and searches for a master for three years, and a master will test the disciple for three years." It also says: "A disciple would rather spend three years looking for a good master than learn three years from an unqualified master." A good master who comprehends the art and teaches it to his students is the key to changing a rock into a piece of gold. It is the teacher who can guide you to the doorway by the shortest path possible and help you avoid wasting your time and energy. It is said: "To enter the door and be led along the way, one needs oral instruction; practice without ceasing, the way is through self-practice" (See Appendix A-15). It is also said: "Famous masters create great disciples." On the other hand, a good master will also judge if a disciple is worth his spending the time and energy to teach. A student can be intelligent and practice hard in the beginning, and change his attitude later on. A student who practices, ponders, humbly asks, and researches on his own will naturally be a good successor to the style. Usually a master needs three years to see through a student's personality and know whether he is likely to persevere in his studies and maintain a good moral character.

In the fifty years since *Taijiquan* has been popularized, many good *Taiji* books and documents have been published (see Bibliography). A sincere *Taiji* practitioner should collect and read them. Books are the recording of many years of learning, study, and research. If you do not know how to use this literature to your advantage, you will surely waste more time and energy wandering in confusion. However, you should not completely believe what any book says. What is written is only the author's opinions and personal experience. You should read widely, investigate, and then clearly discriminate between the worthwhile and the not-so-worthwhile in what you have read. If you do this well you can minimize confusion and avoid straying too far from the right path.

In addition, you should take advantage of seminars, summer camps, and other ways to come in touch with experienced masters. In this way you will be able to catch many key points and gain a "feeling" for many things which you may have only read about. But remember, you must research on your own in great detail in order to achieve a deeper understanding of the art. Thus it is said "You don't ever want to give up your throat; question every talented person in heaven and earth. If (you are) asked: how can one attain this great achievement, (the answer is) outside and inside, fine and coarse, nothing must not be touched upon" (see Appendix A-5B).

Training Sequence:

Every *Taiji* master has his own sequence of training, emphasizing his methods and content. In this section, the author will list the general training procedures according to his learning experience with three *Taiji* masters and his teaching experience of more than twenty years. This section is a guide only to the barehand training procedures of *Taijiquan*.

The general sequence of *Taijiquan* training is as follows:

1. Understanding the fundamental theory of *Taijiquan*.
2. Relaxation, calmness, and concentration practice.
3. Breath training.
4. Experiencing and generating *Qi*.
5. *Qi* circulation and breathing.
6. Still meditation.
7. Fundamental stances.
8. Breath coordination drills.
9. Fundamental moving drills.
10. Solo *Taijiquan*.
11. Analysis of the martial applications of the sequence.
12. Beginning *Taiji* pushing hands.
13. Fundamental forms of *Taiji Jin* training.
14. Hen and Ha sound training.
15. Fast *Taijiquan*.
16. Advanced *Taiji* pushing hands.
17. Advanced *Taiji Jin* training.
18. *Qi* expansion and transportation training.
19. Martial applications of *Taiji* pushing hands.
20. Free pushing hands.
21. *Taiji* fighting set.
22. *Taiji* free fighting.

Before the *Taiji* beginner starts training, he should ask himself several questions: Why do I want to learn *Taiji*? What benefits do I hope to gain? Am I likely to continue training for a long time? After you have answered these questions you should then ask: Does this *Taiji* style offer what I want? Is this master qualified? Does this master have a training schedule? How long and how deep can this master teach me? Will this master teach me everything he knows or will he keep secrets when I approach a certain level? After I have studied for many years, will I be able to find an advanced master to continue my study? In order to answer these question you have to survey and investigate. You have to know the historical background of the style and the master's experience. Once you have answered the above questions, then you can start your *Taiji* study without any doubt or confusion.

The first step in learning *Taijiquan* is to understand the fundamental theory and principles through discussion with your master, reading the available books, studying with classmates, and then pondering on your own. You should ask yourself: How does *Taijiquan* benefit the body and improve health? How can *Taiji* be used for martial purposes? What are the differences between *Taijiquan* and other martial styles? Once you have answers to these questions, you should have a picture of the art, and an idea of where you are going. The next question to arise should be: How do I train the relaxation, calmness, and concentration which are the most basic and important aspects of *Taijiquan*? This leads you to the second step of the training.

Usually, if you have the right methods and concepts, you can train your mind to be calm and concentrated and can relax physically in a short time. Keeping this meditative attitude is very important for beginning training. The next step is to train your breathing. The breathing must be deep, natural, and long. If you are interested in health only, you can use Buddhist, or normal breathing. However, if you want to advance to martial applications, you should train and master Daoist, or reverse breathing. You should be able to expand and withdraw the muscles of the abdomen area easily. After you have trained your breath correctly, you should then begin to sense the *Qi* in your abdomen and *Dan Tian*. This will lead to the fourth step - generating and experiencing *Qi*. If you are interested in knowing more about *Taijiquan* and breathing, please refer to the book: **The Essence of Tai Chi Chi Kung**, by YMAA.

Usually, *Qi* can be generated in two ways: externally and internally. To generate *Qi* externally is called *Wai Dan*, and when it is generated internally it is called *Nei Dan*. Interested readers should refer to the author's book: **Chi Kung - Health and Martial Arts.** Through training *Qi* generation you will gradually realize what *Qi* is and why smooth *Qi* circulation benefits the body. You will also build up your sensitivity to the movement of *Qi*. The more you train, the more sensitive you will become. After a time, you should then go to the next step - circulating *Qi*. This is best practiced through still meditation, which will enhance your *Qi* generation and circulation. *Qi* circulation is guided by the calm mind and made possible by a relaxed body. You must train your mind to guide the *Qi* wherever you wish in coordination with correct breathing. First you should develop Small Circulation, which moves the *Qi* up the spine and down the center of the front of the body. Eventually you should develop Grand Circulation whereby *Qi* is circulated to every part of your body. When you have completed the above six steps, you should have built a firm foundation for *Taiji* practice. With correct instruction, it should take less than six months to complete the above training (except Grand Circulation).

The above six steps are purely mental training. When you practice these, you can simultaneously practice the fundamental stances, which build the root for the *Taiji* forms. You should be familiar with all the stances and should practice them statically to strengthen your legs. Also, at this stage you can begin fundamental breath coordination drills. These drills are designed for the beginning student to train: 1. coordination of breathing and movement; 2. coordination of *Qi* circulation and the forms; 3. smoothness and continuity; 4. relaxation; and 5. calmness and concentration of the mind. These drills will help you experience *Qi* circulation and the mood or atmosphere of *Taiji* practice. After you have mastered the fundamental stances and fundamental drills, you should then go on to the fundamental moving drills.

In fundamental moving drills, a few typical forms are selected from the *Taiji* sequence to train proper movement, in addition to the five points mentioned above. These drills are discussed in the author's first *Taiji* book. This step leads the student to the door of the *Taiji* solo sequence.

The *Taiji* solo sequence is constructed with about forty apparent techniques and more than two hundred hidden techniques. It is practiced to enhance *Qi* circulation and improve health, and is the foundation of all *Taiji* martial techniques. It usually takes from six months to three years to learn this sequence depending on the instructor, the length of the sequence, and the talent of the student. After a student has learned this sequence, it will usually take another three years to attain a degree of calmness and relaxation, and to internalize the proper coordination of the breathing. When practicing, not only the whole of your attention, but also your feelings, emotions, and mood should be on the sequence. It is just like when a musician or a dancer performs his or her art - their emotions and total being must be melted into the art. If they hold anything back, then even if their skill is very great, their art will be dead.

When you finish learning the solo sequence, you should then start discussing and investigating the martial applications of the postures. This is a necessary part of the training of a martial arts practitioner, but it will also help the non-martial artist to better understand the sequence and circulate *Qi*. With the instruction of a qualified master, it will take at least two or three years to understand and master the techniques. While this stage of analysis is going on, you should begin to pick up fundamental (fixed step) pushing hands.

Pushing hands trains you to listen (to feel) the opponent's *Jin*, understand it, neutralize it, and then counterattack. There are two aspects of pushing hands training. The first emphasizes feeling the opponent's *Jin* and then neutralizing it, and the second aspect emphasizes understanding the emitting of *Jin* and its applications. Therefore, when you start the fundamental pushing hands, you should also start fundamental *Jin* training. *Jin* training is usually difficult to practice and understand. A qualified master is extremely important. While training *Jin*, the coordination of the sounds Hen and Ha become very important. Uttering Hen and Ha can enable you to emit or withdraw your *Jin* to the maximum and coordinate the *Qi* with it, and can also help to raise your Spirit of Vitality.

When you finish your analysis of the sequence, you have established the martial foundation of *Taijiquan*. You should then start to train speeding up the solo sequence, training *Jin* in every movement. In fast *Taiji* training, practice emitting *Jin* in pulses with a firm root, proper waist control, and *Qi* support. In addition, develop the feeling of having an enemy in front of you while you are doing the form, This will help you learn to apply the techniques naturally and to react automatically. After practicing this for a few years, you should have grasped the basics of *Jin*, and should start advanced pushing hands and *Jin* training.

Advanced (moving step) pushing hands will train you to step smoothly and correctly in coordination with your techniques and fighting strategy. This training builds the foundation of free pushing hands and free fighting. Advanced *Jin* training enables you to understand the higher level of *Jin* application and covers the entire range of *Jin*. During these two steps of training, you should continue your *Qi* enhancement, expansion, and transportation training to strengthen the *Qi* support of your *Jin*. The martial applications of pushing hands should be analyzed, and discussed. This is the bridge that connects the techniques learned in the sequence to the real applications. When you understand all the techniques thoroughly, you should then get involved in free pushing hands and learn the two-person fighting set.

The *Taiji* fighting set was designed to train the use of techniques in a way that resembles real fighting. Proper footwork is very important. Once you are moving and interacting fluidly, you can begin to use *Jin*. The final step in training is free fighting with different partners. The more partners you practice with, the more experience you will gain. The more time and energy you spend, the more skillful you will become.

The most important thing in all this training is your attitude. Remember to study widely, question humbly, investigate, discriminate, and work perseveringly. This is the way to success.

1-7. The Real Meaning of Taijiquan

People practice *Taijiquan* for different reasons. Some practice for health, to cure an illness, for defense, relaxation, or solely for fun. However, when you approach the highest level of *Taijiquan*, you will probably feel that the above reasons are not really important any more. At this time, you must seek the real meaning of the practice, otherwise you will soon become satisfied with your achievement and lose enthusiasm for further research. You must ponder what is really behind this highly meditative art. Many religious Daoists practice *Taiji* in their striving to eliminate their grosser elements and become immortal. Many non-religious people practice *Taiji* to gain a peaceful mind and reinvigorate their lives.

However, you should understand that *Taijiquan* emphasizes meditation both in movement and in stillness. Through this meditation a *Taiji* practitioner, like a Buddhist priest, trains himself to be calm and concentrated. It is possible to achieve a state of peace and centeredness which allows one to judge things and events in a neutral way, without emotional disturbance. When your mind is truly clear and calm, the spiritual side of things starts to open up. You start to see more deeply into things. A skilled practitioner can sense a person's intentions before they are expressed, and they often develop the ability to look more deeply into people and events in non-martial ways too. Many martial arts masters came to be considered wise men, and were consulted for their insight into the meaning of human life, this world, and the universe. They learned to live in this world without confusion or doubt, and to find peace and happiness. All of this comes through meditation and continuous pondering.

There is a song passed down since ancient times about the real meaning of *Taijiquan* (see Appendix A-8). It says: 1. "No shape, no shadow." This means that when you have approached the higher levels of *Taiji* meditation, you find your physical body seems not to exist - you feel that you are a ball of energy, part of the natural world and inseparable from it. Your actions and Self are part of the natural order of things, fitting in smoothly and unobstrusively, seeming to have no independent shape of their own, casting no shadow. 2. "Entire body transparent and empty." When you feel you are only a ball of energy, there is nothing in your mind, no desire or intention. Since your mind and ego are not there to interfere, you can see clearly and respond correctly. 3. "Forget your surroundings and be natural." Once you are transparent you will easily forget your surroundings and your energy flow will be smooth and natural. 4. "Like a stone chime suspended from West Mountain." This implies that your mind is wide open, free, and unrestricted. Like a stone chime suspended from the mountain, all things are clear under you, while your mind is still controlled by you just as the thread suspends the stone chime. 5. "Tigers roaring, monkeys screeching." When you move the energy you have cultivated it can be as strong as a tiger's roar and reach as far as a monkey's screech. 6. "Clear fountain, peaceful water." Even when your energy is strong, your mind is clear, still, and peaceful. 7. "Turbulent river, stormy ocean." In *Taiji*, if you have to use your energy it can be strong and continuous like a turbulent river or the stormy ocean. 8. "With your whole being, develop your life." During all your practice and meditation, you must concentrate your whole attention in order to develop the highest level of the art. This dedication and concentration carry over to the rest of your life, and the striving for perfection becomes the real inner meaning of *Taiji*.

BIBLIOGRAPHY

1. 太極拳學 *(Study of Tai Chi Chuan),* J. J. Soong, Taipei, Taiwan, 1970.

2. *Taiji Touchstones: Yang Family Secret Transmissions,* ed. and trans. by Douglas Wile, Sweet Chi Press, 1983.

3. *Tao of Tai Chi Chuan,* Jou, Tsung-Hwa, *Taiji* Foundation, 1981.

4. *Tao of Meditation,* Jou, Tsung-Hwa, *Taiji* Foundation, 1983.

5. *Tao of I Ching,* Jou, Tsung-Hwa, *Taiji* Foundation, 1984.

6. *Taiji Chuan* - *A Simplified Method of Calisthenics for Health & Self Defense,* Cheng, Man-Ching, North Atlantic Books, 1981.

7. *Master Cheng's Thirteen Chapters on Tai Chi Chuan,* Cheng, Man-Ching, trans. by Douglas Wile, Sweet Chi Press, 1982.

8. *Tai Chi Chuan* - *For Health and Self-Defense,* T. T. Liang, Vintage Books, 1974.

9. *Tai Chi Chuan Principles and Practice,* C. K. Chu, Sunflower Press, 1981.

10. *Yang Style Tai Chi Chuan* Dr. Yang, Jwing-Ming, Unique Publications, 1981.

11. 太極拳，刀、劍、桿、散手合編 *(Tai Chi Chuan: Saber, Sword, Staff, and Sparring),* Chen, Yan-Lin (陳炎林), Reprinted in Taipei, Taiwan, 1943.

Chapter 2
Qi and Taijiquan

氣與太極拳

2-1. Introduction

Once you have learned the postures of the sequence and the basic principles of *Taiji* movement, the next step is to start working on *Qi*, *Yi* (Mind), and *Jin* (power). This chapter discusses *Qi*, its relationship to health and the martial arts, and how it is controlled by the mind. The role of *Qi* in *Taijiquan* is discussed, as is its relationship with breathing, Spirit, and the Mind. The chapter concludes with general rules of posture, and recommendations for practicing the sequence.

2-2. Qi

General Concepts:

Qi in Chinese has two different meanings. The first refers to *Kong Qi* (空氣), meaning air. The second is *Qi* meaning energy. Many Chinese believe that everything in the universe has its own energy field - every animal and plant, and even inanimate objects like rocks. Living things have a particularly strong energy field circulating through them. When this circulation is disturbed, illness results, and when it stops, there is death. *Qi* can be transferred from one object to another. In animals this *Qi*, which is often translated "intrinsic energy," circulates throughout the body to keep every part vital and alive. *Qi* can be affected by the weather, the season, the food you eat, your mood and thoughts.

Qi is often associated with a feeling of warmth or tingling which many people experience. Some *Qigong* practitioners misunderstand this and believe that *Qi* is heat, and that this is why they feel warm during meditation or *Qigong* practice. Actually, warmth is an indication of the existence of *Qi*, but it is not *Qi* itself. This is just like electricity in a wire. Without a meter, you cannot tell if there is an electric current in a wire unless you sense some phenomenon such as heat or magnetic force. Neither heat nor magnetic force is electric current; rather they are indications of the existence of this current. In the same way, you cannot feel *Qi* directly, but you can sense the presence of *Qi* from the symptoms of your body's reaction to it, such as warmth or tingling.

The Chinese have researched human *Qi* and its relationship with nature for more than four thousand years. This has resulted in acupuncture and in the many exercises and practices which can be used to strengthen the body and improve health and life. *Taijiquan* is only one of the many available systems.

Qi and Health:

If you understand the relationship of *Qi* to health, you will then realize why *Taijiquan* is so beneficial. In human or animal bodies, there are two major types of circulation. One is the blood circulation, commonly known in the Western world. Blood vessels and capillaries carry the blood to every part of the body in order to supply oxygen and nutrients, and to carry away waste. The other major circulatory system is that of *Qi* (internal energy). This *Qi* circulation supplies energy to the organs and to every cell of the body. There are twelve major pairs of *Qi* channels (*Jing*, 經) and eight *Qi* vessels (*Mai*, 脈). The twelve channels are related to the internal organs, which will function normally when *Qi* is circulating smoothly, but will degenerate or malfunction when the circulation is disturbed. Of the eight vessels, two are particularly important. These are the Governing Vessel (*Du Mai*, 督脈), which goes up the spine and over the head, and the Conception Vessel (*Ren Mai*, 任脈), which runs down the center of the front of the body. In addition to the twelve channels and eight vessels, there are numerous small channels called *Luo* (絡) which are similar to capillaries. These carry *Qi* from the major channels to the skin and to every cell of the body. Some of these small channels bring *Qi* from the main channels to the marrow of the bones, which are also alive and need *Qi* and blood for growth and repair. Figure 2-1 is an example of a *Qi* channel (*Jing*), showing the branches (*Luo*) through which the *Qi* can flow laterally to the surface of the skin and deep into the marrow.

In order to maintain and enhance health, the *Qi* must circulate smoothly and strongly, and it must be balanced. When the *Qi* circulation loses its balance through stagnation or accumulation in one area, you may become ill. There are many "knots" along the paths of the *Qi* channels, both the *Jing* and the *Luo*, where the flow is constricted. These knots can slow down the *Qi* circulation and cause serious problems. In addition, stress or injury will cause an accumulation of *Qi* in the affected area. To heal this, the channels must be opened up and the stagnation removed. The training and practices used to open these knots and strengthen *Qi* circulation are called *Qigong*. *Taijiquan* is a form of *Qigong*, and has been proven to be a safe and effective way to maintain and improve health.

Often imbalances will clear up by themselves, because **Qi always seeks to balance itself**. However, it is wise to pay attention to your training and to any activity in your life which influences your *Qi* circulation. Be careful of anything which may disturb the body's natural circulation pattern, and avoid anything which causes imbalance. For example, if you build up the *Qi* in your right arm, you should also build up the *Qi* in your left arm.

Figure 2-1. A Qi channel and its branches.

Qi Generation:

Generally speaking, there are two ways to generate *Qi*: externally (called *Wai Dan*) and internally (*Nei Dan*). External *Qi* generation comes from stimulating a part of the body, such as the arms, in order to build up *Qi* in that area, and then circulating it throughout the body. This circulation is done either through conscious control, or by letting it happen spontaneously.

Methods of external *Qi* generation include muscular tension, massage or acupressure, and acupuncture:

1. **Muscular tension:**

   The most famous way of generating *Qi* by muscular tension is Da Mo's system, explained in his book ***Yi Jin Jing (Muscle/Tendon Change Classic)***. In these exercises, the practitioner will repeatedly tense and relax some part of the body, such as the forearms or wrists. When the muscles of a part of the body are tensed, *Qi* is built up in that area. This accumulation is most commonly felt as warmth. When the muscles are then completely relaxed, the *Qi* will naturally start to flow to other parts of the body.

2. **Massage, Rubbing, and Acupressure:**

   This approach uses external force to stimulate the muscles, skin, or points on the *Qi* channels in order to normalize or balance the *Qi* circulation.

3. **Acupuncture:**

   This is one of the most common methods in China for adjusting *Qi* circulation. Needling and other methods are used to balance the system, increasing or decreasing the flow of *Qi*.

Internal *Qi* generation comes from exercising the *Dan Tian*, and uses the mind to guide the *Qi*:

1. **Dan Tian Exercises:**

   The generation of *Qi* from the *Dan Tian* has been used by *Qigong* practitioners both for maintaining health and for increasing martial ability. In these exercises, *Qi* is generated in the *Dan Tian* by the continual in and out motion of the abdomen. When the *Qi* has accumulated there to a certain level, the concentrated mind circulates it up the back and down the front of the body, which is called "Small Circulation" (*Xiao Zhou Tian*, 小周天). In the next step, called "Grand Circulation" (*Da Zhou Tian*, 大周天), the *Qi* is circulated throughout the whole body.

2. **The Mind:**

   The concentrated mind is crucial for generating *Qi*, and the will and intention lead the *Qi* throughout the body. A person with extensive *Qigong* experience can concentrate his mind at some area of the body and generate *Qi* there purely by thinking. The *Qi* can be affected or disturbed when a person gets nervous, worried, uptight, or in shock. However, this kind of *Qi* generation is not caused by conscious control and cannot be called *Qigong*.

Qi and the Mind:

Yi has been popularly translated "Mind." However, another Chinese word, *Xin* (心), is also translated "Mind." You must understand and distinguish between them in order to be able to grasp the meaning of the ancient poems and songs translated in Appendix A.

In China, the heart is considered the most vital organ. The direct translation of *Xin* is "heart." When Chinese say *Zhuan-Xin* (專心), literally "single heart," they mean "single-minded, with one mind." It is often translated as "concentrated mind." *Xin* commonly means "intention, idea, or thought," referring to an idea which is not yet expressed, which lacks the full intention necessary to express it. When this idea is shown or expressed in some way, it is called *Yi* (意), and has the meaning of "purpose, intention, or desire." The reader should understand that a person must have *Xin* first and then *Yi*, because *Xin* is the source of *Yi*. If you want to do something, that is called *Xin*. When you want it and fully intend to do it, or actually do it, this is called *Yi*. Sometimes the words are put together: *Xin-Yi* (心意). This can be translated "mind" or "intention," and also refers to the intention to do something specific.

The *Taiji* master Chen, Yan-Lin wrote: "Somebody said that *Yi* is *Xin*, and *Xin* is *Yi*. As matter of fact, there is some difference between them. *Xin* is the master of *Yi*. *Yi* is the chancellor of *Xin*. When *Xin* generates an idea, the *Yi* is then raised. When *Yi* is generated, the *Qi* then follows. In other words, there is linkage and a mutual relationship between *Xin*, *Yi*, and *Qi*. When *Xin* is scattered, the *Yi* is then dispersed. When *Yi* is dispersed, then the *Qi* will float. Conversely, when the *Qi* is sunken, then *Yi* is strong; when *Yi* is strong, then *Xin* is steady. Therefore, all three are interrelated and inseparable."

As mentioned, *Qi* can be affected by your thinking. Consequently, all *Qigong* styles emphasize calming down the mind and using it to guide the *Qi* circulation. Therefore, it is said: "Use your mind to lead your *Qi*" (*Yi Yi Yin Qi*, 以意引氣). Sometimes when you concentrate your mind on the *Qi* you will find that your body tenses up and adversely affects the *Qi* circulation. This is because your mind is not calm and relaxed. Remember that your body can only be relaxed if your mind is.

In *Qigong* and *Taijiquan*, *Yi* is probably the most important key to success. If you cannot concentrate your *Yi* and use it to lead the *Qi*, all your practice will be in vain.

Qi and the Martial Arts

According to Chinese history, *Qi* was first noticed four thousand years ago. Later, when its importance to health was realized, methods were researched to enhance its circulation. The Chinese people have used these methods for more than two thousand years to improve their health. Eventually it was realized that this enhanced *Qi* circulation could be used in the martial arts to support the muscles and strengthen offensive and defensive techniques.

Almost every Chinese martial style trains *Qi* through *Wai Dan*, *Nei Dan*, or both. When *Qi* is used to support either the muscles (in external styles) or the sinews (in internal styles), the power generated will be greater than if you used only unaided muscular strength. *Taijiquan* is an internal martial style and specializes in using *Qi* to support the *Jin* which is emitted from the joints, tendons, and sinews, and which is controlled by the waist. The next chapter will focus on the principles of *Jin* and various training methods.

Qi is also used in *Jin Zhong Zhao* (Golden Bell Cover, 金鐘罩) and *Tie Bu Shan* (Iron Shirt, 鐵布衫) to train the body to resist strikes without injury. Methods such as *Yi Zhi Chan* (One Finger Contemplation, 一指禪) and *Jin Gang Zhi* (Gold-Steel Finger, 金剛指) have been developed to build up high levels of *Qi* in the fingers. This was used for cavity press (*Dian Xue*, 點穴) whereby a touch to the appropriate cavity could kill or injure an opponent.

Qi and Hand Forms:

Hand forms play a very important role in *Qigong* and the martial arts. Different hand forms are used for different purposes, and various styles emphasize different forms. It is through your hands that you express your will, whether for martial arts, for health, or for healing. Your hands are the furthest point to which your *Qi* moves inside your body, and how they are held, and whether any muscles are tensed, influences the flow of energy.

There are six main energy channels which end in the fingers. The thumb and middle fingers each carry a *Yin* channel (Hand *Taiyin* Lung and Hand *Jueyin* Pericardium channels respectively, 手太陰肺：手厥陰包絡) and the index and ring fingers each carry a *Yang* channel (Hand *Yangming* Large Intestine and Hand *Shaoyang* Triple Burner channels respectively, 手陽明大腸：手少陽三焦). The little finger has both *Yin* and *Yang* channels (Hand *Shaoyin* Heart *Xin* and Hand *Taiyang* Small Intestine channels respectively, 手少陰心：手太陽小腸). Normally, when your *Yi* leads *Qi* to your hands, the *Qi* will be distributed to all the fingers. However, often you would like to concentrate your *Qi* in specific fingers for some special purpose. For example, you might wish to concentrate the *Qi* in the index finger for cavity press. In order to do this, a special hand form is used to narrow the other channels while leaving the channel in the index finger open.

Generally speaking, when a finger is extended the *Qi* will circulate easily to the fingertip and out. This emission of *Qi* is useful for attacking an enemy's vulnerable points, as well as for healing. An extended finger is usually offensive and is classified as a *Yang* finger. When the finger is bent and touching the palm, the *Qi* is less active and will flow back to the palm. This is usually classified as a *Yin* finger. Sometimes the bent fingers are stiffened to slow down their *Qi* circulation and make the extended finger(s) stronger. The extended fingers may also be stiffened. This is often seen in external styles where a muscular type of *Jin* predominates. Conversely, when the extended fingers are relaxed the *Qi* can move strongly. This is commonly seen in the internal styles where *Qi* plays a more important role in emitting *Jin*.

In *Qi* transportation training, both hands are usually held in the same form in order to keep the *Yi* and *Qi* balanced and symmetrical. The exception to this is when one hand is holding a weapon.

Figure 2-2. One Finger Contemplation (一指禪).

We will now discuss the more common hand forms. Most of their names contain the word *Jin* because they use *Qi*, in coordination with breathing, to generate a flow of energy for either healing or martial purposes. These forms range from ones which only direct *Qi*, to those which use *Qi* to support the muscles, and to those in which muscular strength predominates. This will be discussed further in Chapter 3.

A. Yi Zhi Chan (One Finger Contemplation): 一指禪

Yi Zhi Chan is used in both internal and external styles. In this hand form (Figure 2-2), the index finger is straight to allow the free passage of *Qi*, while the other fingers are bent to slightly restrict the flow. The thumb touching the bent fingers enables the *Qi* to circle through them, and also helps the *Qi* to flow strongly to the straight finger. This form is commonly used in cavity press. External styles use special training to stiffen the finger without losing *Qi* concentration, while internal styles emphasize *Qi* circulation and minimize the use of the muscles. This form is sometimes also used in healing.

B. Bao Pu Jin (Rushing Panther Jin): 豹扑勁

This hand form is said to resemble a panther rushing at something (Figure 2-3). The thumb is separated from the other four extended fingers, dividing the *Qi* into two major flows - one to the thumb, and the other to the rest of the fingers. This form is commonly used for massage.

C. Ya Zui Jin (Duck's Beak Jin): 鴨嘴勁

In the *Ya Zui Jin* hand form (Figure 2-4), all the fingers except the thumb are held tightly closed. The channel to the thumb

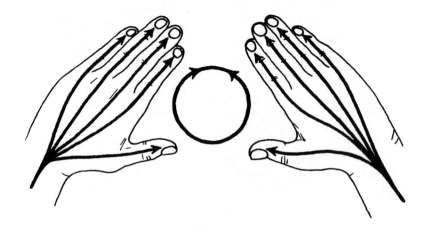

Figure 2-3. Rushing Panther Jin (豹扑勁).

Figure 2-4. Duck's Beak Jin (鴨嘴勁).

is kept wide open, while the flow to the other fingers is restricted. The thumb in this form is commonly used for cavity press, although it is also often used in massage and *Qigong* healing.

D. He Zui Jin (Crane's Beak Jin): 鶴嘴勁

There are two forms called *He Zui Jin*. In the first, commonly used in the Crane martial style, the thumb and index fingers touch while the other three fingers are gently closed (Figure 2-5). *Qi* is concentrated in the thumb and, index finger, while a lesser flow circles through the other three fingers. The second crane's beak form is similar to the first except that the middle, ring, and little fingers are now open (Figure 2-6). *Qi* is not concentrated as strongly in the thumb and index finger as is the case with the martial crane's beak form. This form is commonly used in *Qigong* healing.

Figure 2-5. Crane's Beak Jin used in the martial arts (鶴嘴勁一).

Figure 2-6. Crane's Beak Jin used in Qigong healing (鶴嘴勁二).

E. Tong Tian Jin (Reach the Heaven Jin): 通天勁

In this form, the middle finger is extended, allowing *Qi* to reach the tip, while all the other fingers are closed, circling and conserving the *Qi* (Figure, 2-7). The *Qi* in the middle finger is usually stronger and can reach further than is the case with *Yi Zhi Chan*. This form is commonly used for healing although it is sometimes seen in the martial arts.

F. Long Xian Zhu Jin (Dragon Holding a Pearl in its Mouth Jin): 龍銜珠勁

This form is said to resemble a dragon holding a pearl in its mouth (Figure 2-8). All the fingers except the little one are extended. The *Qi* is divided into two flows; one to the thumb and the other to the index, middle, and ring fingers. This form is used for attacking the eyes, throat, or armpit, and is also commonly used in massage.

Figure 2-7. Reach the Heaven Jin (通天勁).

Figure 2-8. Dragon Holding a Pearl in its Mouth Jin (龍銜珠勁).

G. Jian Jue Kai Qi Jin (Secret Sword Opening the Qi Jin):
劍訣開氣勁

In this hand form, the index and middle fingers are extended, while the other three are closed with the fingertips touching (Figure 2-9). If the palm faces sideward or upward, it is a *Yang Jin*, and if the palm faces downward, it is a *Yin Jin*. This form extends *Qi* to the two straight fingers while allowing a second flow to move through the other three fingers and recirculate. In sword training it is very important to transport *Qi* to the end of the sword. In order to do this, while one hand is holding the sword, the other should be in this form to balance the *Qi* and extend it symmetrically. Without this hand form it is very difficult for the *Qi* to reach the tip of the sword. *Jian Jue* is also commonly used for cavity press and some healing purposes.

H. She Tou Jin (Snake Head Jin): 蛇頭勁

In *She Tou Jin* the hand is formed like a snake's head. The index, ring, and little fingers are closed while the thumb and middle finger are extended (Figure 2-10). This form is commonly used in *Qigong* healing.

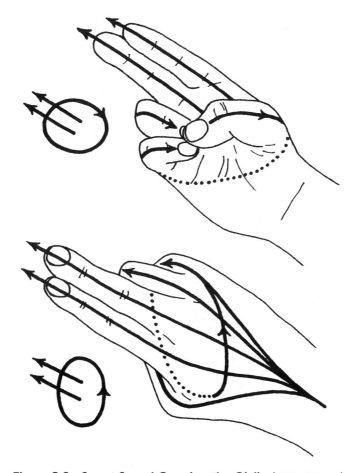

Figure 2-9. Secret Sword Opening the Qi Jin (劍訣開氣勁).

Figure 2-10. Snake Head Jin (蛇頭勁).

Figure 2-11. Flat Finger Jin (平指勁**).**

Figure 2-12. Eight Trigram Palm (八卦掌**).**

I. Ping Zhi Jin (Flat Finger Jin): 平指勁

Ping Zhi Jin is almost the same as Dragon Holding a Pearl in its Mouth *Jin* mentioned above with one difference: the little finger is also extended (Figure 2-11). It is used to grab the throat, or the muscles located in the armpit or waist area. In order to make the grabbing effective, the *Qi* is divided into two flows: one to the thumb and the other to the rest of the fingers. This form is also commonly used in massage and *Qigong* healing.

J. Baguazhang (Eight Trigram Palm): 八卦掌

Baguazhang is used by the *Bagua* internal martial style, which specializes in using several varieties of this form. In order to make strikes effective, the *Qi* must be concentrated in the palm. To do this, the fingers are kept extended, and tightened somewhat (Figure 2-12).

Figure 2-13. Eagle Claw Jin (鷹爪勁 **).**

Figure 2-14. Crane Claw Jin (鶴爪勁**).**   **Figure 2-15. Tiger Claw Jin (** 虎爪勁 **).**

K. Ying Zhua Jin (Eagle Claw Jin): 鷹爪勁

This is a specialty of the Eagle Claw style, and is used for grabbing. The thumb and fingers are spread and bent like an eagle's claw (Figure 2-13). When this hand form is used for grabbing, the *Qi* and strength are held in the palm and fingers.

L. He Zhua Jin (Crane Claw Jin): 鶴爪勁

As with Eagle Claw *Jin*, this *Jin* is used by the Crane style for grabbing. The thumb, index and middle fingers are shaped like a crane's claw (Figure 2-14).

M. Hu Zhua Jin (Tiger Claw Jin): 虎爪勁

Tiger Claw *Jin* is used by the Tiger Claw style for grabbing and clawing. The five fingers are formed like a tiger's claw and tensed to hold the *Qi* in them (Figure, 2-15).

Figure 2-16. Praying Mantis Hand (螳螂手).

Figure 2-17. Buddha Hand (佛手).

N. Tang Lang Shou (Praying Mantis Hand): 螳螂手

This hand form is used by the Praying Mantis style to hook and grab the enemy. It is also used to attack the opponent's eyes and cavities. The Praying Mantis Hand is formed with the thumb touching the first knuckle of the index finger while the other three fingers are lightly held in (Figure 2-16).

O. Fo Shou (Buddha Hand): 佛手

Buddha Hand is popularly used in meditation. It is formed with the thumb and middle fingers touching each other to circulate the *Qi* back to the body, while the other three fingers are slightly bent (Figure 2-17).

There are many other hand forms used in different martial styles, in meditation, and in healing. *Taijiquan* also has its special hand forms. These will be discussed in a later section.

Figure 2-18

2-3. Qi and Taijiquan

There are several questions which *Taiji* practitioners frequently ask, such as: How do I experience *Qi* in *Taijiquan*? How do I generate *Qi*? How can *Taijiquan* benefit the body and bring me health? How is *Qi* circulated in *Taijiquan*? How do I use my *Qi* in the martial applications of *Taijiquan*? What is the relationship of *Qi* to *Jin*? All these questions are very important for the practitioner who wishes to approach the higher levels of *Taijiquan*.

Qi Generation and Transportation in Taijiquan

Taijiquan is a style of martial *Qigong* training, so naturally *Qi* is extremely important. In Chinese martial society there is a saying: "Train muscles, bones, and skin externally, and train *Qi* internally" (*Wai lian Jin gu pi, nei lian yi kou Qi*, 外練筋骨皮，內練一口氣). However, this raises the questions: How do I generate *Qi* and how do I experience it?

Qi in *Taijiquan* is generated both externally and internally. It is recommended that you do certain exercises, in addition to the sequence, which will help you to understand and develop *Qi*. An exercise called *Gong Sho* (Arcing the Arms, 拱手)(Figure 2-18) is commonly used to help beginners generate *Qi* in the shoulders and back. For this exercise, stand in the False Stance with one leg rooted on the ground and the other in from of it, with only the toes touching the ground. Both arms are held in front of the chest, forming a horizontal circle, with the fingertips almost touching. The tongue should touch the roof of the mouth to connect the *Yin* and *Yang Qi* Vessels (Conception and Governing Vessels respectively). The mind should be calm and relaxed and concentrated on the shoulders; breathing should be deep and regular.

When you stand in this posture for about three minutes, your arms and one side of your back should feel sore and warm. Because the arms are held extended, the muscles and nerves are stressed and tense. *Qi* will build up in this area and heat will be generated. Also, because one leg carries all the weight, the muscles and nerves in that leg and in one side of the back will be tense and will thereby generate *Qi*. Because this *Qi* is generated in the shoulders and legs rather than in the *Dan Tian*, it is considered "local *Qi*." In order to keep the *Qi* generation and the flow in the back balanced, after three minutes change your legs without moving the

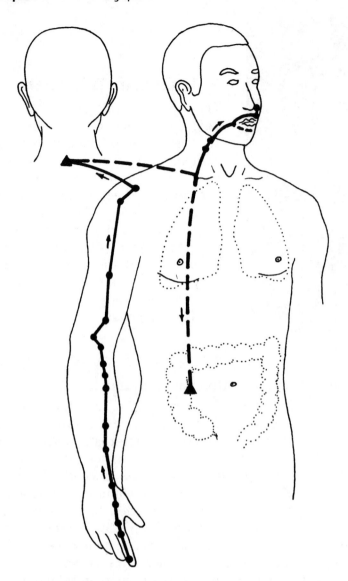

Figure 2-19. Hand Yangming Large Intestine Channel

arms and stand this way for another three minutes. After the six minutes, put both feet flat on the floor, shoulder-width apart, and lower your arms slowly. The withheld *Qi* will then flow out naturally and strongly. It is just like a dam which, after accumulating a large amount of water, releases it and lets it flow out. At this time, concentrate and calm the mind and look for the feeling of *Qi* flowing from the shoulders to the palms and fingertips. Beginners can usually sense this *Qi* flow, which is typically felt as warmth or a slight numbness.

Sometimes *Qi* is felt on the upper lip. This is because there is a channel (Hand *Yangming* Large Intestine) which runs over the top of the shoulder to the upper lip (Figure 2-19). However, the feeling is usually stronger in the palms and fingers than in the lip, because there are six *Qi* channels which pass through the shoulder to end in the hand, but

Figure 2-20

there is only one channel connecting the lip and shoulder. Once you experience *Qi* flowing in your arms and shoulders during this exercise, you should also find that you can sense it in your back.

After you have developed your *Qi* circulation you should practice directing it into both arms as you exhale. The energy goes out each arm, exchanges at the fingertips, and comes in through the opposite arm as you inhale, circling in both directions simultaneously. Because the arms and hands form a circle, the *Qi* is always flowing from each hand into the other and back to the body. Since the energy is withheld or conserved within the body, the *Gong Shou* posture is considered *Yin*. In addition to increasing the circulation of *Qi* in the arms and shoulders, the *Gong Shou* exercise will also improve the flow in the spine, which is particularly important in *Taijiquan*.

This exercise is one of the most common practices for leading the beginner to experience the flow of *Qi*, and some *Taiji* styles place great emphasis on it. If a *Taiji* practitioner does not know and experience the feeling of *Qi* flow, how can he really understand *Qi*?

Another common form is called *Tuo Tian* (Supporting the Heavens, 托天)(Figure 2-20). This exercise has been discussed in the author's first *Taiji* book **Yang Style Tai Chi Chuan,** and will not be repeated here. There are many other forms which are used to teach beginners about *Qi*. The reader should consult different *Taiji* and *Qigong* books for further ideas.

After you understand what you are looking for, there are two basic sets of exercises you should practice. These exercises increase the generation of *Qi*, balance it, and train the coordination of breath with movement and the transporting of *Qi*. The mind is all-important, and the beginner will find visualizations extremely helpful. For the beginner, **the generation and transporting of *Qi* comes from the concentrated imagining that you are pushing a heavy object with relaxed muscles.** At first, most beginners will not feel the energy flow, but with time and practice most will start feeling warmth in the palms. It is important also to **keep the *Yi* further than the *Qi*.** You know that when you walk you must keep your *Yi* (mind, attention, intention) ahead of you, rather than on your feet, or else you won't be able to take the first step. Similarly, when you want to transport *Qi* you must keep your *Yi* ahead of where the *Qi* is in order to move it.

The first set of these exercises trains the coordination of *Qi* and breath, balances energy, and opens up the *Qi* channels in the arms and legs. The exercise consists of standing stationary and moving the arms in simple movements - up and down, in and out- in coordination with the breathing. This set has been mentioned in the author's first *Taiji* book and will not repeated here.

After you have practiced this set for a while and can move *Qi* to your limbs, you can start the second set, which coils the *Qi* throughout your body and out to the skin. In these exercises, your muscles are tensed by the twisting of your limbs and body, and then relaxed. The *Qi* which is generated in these tensed areas is led by the mind to coil out to the extremities and spiral out to the skin. This coiling motion helps to increase the penetration of your *Jin* and brings the *Qi* out to the skin, opening all the little *Qi* channels (*Luo*, 絡). This slows degeneration and increases the efficiency of your muscles. This is what is meant by the saying: "Transport *Qi* as though through a pearl with a 'nine-curved hole,' not even the tiniest place won't be reached" (Appendix A-3).

In pushing hands and in fighting, victory is frequently decided by who has the greatest skill in what is called "listening." When *Qi* is circulating smoothly to your skin, you will be able to sense or "listen" to your enemy's power and intention. Also, after many years of *Qi* development, you may be able to pass your *Qi* into another person's body through the cavities on his *Qi* channels in order to injure or heal.

Once you have accomplished Grand Circulation, you can use these exercises to circulate energy from the *Dan Tian* out to the extremities, instead of just using local energy.

Before starting this exercise, calm down and meditate for a minute. The tongue should be touching the roof of the mouth, and the entire body should remain relaxed throughout the exercises. The thumbs and little fingers should be pulled back slightly to direct the *Qi* to the palms. In order to build the *Qi* to a high level, repeat each form ten to twenty times, then go on to the next form without stopping.

In these exercises, inhale as you bring your hands toward your shoulders, and exhale as you move your hands away from your shoulders. As in all of *Taiji*, the arms are never extended fully - you should always maintain a slight bend in the elbow. As you inhale, imagine that you are drawing energy in through your hands and feet, and condensing it in your *Dan Tian* and spine. As you exhale, move the *Qi* from your *Dan Tian* and spine out through your hands and feet. When you exhale you should notice six flows of *Qi* - two out of the palms (*Laogong*, P-8, 勞宮), two out of the feet (*Yongquan*, K-1, 湧泉), one from the *Dan Tian* down to the place between the anus and groin (*Huiyin*, Co-1, 會陰), and one from the *Dan Tian* through the spinal cord to the crown of the head (*Baihui*, Gv-20, 百會). As always, imagine that you are moving against resistance, and that your feet are pushing against the floor.

Figure 2-21

Figure 2-22

Qi Coiling Exercises:

Form 1: (Figures 2-21 and 2-22)

This is the beginning warm-up form. Hold both arms extended in front of the chest. Rotate your palms downward as you inhale, and imagine drawing energy into your bones. Rotate the palms upward, exhaling and using the mind to lead the *Qi* from deep inside of the arms to the surface in a coiling, expanding motion. When a hand faces downward it is considered a *Yin* Palm, and when it faces upward it is a *Yang* Palm. After doing this form ten to twenty times, you should feel your forearms and shoulders getting warm. This form helps you to generate a feeling of coiling *Qi* from inside your arms to the surface of the skin.

Form 2: (Figures 2-23 and 2-24)

This is the second warm-up form. Continuing from the last exhale form, inhale and bring the hands in to the chest in a twisting motion. Then exhale, stretching the hands out in a screwing motion. The right hand moves in a regular screwing motion, clockwise forward and counterclockwise backward, while the left hand reverses this, twisting counterclockwise forward and clockwise backward. Finish this form with the arms in and both palms facing down. This form practices a forward drilling motion in addition to the coiling motion of the first exercise.

Figure 2-23

Figure 2-24

Figure 2-25

Figure 2-26

Form 3: (Figures 2-25 and 2-26)

Continuing from the last inhale form, keep the palms down and exhale as you lower your hands to the waist. Imagine that you are pushing something downward, but do not tense your muscles. Turn your palms up and raise them to the chest as you inhale. Turn the palms down and repeat. In this form keep the fingers and palms of both hands in a line with each other, rather than pointing out to the front. This increases the twist-

Figure 2-27

Figure 2-28

Figure 2-29

ing motion. This form builds up *Qi* in the forearms through the alternate twisting and relaxing of the muscles. The *Qi* thus generated is coiled outward to the surface of the skin.

Form 4: (Figures 2-27 to 2-29)

After the last inhale of the previous form, exhale and push the arms out in front of the chest while rotating the palms forward. Inhale and bring the hands in, palms facing the chest, then exhale and let the hands sink down, palms down. Raise them again, palms up, as you inhale. This form has two complete breaths and four motions: forward, back, downward, and upward. Keep the fingers of both hands in line while moving the hands upward, forward, and back, but let them relax to a natural angle while sinking. When you are moving your hands forward, imagine that you are pushing a heavy object, and also visualize the counterforce into your feet.

Figure 2-30

Figure 2-31

Figure 2-32

Figure 2-33

Form 5: (Figures 2-30 to 2-33)

Continuing from the last exhale form, inhale and raise the hands to the chest, palms up, fingers pointing forward. Exhale and extend your arms forward until they are almost straight, with the palms facing sideward. Inhale and move your arms in a big circle out, back, and forward again to your chest. Exhale while extending the arms forward, continuing the exercise in a swimming motion. When you exhale, you should have a flow of *Qi* reaching out through the fingertips of both hands in a drilling or screwing motion.

Figure 2-34

Figure 2-35

Figure 2-36

Figure 2-37

Form 6: (Figures 2-34 to 2-37)

After the last inhale form, exhale and push your hands over your head, palms up. As you inhale, turn the palms down and bring them to your chest. Exhale and lower your hands to your waist, inhale and raise them again to your chest. This form has two complete breaths and four motions.

Figure 2-38

Figure 2-39

Figure 2-40

Figure 2-41

Form 7: (Figures 2-38 to 2-41)

When the last inhale form is finished, exhale and separate your palms. One palm continues to push upward while the other pushes downward in front of the abdomen. Inhale and draw both hands toward each other, exhale and repeat the motion with the opposite hands raising and lowering. Inhale and draw both hands toward each other. This form trains the *Qi* to balance in both arms.

Figure 2-42

Figure 2-43

Figure 2-44

Form 8: (Figures 2-42 to 2-44)

Continue the same motion as the last form except this time the lower hand goes behind the body in the hip area, palm down. This twists the shoulder of the back hand and coils the *Qi* through it.

51

Figure 2-45

Figure 2-46

Figure 2-47

Figure 2-48

Form 9: (Figures 2-45 to 2-48)

Continue the previous exercise with one addition — rotate the body in the direction the upper hand is moving. While the right hand is rising, rotate the body to the left as far as possible. Similarly, while the left hand is rising, rotate the body to the right. As you twist your body to the rear, exhale and extend your *Qi* out through your fingertips, rather than your palms. This is similar to the last form, except that twisting the body coils the *Qi* around the body.

Figure 2-49

Figure 2-50

Figure 2-51

Figure 2-52

Form 10: (Figures 2-49 to 2-52)

Continuing from the last inhale form, extend the legs somewhat wider than shoulder width. This exercise is essentially
the same as the last form, except that when you turn to the
side, let the feet turn into a Bow and Arrow stance, and tilt the
body. This form coils the energy around the whole body even
more than the previous form.

Figure 2-53

Figure 2-54

Figure 2-55

Figure 2-56

Form 11: (Figures 2-53 to 2-62)

After the last exhale form, inhale and rotate your body to the front while bringing the legs back to shoulder width, and return both hands to the waist, palms up. Exhale while raising the hands and turning the palms forward. Inhale, and rotate the body all the way to the rear into the Sitting on Crossed Legs stance, while bringing the hands to the chest, palms fac-

Figure 2-57

Figure 2-58

Figure 2-59

Figure 2-60

ing in. Exhale while turning and lifting the body to the front and raising the hands above the head, palms forward. Inhale and repeat the same motion, turning to the other side, and on the exhale return again to the front. This form trains coiling *Qi* through the whole body as well as screwing the body up and down.

Figure 2-61

Figure 2-62

Figure 2-63

Figure 2-64

Form 12: (Figures 2-63 and 2-64)

After completing the above exercises, you should have built up and transported quite an amount of *Qi* to your skin. Let your hands drop down naturally and rotate them in both directions in coordination with your breathing for a minute or so to continue feeling the *Qi* flow. This form will help you to balance your energy after the exercises.

With continued practice, these *Qi* transportation exercises will teach you to build up and circulate *Qi* in the local areas which are being stressed. After a while you should be able to apply the principles of these *Wai Dan Qigong* exercises to the *Taiji* solo sequence. However, this is only a part of the *Qigong* training which *Taijiquan* uses. A skilled *Taiji* artist generates *Qi* in the *Dan Tian* and circulates it throughout his body. This is called *Nei Dan* (a Daoist term meaning Internal Elixir), and is the foundation of *Taijiquan*. The classics refer to this frequently: "The *Qi* is sunk to the *Dan Tian*" (Appendix A-2), "Grasp and hold the *Dan Tian* to train internal *Gongfu*" (Appendix A-13), and "The *Dan Tian* is the first chancellor" (Appendix A-5A). If you keep part of your attention on your *Dan Tian* while doing the sequence, you will gradually build up your internal circulation from this area. If you want to learn more about *Taiji Qigong* or Martial *Qigong*, please refer to author's books: **The Essence of Tai Chi Chi Kung** and **The Essence of Shaolin White Crane**.

Once you can generate *Qi* in the *Dan Tian*, you begin circulating it through the Small Circulation (the Conception and Governing Vessels). After you have accomplished this, you can work on Grand Circulation, which circulates *Qi* through the arms and legs and clears obstructions in the twelve primary *Qi* channels. One of the best ways to do this is through doing the *Taiji* sequence. The final step is to move the *Qi* from the channels to the skin through the small channels (*Luo*). The *Qi* flow should be smooth, continuous, strong, and animated, but yet condensed. There are many references to this in the classics: "*Qi* should be full and stimulated" (Appendix A-1); "(You) want the entire body's *Qi* to circulate smoothly, (it) must be continuous and non-stop" (Appendix A-5B); "Don't be broken and then continuous, refine your one *Qi*" (Appendix A-13); "*Qi* (circulates) in the entire body without the slightest stagnation" (Appendix A-15); "Third saying: *Qi* condenses. When the appearance of *Qi* is dispersed and diffused, then it is not conserved, and the body can easily be scattered and disordered. In order to make *Qi* condense into the bones your exhalation and inhalation must flow agilely (smoothly). The entire body is without gap" (Appendix A-12).

Once you have built up your *Qi* circulation you should begin to train using it to support your fighting techniques. For this the *Qi* must be able to flow readily to the arms and legs in coordination with the breath. This will be discussed in the next section.

After you have worked for a while on circulating your *Qi* with the exercises mentioned above, you should start practicing individual forms from the sequence. Wardoff, Rollback, Press, and Push can be practiced together as a unit. You can also use Brush Knee and Step Forward, Diagonal Flying, Wave Hands in Clouds, Step Back and Repulse Monkey, and Step Forward, Deflect Downward, Parry and Punch. Individual forms should be practiced repeatedly, emphasizing root, stability, and balancing the *Qi*.

It is important to balance the *Qi* accurately so that the *Jin* will be able to reach its maximum. In order to do this, the *Yi* must be balanced first. You know that when you push a heavy object, you must push the rear leg back in order to push the object forward. In the same way, when you wish to lead *Qi* forward, you must think of the rear foot in order to lead the *Qi* forward efficiently. It is very important to remember: **the *Qi* must be balanced to the opposite side, or it will be weak and inefficient**. Thus it is said: "If there is a top, there is a bottom; if there is a front, there is a back; if there is a left, there is a right" (Appendix A-1). Therefore, in the beginning, the mind should concentrate on balancing the *Qi* flows. If you persevere in this practice, the balancing will begin to occur naturally, and you will no longer have to think about it. When you use this balanced *Qi* to support *Jin*, the *Jin* will be able to reach its maximum.

In conclusion, *Taijiquan* uses both *Wai Dan* (external) and *Nei Dan* (internal) *Qi* circulation. A wise *Taiji* practitioner will use *Wai Dan* to open the channels and branches locally in the limbs, and at the same time build up his internal *Nei Dan Qi* in the *Dan Tian*. One day, when he has completed the Small Circulation, he will be able to accomplish Grand Circulation quickly and easily because he has already opened the channels in the limbs. Remember, even if you don't have internal (*Nei Dan*) *Qi* circulation, you can still circulate *Qi* locally in the limbs with the *Wai Dan* exercises. This will benefit your internal organs, though not as much as the internal *Nei Dan* circulation will.

Qi and Breathing

Breathing plays a very important role in *Qigong* and *Taiji* practice. Breathing with the right method calms down the mind and relaxes the body. This makes it possible for the *Qi* to circulate smoothly, and helps the *Yi* to generate and lead *Qi* wherever desired. Breathing should be deep, relaxed, and regular. In *Qigong*, there are two common ways of breathing. The Buddhist method uses the normal breathing in which the abdomen expands as you inhale, whereas the Daoist method uses "reverse" breathing in which the abdomen expands as you exhale. *Taijiquan* was developed according to the Daoist method and therefore uses reverse breathing. Because detailed theory and training methods have been discussed in the author's books **Yang Style Tai Chi Chuan, Chi Kung - Health and Martial Arts, The Essence of Tai Chi Chi Kung, and The Essence of Shaolin White Crane**, we will not repeat them here. We will only discuss the essential points of breathing in *Taiji* practice.

In *Taiji*, the breathing coordinates with *Qi* and the fighting techniques. There are several stages of coordinating breath and *Qi*. The first stage uses meditation, usually sitting, to develop Small Circulation. This trains you to bring the *Qi* up the Governing Vessel from the tailbone to the roof of the mouth and down the Conception Vessel from the tongue to the tailbone. This can be done with either two cycles of inhalation and exhalation (Figure 2-65) or only one cycle (Figure 2-66).

In the second stage, after you have developed Grand Circulation,

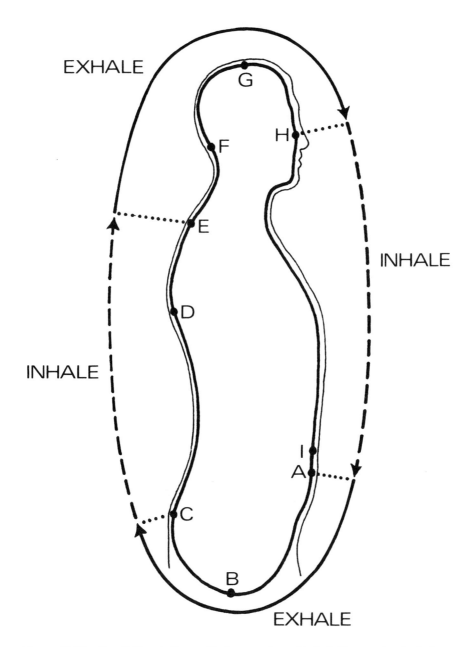

Figure 2-65. Small Circulation with two cycles of inhalation and exhalation.

you can coordinate *Qi* with your technique. On the inhale, bring *Qi* up the spine from the tailbone to the point between the shoulder blades, and also from the roof of the mouth down to the *Dan Tian* (Figure 2-67). In this way you are accumulating energy in the back and *Dan Tian*. When you exhale, bring *Qi* from your back out your arms, and from your *Dan Tian* out your legs. On the exhale the *Qi* also moves over your head and from the *Dan Tian* to the tailbone to complete the circuit of the Small Circulation. This method is considerably more complicated than the

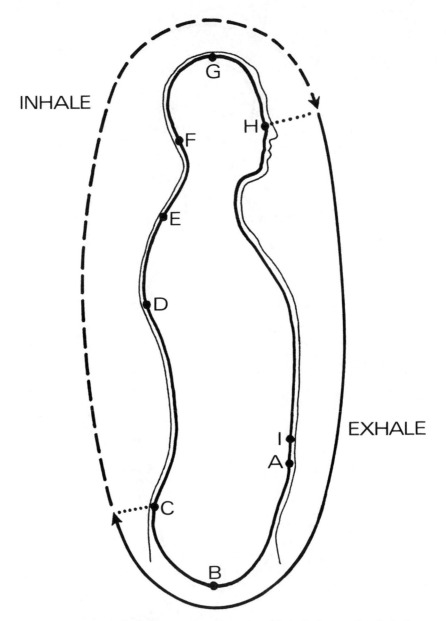

INHALE

EXHALE

Figure 2-66. Small Circulation with one cycle of inhalation and exhalation.

Small Circulation because there is more than one single focus point of attention and *Qi*.

In the third stage, once the *Qi* moves quickly and easily wherever you want it, you can use a much simpler visualization. When you do a defensive move, inhale and accumulate energy in your *Dan Tian* and spine. When you do an offensive technique, exhale and send *Qi* out your arms and legs. Your abdomen becomes firm as you move *Qi* in both directions. It is said: "Inhalation is storage, and exhalation is emitting. That is because inhalation lifts up naturally (the Spirit of Vitality). It can also lift (control) the opponent. (When you) exhale, then (your *Qi*) can

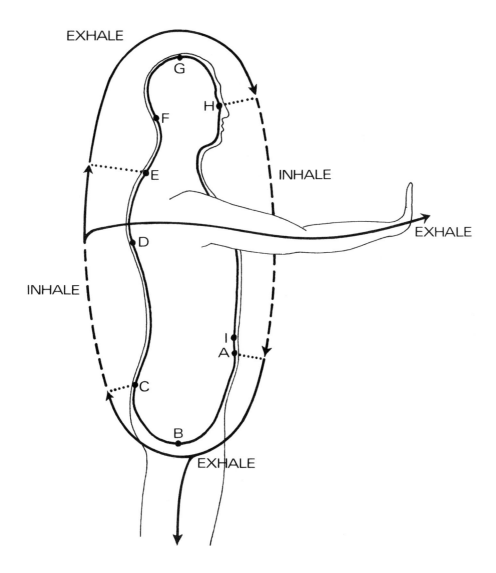

Figure 2-67. Grand Circulation — coordinating Qi with your techniques.

sink naturally. (You) also can release (*Jin*) out to the opponent. That means use *Yi* (your mind) to move your *Qi*, don't use *Li* (strength)" (Appendix A-12).

It is said: "Every form of every posture follows smoothly; no forcing, no opposition, the entire body is comfortable. Each form smooth" (Appendix A-10). In the sequence, breathing coordinates with the forms. Since some of the forms are long and some are short, you must vary the length of your breaths to keep the speed of the sequence uniform. If a form in the sequence is too long for one breath, add another. **Your**

breathing should be relaxed - do not hold it, do not force it. Don't hold your breath, because your lungs will tighten and your body will tense. This not only slows the *Qi* circulation, but also damages lung cells.

Once your breathing naturally coordinates with the movements, you should no longer pay attention to your breathing. It says in the classics: "(Throughout your) entire body, your mind is on the Spirit of Vitality (*Jing-Shen*), not on the breath. If concentrated) on the breath, then stagnation. A person who concentrates on breath has no Li (strength); a person who cultivates *Qi* (develops) pure hardness (power)" (Appendix A-3). The reason for this is that the mind must be ahead of the *Qi* in order to lead it, and you cannot do this if your mind is on your breathing. If you develop a sense of having an enemy in front of you, the Spirit of Vitality is raised and the mind is kept ahead of the *Qi*, leading it naturally in support of your movements.

Qi and Shen

Before we discuss the relationship of *Qi* and *Shen*, the reader should understand three concepts: *Shen* (神), *Jing* (精), and *Jing-Shen* (精神).

In China, *Shen* means Spirit, one's higher nature, or the soul. *Shen* is the divine part of man, his inner nature which is in contact with the divine nature. When you act in harmony with your *Shen*, you are in harmony with yourself and all around you. *Shen* is the vital part of your being, the alert aliveness, the consciousness within which the mind and thought function. It is the force behind your attitudes, thoughts and actions. The Chinese believe that when a person with a strong will and Spirit dies, his *Shen* lives on. Many Chinese still worship these spirits of the dead. A person's Spirit may be good or evil, and this will carry over into death.

Jing in Chinese means essence. It is what is left after something has been refined and purified. In Chinese medicine, *Jing* can mean semen, but generally refers to the basic substance of the body which the *Qi* and Spirit enliven. *Jing* is inherited from your parents, and the amount of *Jing* that you have inherited determines the strength of your constitution. Generally speaking, the amount of *Jing* is fixed, although it can be weakened by illness or dissipation, and it can be augmented through diet and certain meditation practices, including *Taiji*.

When the term *Jing-Shen* is used in *Taiji* it means "the essence of the Spirit," and is sometimes translated "Spirit of Vitality." The Chinese also commonly use just *Shen* to express *Jing-Shen*. When a person has a strong *Jing-Shen* it is usually visible in how he holds himself and moves. He is concentrated, active, alive, vigorous, and often highly spiritual. Strong Spirit often shows in the brightness and alertness of a person's eyes. When a person lacks *Jing-Shen* he is dull and listless, without will or enthusiasm.

In China, *Jing*, *Qi*, and *Shen* are called the *San Bao* (三寶) or Three Treasures, because they are so important. In *Taiji* practice, the highest of these is *Shen*, because it can control the others. It is the Spirit which stimulates the *Qi*, causing it to condense, and which guides it throughout the body. This is especially important when *Taiji* is used for fighting. A person who has a strong *Jing Shen* will be able to use his condensed and stimulated *Qi* to support his *Jin* in a fight.

It is said: "The Spirit of Vitality is threaded and concentrated" (Appendix A-12). Just as you must thread your *Qi* throughout your body, so too must you thread your Spirit. You should be able to expand your consciousness to fill your body without any gaps or dark spots. At the same time, you must be able to concentrate your awareness wherever you wish.

It is said: "*Qi* should be full and stimulated, *Shen* (Spirit) should be retained internally" (Appendix A-1). Retaining the Spirit internally means to be centered and to avoid unnecessary actions of the body, mind, and eyes. Thus concentrated, you will be able to use your mind to act quickly and efficiently, and you will avoid betraying your intentions to the opponent.

It is also said: "(If) the *Jing-Shen* (Spirit of Vitality) can be raised, then (there is) no delay or heaviness (clumsiness)" (Appendix A-3). When *Qi* is sunken and concentrated, it is possible for the Spirit of Vitality to rise to the top of the head. This clears the mind and allows the body to move lightly and without inhibition. The Song of Five Key Words talks of the importance of a calm heart, an agile body, condensed *Qi*, and integrated *Jin*, and then goes on to say: "All in all, (if) the above four items (are) totally acquired, it comes down to condensing *Shen* (Spirit). When *Shen* condenses, then one *Qi* (can be) formed, like a drum. Training *Qi* belongs to *Shen*" (Appendix A-12).

Qi and the Mind in Taijiquan

The mind, both *Yi* (Mind) and *Xin* (Heart), controls the actions of the *Qi*, and it is the *Qi* which controls the actions of the body. It is said: "Use the heart (mind) to transport the *Qi*, (the mind) must be sunk (steady) and calm, then (the *Qi*) can condense (deep) into the bones. Circulate the *Qi* throughout the body, it (*Qi*) must be smooth and fluid, then it can easily follow the mind.....*Yi* (Mind) and *Qi* must exchange skillfully, then you have gained the marvelous trick of roundness and aliveness....The *Xin* (heart, mind) is the order, the *Qi* is the message flag" (Appendix A-3). It is also said: "If asked, what is the standard (criteria) of its (thirteen postures) application, (the answer is) *Yi* (mind) and *Qi* are the master, and the bones and muscles are the chancellor" (Appendix A-15).

From the above sayings, it is clear that the ancient masters placed great emphasis on the mind and *Qi*. A *Qigong* proverb says "Use your mind to lead your *Qi*" (*Yi Yi Yin Qi*, 以意引氣). This is the key to using *Qi*, because it tells you that if you want to move your *Qi* somewhere, your mind must go there first. **Remember: first there is *Yi*, then there is *Qi*.**

The Highest Level of Qi Transportation

Once you have achieved Grand Circulation you have opened up the twelve primary *Qi* channels and the two major vessels, but this doesn't mean that you have opened up all the channels in your body. There are the thousands of small *Qi* branches (*Luo*) which spread from the main channels out to the skin and in to every part of the body. The benefits of opening these branches can be explained from both the health and martial arts points of view.

From the point of view of health, the stagnation of *Qi* in the *Luo* will not significantly affect the functioning of the organs, but it will affect your overall health in some ways. If there is stagnation in some of the *Luo*, the *Qi* may not be able to reach the skin, and this will be reflected in the condition of the skin. For example, when people get old, *Qi* is not easily transported to the skin, and this shows as age spots. In Chinese medical diagnosis, the appearance of the skin is commonly used to judge a person's health and the balance of his *Qi*. When a person is sick his *Qi* flow loses its balance. Since the *Luo* are connected to the *Qi* channels, the appearance of the skin will then show symptoms of the illness. Conversely, because the main channels are connected by these branches to the skin, stimulation of the skin is commonly used to generate *Qi* to compensate for imbalances in the channels and organs. A common method is rubbing the skin, as in massage.

In order to be healthy your *Qi* should reach every cell of your body, from deep inside the bones out to the skin. It is believed that if you can circulate *Qi* smoothly throughout the body, there will be no danger of getting cancer. One of the leading causes of death in this country, cancer, is the uncontrolled growth of certain cells in the body. It is believed that this is caused by unbalanced *Qi* flow. For further discussion, interested readers should refer to the author's *Qigong* books. Once you can transport *Qi* to your skin, you may then start developing the ability to transport it beyond your body. When this goal is reached, you can then use your *Qi* for healing by removing excess *Qi* from a person or by reinforcing his deficient *Qi*.

For the martial artist, there are two reasons for circulating *Qi* to the skin: defense and offense. In defense, a *Taiji* martial artist must build the sensitivity of his skin to "listen" to his enemy's *Jin*. Listening *Jin* is one of the most decisive factors in *Taiji* fighting. The better a *Taiji* fighter's ability to sense the enemy, the better his fighting art will be. When two *Taiji* artists fight, skill in "Listening *Jin*" is usually the main factor in deciding the winner. It is said that when your *Qi* can be transported strongly to your skin, it will cover the body like a cloud of energy. The better you are, the thicker this cloud will be.

For offensive purposes, a martial artist wants to build up his *Qi* as much as possible, both to support his *Jin* and also for use in cavity strikes. The highest level of *Taiji* martial application is to have your *Qi* overflow into the opponent's body when you touch one of his cavities. For example, if you can transport *Qi* beyond your skin, you can strike or touch the cavity in the opponent's armpit and shock his heart through the heart channel. It takes many years of correct practice to reach this level.

When you can extend *Qi* beyond your body, you can also move it to the tip of weapons such as the sword or spear. It is said that the sword is king of the short weapons and the spear is leader of the long weapons. This is because these two weapons require *Qi* rather than muscle for the higher levels of the art.

Now let us discuss how to transport *Qi* to your skin. First, you must open as many of the *Luo* as possible. Most of these branches are already open, but if you use only these branches to transport your *Qi* to the skin you will be no different than any run-of-the-mill martial artist. But how do you open these branches? You must build up your *Qi* so that the branches which are already open cannot handle the flow, and the *Qi* overflows into the other branches and opens them. The stronger your *Qi* is, the more branches you will open. In order to strengthen your *Qi*, you must train your *Dan Tian* continuously so that it is full of *Qi* like a drum or a balloon. You must also train your *Qi* to extend out to the furthest parts of your body, to fill every nook and cranny, to extend from the marrow of the bones to beyond the skin. Thus, it is said: "Transport *Qi* as though through a pearl with a 'nine-curved hole,' not even the tiniest place won't be reached" (Appendix A-3).

There are several ways to work at expanding your *Qi* out to the skin, but in every method the most important point is to use your *Yi*. Do the *Qi* coiling exercises and visualize the *Qi* spiraling out to the skin. Another good method that you can use while doing the form, meditating, sitting at work, or just walking down the street, is to feel when you exhale that *Qi* is expanding from the *Dan Tian* into a sphere which is larger than your body. You can also visualize that you are inflated with *Qi*, and your limbs and body are rounded and full like a balloon. An especially good way to train extending your *Qi* further is to increase the length of your breath. When you coordinate your *Yi*, *Qi* and breath, the longer your breath is, the further your *Qi* will extend. This is why the solo *Taiji* sequence is normally done so as to take 18 to 20 minutes. The breath is coordinated with each movement, and the mind leads the *Qi* inward with each inhale and extends it outward to the maximum with each exhale. To train and extend the *Qi* further, the sequence should be done slower, without adding any breaths.

2-4. Posture and Taijiquan

Since *Taijiquan* is an internal *Qigong* martial style, correct posture is essential. Incorrect postures can cause many problems: a tight posture can stagnate the internal *Qi* circulation, wrong postures may expose your vital points to attack, floating shoulders and elbows will break the *Jin* and reduce *Jin* storage.

Taiji students are generally taught to make the postures large at first. This helps the beginner to relax, makes it easier to see and feel the movements, and also helps him to sense the *Qi* flow. Furthermore, because large postures are more expanded and relaxed, the *Qi* flow can be smoother. Large posture *Taiji* was emphasized by *Yang*, Cheng-Fu and has been popularly accepted as the best *Taiji* practice for health.

Large postures also make it easier to train *Jin*. It is more difficult to learn *Jin* with small postures because the moves are smaller and quicker, and they require more subtle sensing *Jins*. Large postures build the defensive circle larger and longer than small postures, which allows you more time to sense the enemy's *Jin* and react. It is best to first master the large circles, and only then to make the circles smaller and increase your speed. Thus, the poem of Thirteen Postures: Comprehending External and Internal Training states: "First look to expanding, then look to compacting, then you approach perfection" (Appendix A-3).

In addition, when you begin *Taiji*, you should first train with low postures and then gradually get higher. When you first start *Taiji* you cannot build your root by leading your *Qi* to the Bubbling Well point (*Yongquan,* K-1) on the soles of your feet. Without this firm foundation you will tend to float and your *Jin* will be weak. To remedy this problem, you should first train with low postures (though not so low as to make you tense), which will give you a root even without *Qi*, and simultaneously develop your *Qi* circulation. Only when you have accomplished Grand Circulation and the *Qi* can reach the Bubbling Well can you use it to build the internal root. This is done by visualizing the *Qi* flowing through your feet and extending into the ground like the roots of a tree. At this time you may start using higher postures and relaxing your leg muscles. This will facilitate the *Qi* flow, which in turn will help you to relax even more. In the higher levels of *Taijiquan*, muscle usage is reduced to the minimum, and all the muscles are soft and relaxed. When this stage is reached, *Qi* is being used efficiently and is the predominant factor in the *Jin*. Usually it takes more than thirty years of correct training to reach this level. Train according to your level of skill - start with the larger and lower postures, and only move to the smaller and higher postures as your skill increases.

To summarize: build your *Qi* both externally and internally, and circulate it through the entire body. After the internal *Qi* can reach the limbs, use this *Qi* to support your *Jin*. Gradually de-emphasize the use of the muscles, and rely more and more on using the mind to guide the *Qi* to lead the body. Train the postures from large to small, low to high, slow to fast, and easy to hard. First build the defensive circle large, then make it smaller. For maximum *Jin*, strengthen the root, develop power in the legs, balance your *Yi* and *Qi*, exercise control through the waist, and express your will through your hands.

Now, let us discuss the general rules of posture:

Hands and Wrists:

The most common hand forms used in *Yang* style barehand practice are the *Taiji* palm and the *Taiji* fist. The open palm hand form is done in two ways, depending on the style one is practicing. In one style, the little finger is pulled slightly back while the thumb is pressed forward (Figure 2-68). The hand should be cupped. The other open palm hand form is similar to the first except that the thumb is pulled back slightly

Figure 2-68. Taiji Palm with little finger back and thumb forward (太極掌一).

Figure 2-69. Taiji Palm with both thumb and little finger back (太極掌二).

instead of pushed forward (Figure 2-69). Here, the hands should be shaped as if you were holding a basketball with the palms, without the thumbs and little fingers touching the ball. In *Yang* style *Taijiquan* this hand form is called *Wa Shou* (Tile Hand, 瓦手) because it is curved like a Chinese roof tile. In both hand forms, the thumbs and little fingers are slightly tensed to restrict the *Qi* flow to these fingers and increase the

Figure 2-70. The Tai Chi fist.

flow to the middle fingers and palms.

The open palm hand form is classified as a *Yang* hand in *Taiji*. When palms are used to attack, the fingers are loosely extended and the wrists settled (dropped slightly) in order to allow the *Jin* to reach the palms and exit easily. It is said: "Settle the wrists, extend the fingers" (Appendix A-10).

The *Taiji* fist should be formed as if you were holding a Ping-Pong ball lightly in the center of the hand (Figure 2-70). When striking, the fist closes momentarily, but the fingers and palms are kept relaxed to allow the *Qi* to circulate. The fist hand form guides the energy back to the palm and is classified as a *Yin* hand in *Taiji*.

Elbows and Shoulders:

The *Taiji* classics say: "Sink the shoulders, drop the elbows" (Appendix A-10). There are several reasons for this - first, it allows the elbows and shoulders to be loose and the muscles relaxed. Second, dropping the elbows seals several vital cavities, such as the armpits. Third, when the elbows and shoulders are sunk, *Jin* can be effectively stored in the postures, as well as emitted naturally from the waist without being broken (see next chapter for a more detailed discussion). Fourth, dropped elbows and shoulders help to keep the postures stable and the mind more centered.

Head:

The head should be upright. It is said: "An insubstantial energy leads the head (upward)" (Appendix A-10). When your head is upright and feels suspended from above, your center will be firm and the Spirit of Vitality will be raised up. In addition, the eyes and mind should concentrate. It is said: "The eye gazes with concentrated Spirit" (Appendix A-10).

Chest:

It is said: "Hold the chest in, arc the back" (Appendix A-10).

Remember that *Yi* leads the *Qi*, so whenever you inhale, pull your chest in and arc your back to store *Jin* in the posture, and visualize as vividly as possible that you are storing *Yi* and *Qi*.

Waist, Hips, and Thighs:

The waist and hips are particularly important in *Taiji* martial applications. The waist is the steering wheel which is used to direct the neutralization of the enemy's attack and the emission of *Jin*. The waist must be relaxed and the hips should be as if sitting, so that the pelvis is level and the lower back straight. This will let your movements be agile and alive. As you move, your waist should generally stay the same distance from the floor - unnecessary up and down movement will disturb your root. The *Dan Tian* in the abdomen is the source of *Qi*. It must be stimulated in order to fill it up with *Qi* so that the abdomen is tight like a drum. However, the muscles in this area must be relaxed in order to pass the *Qi* which you have generated in the *Dan Tian* down to the Sea Bottom cavity, and then up the spine and out to the hands. The hips and thighs connect the waist to the legs where the *Jin* is generated. In order to pass this *Jin* to the waist, the hips and thighs must be relaxed and stable, otherwise the *Jin* will be broken and the *Qi* stagnant. In addition, if the hips and thighs are tight, the *Qi* generated in the *Dan Tian* will have difficulty reaching the legs. Thus, it is said: "Relax your waist and relax your thighs" (Appendix A-10).

Legs, Knees, and Feet:

The legs and knees must be loose and alive, then you can generate *Jin* from the tendons and sinews. The muscles should not be tensed, for this will obstruct the generation of *Jin*. However, the legs and knees cannot be completely loose and relaxed. They must be slightly tensed in order to keep your foundation stable. You should look loose but not be loose, look relaxed but not be relaxed.

When your weight is on the front foot, the rear leg should not be straightened, but should have a slight bend, and the front knee should generally not go past the front toe. The exception to this is when you are emitting *Jin*. In this case the knee may momentarily go past the toe, but should immediately pull back, and the rear leg may momentarily straighten, but should immediately bend again.

In *Taiji*, the weight is almost never distributed evenly on both legs. Rather, it is always more on one foot than the other, and it is always shifting from one foot to the other. Once you learn to use the muscles and tendons in your legs correctly, and learn the exchange of substantial and insubstantial, you will not lose your root, and will be able to generate *Jin* efficiently. Thus, it is said: "The knees look relaxed, but are not relaxed" (Appendix A-10).

The feet are the root of all the postures and the source of mobility. The feet must firmly stick to the ground. It is said: "Soles touch the ground" (or "Feet flat on the ground") (Appendix A-10). In order to do this, your *Yi* must be directed into the ground and the *Qi* must be able to reach the Bubbling Well cavity. It takes a great deal of practice to develop a good root, but gradually you will grasp the trick and your root will grow deeper and deeper.

In conclusion, the entire body must be relaxed, centered, stable, and comfortable, and should not lean forward or backward nor tilt to either side. It is said: "Postures should not be too little or too much (i.e. neither insufficient nor excessive). They (the postures) should seek to be centered and upright" (Appendix A-10). Every form must be continuous, smooth, and uniform, then the Spirit will be calm, the *Yi* concentrated, and the *Qi* will flow smoothly and naturally. Also: "Every form of every posture follows smoothly; no forcing, no opposition, the entire body is comfortable. Each form smooth" (Appendix A-10). Chang, San-Feng's *Taijiquan Treatise* says: "No part should be defective, no part should be deficient or excessive, no part should be disconnected" (Appendix A-1). *Yi, Qi, Jin*, the postures, top and bottom, inside and outside, front and back: all must act as one unit. When you reach this level, you will no doubt be a real *Taiji* expert.

2-5. How to Practice the Taijiquan Sequence

This chapter has discussed the two most basic aspects of *Taijiquan* practice: *Qi* and postures. Normally, it takes at least three years to learn to circulate *Qi* smoothly in coordination with the breathing and postures. You should then learn to transport *Qi*, and develop *Qi* balance. Even after you have accomplished this, there is still more to learn before you can be considered a proficient *Taiji* martial artist. You must learn how to strengthen your *Qi* through practice, you must develop a sense of having an enemy in front of you during the sequence, and lastly, you must learn how to train *Jin* during the sequence.

In *Taijiquan*, *Qi* plays a major role in *Jin*. When *Qi* is strong and full, then the *Jin* will also be strong. An important way to strengthen and extend your *Qi* is to **practice the sequence slower and slower**. If it usually takes 20 minutes to finish the entire sequence, increase the time to 25 minutes, then 30 minutes, and so on. Do not add any more breaths. Everything is the same except that every breath, which is used to lead the *Qi*, gets longer and longer. In order to do this you must be very calm and relaxed, and your *Qi* must be full like a drum or balloon, first in your abdomen, and later in your whole body. If you can extend a sequence which normally takes 20 minutes to one hour, your *Qi* will be very full and fluid, your mind calm, and the postures very relaxed. When you do the sequence at this speed, your pulse and heartbeat will slow down, and you will be in a self-hypnotic state. You will hardly notice your physical body, but instead will feel like a ball of energy.

Even when you can do the form very well, it may still be dead. To make it come alive you must **develop a sense of enemy**. When practicing the solo sequence, you must imagine that there is an enemy in front of you, and you must clearly "feel" his movements and his interaction with you. Your ability to visualize realistically will be greatly aided if you practice the techniques with a partner. There are times when you will not actually use visualizations, but every time you do the sequence your movement must be flavored with this knowledge of how you interact with an opponent. The more you practice with this imaginary enemy before you, the more realistic and useful your practice will be. If you practice with a very vivid sense of enemy, you will learn to apply your *Qi* and *Jin* naturally, and your whole Spirit will melt into the sequence. This is not unlike performing music. If one musician just plays the music, and the other plays it with his whole heart and mind, the two performances are as different as night and day. In one case the music is dead, while in the other it is alive and touches us.

If you don't know how to incorporate *Jin* into the forms, then even if you do the sequence for many years it will still be dead. In order for the sequence to be meaningful, *Jin* and technique must be combined. An important way to do this is to **practice fast *Taijiquan***. Once you can do the sequence of movements automatically, and can coordinate your breathing and *Qi* circulation with the movements, you should practice doing the form faster. Remember, if you ever get into a fight, things are likely to move pretty fast, so you have to be able to respond fast in order to defend yourself effectively. If you only practice slowly, then when you need to move fast your *Qi* will be broken, your postures unstable, and your *Yi* scattered. If any of this happens, you will not be able to use your *Jin* to fight. Therefore, once you have developed your *Qi* circulation you should practice the sequence faster until you can do it at fighting speed. Make sure you don't go too fast too soon, or you will sacrifice the essentials such as *Yi* concentration, *Qi* balance, breath coordination, and the storage of *Jin* in the postures. When doing fast *Taiji*, do not move at a uniform speed. Incorporate the pulsing movement of *Jin* so that you are responding appropriately to the actions of your imaginary enemy. It is difficult to develop the pulsing movement of *Jin* solely by doing the sequence, so you should also do *Jin* training either before or concurrently with the fast *Taiji*. This will be discussed further in Chapter 3.

Chapter 3
Jin

勁

3-1. Introduction

Jin training is a very important part of the Chinese martial arts, but there is almost nothing written on the subject in English, and very little even in Chinese. Many instructors have viewed the higher levels of *Jin* as a secret which should only be passed down to a few trusted students. Also, it is unfortunately the case that many instructors don't understand *Jin* very well themselves. It is a difficult subject to explain and, like the poetry and songs in the appendices, it is even harder to express in English. While the author's understanding of *Jin* is still incomplete, he feels it is better to publicize the available information to help the serious martial artist get on the right track, and to encourage further study and research. Information in this chapter is drawn from the available Chinese literature on the subject, oral instruction from the author's two *Shaolin* masters and three *Taiji* teachers, and from the author's research and discussion with his students. This chapter is not meant to be the final authority on the subject, but rather a catalyst to research. Rather than a monument, this chapter should serve as a stone generating ripples in the minds of the readers.

Many martial artists nowadays do not understand what *Jin* is, or think that it is trained in only a few particular styles. Some even brag that the style they have learned is the only style which has *Jin* training. In fact, almost all Oriental martial styles train *Jin*. The differences lie in the depth to which *Jin* is understood, in the different kinds of *Jin* trained, and in the range and characteristics of the emphasized *Jins*. For example, Tiger Claw style emphasizes hard and strong *Jin*, imitating the tiger's muscular strength; muscles predominate in most of the techniques. White Crane (白鶴), *Xingyi* (形意), and *Bagua* (八卦) are softer styles, and the muscles are used relatively less.

In *Taijiquan* and *Liu He Ba Fa* (六合八法), the softest styles, soft *Jin* is especially emphasized and muscle usage is cut down to a minimum. This often confuses people, and they ask: If the muscles are not used for fighting, where does the power to win the fight come from? Hopefully, once you have read this chapter you will know the answer, and will have grasped the key to the traditional Chinese martial arts.

The application of *Jin* brings us to a major difference between the Oriental martial arts and those of the West. Oriental martial arts traditionally emphasize the training of *Jin*, whereas this concept and training approach are relatively unknown in other parts of the world. In China, martial styles and martial artists are judged by their *Jin*. How deeply is *Jin* understood and how well is it applied? How strong and effective is it, and how is it coordinated with martial technique? When a martial artist performs his art without *Jin* it is called *Hua quan xiu tui* (花拳繡腿) which means "Flower fist and brocade leg." This is to scoff at the martial artist without *Jin* who is weak like a flower and soft like brocade. Like dancing, his art is beautiful but not useful. It is also said *Lian quan bu lian gong, dao lao yi chang kong* (練拳不練功，到老一場空) which means "Train *quan* and not *gong*, when you get old, all emptiness." This means that if a martial artist emphasizes only the beauty and smoothness of his forms and doesn't train his *Gong*, then when he gets old, he will have nothing. The *Gong* here means *Qigong*, 氣功, and refers to the cultivation of *Qi* and its coordination with *Jin* to develop the latter to its maximum, and to make the techniques effective and alive. Therefore, if a martial artist learns his art without training his *Qigong* and *Jin Gong*, 勁功, once he gets old the techniques he has learned will be useless, because he will have lost his muscular strength. The author is saddened to see that for the last thirty years *Jin Gong* has been widely ignored while the beauty of the art has been emphasized. Many of the martial artists today tend to train dance-like forms and acrobatic skills and ignore the major part of *Gongfu* training.

This unfortunate tendency is also common in *Taiji* society today. Since the great majority of people do *Taiji* for health, the martial aspect is being more and more ignored. An example of this is that most people only practice *Taiji* slowly. How can *Jin* be developed this way? How can martial applications be learned? When a person attacks you he will move fast and hard, so unless you have trained with speed and *Jin*, you will be unable to defend yourself.

Jin has been considered a secret transmission in *Taiji* society. This is so not only because it was not revealed to most students, but also because it cannot be passed down with words alone. *Jin* must be experienced. It is said that the master "passes down *Jin*." Once you feel *Jin* done by your master, you know what is meant and are able to work on it by yourself. Without an experienced master it is more difficult, but not impossible, to learn about *Jin*. There are general principles and training methods which an experienced martial artist can use to grasp the keys of this practice. If you read this chapter carefully and practice patiently and perseveringly, and remember to remain humble, to question and ponder, you will no doubt be able to learn *Jin* and become a real master.

Section 2 of this chapter will define *Jin* according to the author's best understanding. *Jin*, *Qi* and *Li* will be compared and contrasted, and the range of *Jin* will be explained. Section 3 will discuss the general theory of *Taiji Jin* and the keys to its generation. Section 4 will discuss the accumulation of *Jin* in your postures. Section 5 is a summary of the key points to *Taiji Jin*. Section 6 will explain the different kinds of *Jin* and offer exercises to help you discover and train your *Jin*. Finally, Section 7 will summarize the training methods which have been explained in the preceding sections.

3-2. General Definition of Jin

Before you can understand *Jin*, you must first understand *Li*. *Li*, which is defined as muscular strength, is usually visible as big muscles. It is considered "post-birth" energy because it goes through the cycle of increasing as you mature and then weakening as you grow old. Muscular *Li* can be long and slow, and can be used to push a car or hold a heavy object. When *Li* is used, the muscles are tensed and stiff.

Now let us define *Jin*. The Chinese dictionary gives two main meanings of *Jin*. The first is "strong, unyielding, muscular," and is usually applied to powerful, inanimate objects. For examples, *Jin Gong* (勁弓) means a strong bow, and *Jin Feng* (勁風) means a strong wind. It can also be applied to more abstract feelings of strength, as in *Jin Di* (勁敵) which means a strong enemy. These examples illustrate the first difference between *Jin* and *Li*. *Li* is explicit and is shown externally, while *Jin* is more implicit and internal - you must feel it to sense its strength. You can't tell the strength of a bow by looking at it, rather you must pull it to see if it has the potential to generate a lot of power. Once it releases an arrow, the strength of its *Jin* is shown by the power (*Li*) of the arrow. (For inanimate objects, *Li* refers to manifest strength or power). Another quality often associated with *Jin* is the feeling of a strong, pulsed, flow. An example is *Jin Feng* (a strong wind) - never steady, it moves this way and that, over and around obstacles, and when it surges, trees bend and houses are knocked down.

The second dictionary definition of *Jin* is *Qi-Li* (氣力)(or *Li-Qi*), which refers to muscles which are supported by *Qi*. Using only your muscles is considered *Li*. However, when you use your *Yi* (mind) and concentration to lead the muscles to do something, *Qi* will flow to where you are concentrating and enliven the muscles. This is considered *Jin*. The Chinese martial arts emphasize using *Yi* and concentration, so whenever *Jin* is mentioned in this book, it means *Qi-Li*.

There are many types of *Jin*, but the one thing they all have in common is that they all deal with the flow of energy, one aspect of which is *Qi*. The most obvious type of *Jin* is "manifest *Jin*," where you can see something happening, as when you push someone. Sensing another person's motion or energy is also considered a type of *Jin*. In fact, in the highest levels of the "sensing *Jin*" you actually sense the *Qi* flow of your opponent and, thereby know his intentions. These sensing *Jins* are enhanced by increasing the *Qi* flow to your skin. Many of the hand forms described in Chapter 2 are called *Jins* — they direct the *Qi* flow in particular ways, or rely on *Qi* support for use in martial techniques. In general, the higher the level of *Jin*, the more *Qi* and the less *Li* is used.

In the martial arts, it is said that *Jin* is not *Li*. This means that although you must use your muscles (*Li*) every time you move, *Jin* is more than just muscular strength. There are several different kinds of manifested *Jin*. When you rely primarily on muscular strength, but also use *Qi* and your concentrated mind, it is considered "hard" *Jin*. This kind of *Jin* is usually easily visible as tensed muscles. When muscle usage is reduced, and both *Qi* and muscles play equal roles in the *Jin*, it is called "soft-hard" *Jin*. When muscle usage is reduced to a minimum, and *Qi* plays the major role, it is called "soft *Jin*." Soft-hard *Jin*, and especially soft *Jin*, are usually expressed in a pulse. Soft *Jin* is often compared to a whip, which can express a great deal of force in a very short time, concentrated in a very small area. When you snap a whip, it stays loose as it transmits a wave or pulse of energy along its length to the tip. In the same way, when you use soft *Jin* your muscles stay relatively relaxed as you transmit a pulse of energy through your body. This is done with the tendons and the ends of the muscles, supported by *Qi*. A more detailed discussion of this will be given later in this section.

Most of the *Taiji Jins* are of the soft variety. The emission of *Jin* is a relatively short, smooth, and relaxed pulse of energy, without any angular changes in direction. The pulse can be long or short, near the body or at a distance. It can be a sudden contraction and expansion as you bounce the opponent away, or an even sharper "spasm" as you strike or break something. In all of this, *Jin* uses *Li*, because *Li* is necessary any time you move, but the muscles must be supported by *Qi*.

Figure 3-1 may help you understand the difference between *Jin* and *Li*. In this figure, the vertical coordinate represents the depth to which power can penetrate, and the horizontal coordinate represents the elapsed time. The areas under the curves represent the power generated for each curve. We assume that the areas under the curves are the same, i.e., the power generated for each curve is equal. In curve 1, the power is generated, reaches its maximum, stays at the maximum for the time t^1, and then drops to zero. Without *Qi*, this is a typical example of *Li* - muscular strength predominates and penetration is limited. With *Qi*, it is considered "hard" *Jin*. In curve 2, both muscles and *Qi* are involved, and the power is at its maximum for the shorter time t^2. Since the power generated is the same as with curve 1, the peak has to reach higher, which means there is greater penetration. In order to do this, the muscles must be relaxed to allow the *Qi* from either the local area or the *Dan Tian* to flow smoothly to support them. This is the general idea of "soft-hard" *Jin*. In curve 3, the time t^3 in which the power is generated is even shorter. The muscles must be extremely relaxed to generate and express this sharply penetrating power. Naturally, *Qi* plays the predominant role in this "soft" *Jin*. Curve 3 is typical of *Taiji Jin*. From the point of view of muscle usage, curve 1 is like a wooden staff, curve 2 is like a rattan staff, and curve 3 is like a whip. The wooden staff is stiff like tensed muscles, the rattan is more flexible, and the whip is soft, its power sharp and focused.

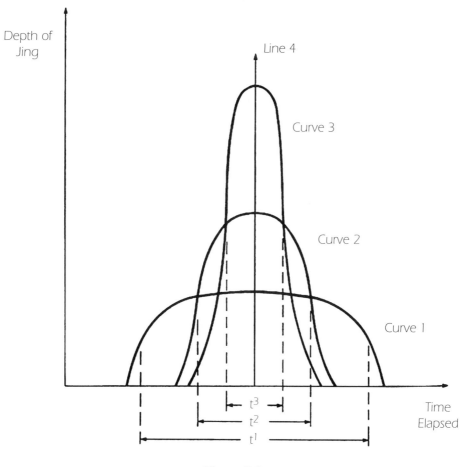

Figure 3-1.

Even curve 3, which is a very high level of power, is still not the highest power in the martial arts. As mentioned in the last chapter, this is when pure *Qi* is used, which can be represented by line 4. When a martial artist has reached this level, he can transport his *Qi* into his enemy's body through the acupuncture cavities to shock the organs and cause damage or death instantly. The time used is extremely short and the penetration is deeper than is possible with *Jin* or *Li.*

The Difference between Jin and Li

Li is said to derive from the bones and muscles. Jin comes from the tendons, and is supported by Qi which is generated either in the Dan Tian or the local area. Since the tendons are emphasized, the muscle fibers are able to be relaxed, allowing the *Qi* to flow through them and support them. If your force is derived from the bones, there is a strong tendency for you to resist and meet your opponent's force directly. When your force is derived from the tendons it is easier to be flexible and elusive, to disappear in front of the opponent's attack and to appear at his weak spot.

Li **has shape, while** *Jin* **has no shape or form**. This means that *Li* can be seen, but *Jin* must be felt. The storing of energy and the preparation for moves, as well as the actual emission of energy, can be more subtle with *Jin* because it is done with the body and *Dan Tian* rather than the arms. With *Li* the muscles of the arms and shoulders tend to be the source of energy, and this is more easily seen.

Li **is square, whereas** *Jin* **is round**. In Chinese, square means clumsy, stiff, stubborn, and straightforward; whereas round implies smooth, flexible, alive, and tricky. This means when *Li* is used, it is sluggish and stiff, whereas when *Jin* is used, it is smooth, agile and alive.

It is said that *Li* **is stagnant and** *Jin* **is fluid**. It is also said that *Li* is slow, but *Jin* is swift. Because *Li* emphasizes muscular contraction, the muscles are stiffer and respond more slowly. Since *Jin* is more relaxed it is easier to change direction. The actual emission of energy is more restrained and controlled, so you can be more subtle and can deal more easily with changes in the situation.

With *Li*, **power is diffuse, but the power of** *Jin* **is concentrated**. When using just the muscles, it is hard to concentrate the energy. When you train *Jin* you emphasize relaxation and moving from the center of your being. This allows you to concentrate all of your energy into a very small space and time.

It is said that *Li* **floats, but** *Jin* **is sunken**. This has two interpretations. First, when you use muscular strength you emphasize the arms and shoulders, and your movements tend to be angular and jerky. This makes it easier to lose your connection with the ground. With *Jin*, especially in *Taijiquan*, the arms and body are relaxed, and energy is derived from the waist, legs, and *Dan Tian*. When your attention is on your legs, it is easier to keep firmly in contact with the ground. Since your center and source of motion are more removed from the opponent than is the case with *Li*, it is easier to avoid throwing yourself at the opponent, which would break your root. A second interpretation of this saying is that with *Li* the power is more from the surface, while with *Jin* the power is more internal. That is, the tendons, from which *Jin* is derived, are relatively more internal than the muscles. After long training, the *Qi* which supports *Jin* comes from deep within the body.

Finally, it is said that *Li* **is dull, but** *Jin* **is sharp**. This implies that *Li*'s power stays on the surface while *Jin* penetrates deeply. Since the approach and the methods of training *Jin* are more refined and internal than is the case with *Li*, it is possible to be more precise in the application of force, and to have the force penetrate more deeply into the opponent.

The Range of Jin

The concept of *Jin* covers quite a wide range. As mentioned before, when muscles are used without any particular *Qi* support, the power generated is called *Li*. This is the most basic power, the post-birth strength which grows as you grow and reaches its maximum when the muscles have developed to their maximum. When you get older, the strength of the muscles lessens, and *Li* is lost. However, if you learn to concentrate your *Yi* (mind) on the muscles used, the *Qi* will be generated naturally in the local area, i.e., the muscles being used. *Qi* is the pre-birth energy which flows in the human body. When you concentrate your *Yi*, the *Qi* will naturally follow, invigorating the muscles being used and raising them to maximum energy. When this pre-birth energy is involved, the force produced is called *Jin*. If the muscles predominate, it is considered a low level of *Jin*. This energy, which still shows most of the characteristics of *Li*, is called *Ying Jin* (hard *Jin*, 硬勁). Tiger Claw is a typical example of a martial style which specializes in hard *Jin*.

External stylists frequently train their local *Qi* to support the muscles. This training can not only enable the muscles to express power more efficiently, but can also enable the *Qi*-filled muscles to resist blows without injury. The latter training is called "Iron Shirt" or "Golden Bell Cover."

If you know how to train your *Yi* to become stronger and stronger, your *Qi* will also become correspondingly stronger. In order to have this stronger *Qi* flow smoothly in support of the muscles, the muscles must be relaxed. The more the muscles are relaxed, the more easily the *Qi* can flow, allowing the muscles to do the job more efficiently. After many years of training, you will rely primarily on the ends of the muscles near the tendons, which allows the bulk of the muscle to stay relaxed and soft. In China it is not uncommon to see old men do feats of strength with apparently soft muscles. This is only possible after long years of *Jin* training which develops *Yi*, *Li*, and *Qi*. Such skills can grow with age, which makes it possible for an old man to successfully defend himself against a strong, young man. The main factor in such a victory remains, however, the ability to concentrate *Yi* and *Qi* sufficiently so that the muscles can reach maximum efficiency. You have probably experienced trying to push a heavy object that seemed immovable. If you stop for a moment, relax your muscles, and visualize the object moving, you will often find that you can now move. it. This is because *Qi* is now playing a greater role.

When *Qi* and the muscles are involved in equal amounts, the *Jin* is considered mid-level and is called *Ruan Ying Jin* (soft-hard *Jin*, 軟硬勁). This is considered a higher level of *Jin* expression than hard *Jin*, both in theory and technique. When using this *Jin*, the muscles are entirely relaxed to allow the *Qi* to flow. Right before the target is reached, the muscles are suddenly tensed to get the stored *Jin* out. Some martial styles specializing in this kind of *Jin* are White Crane, Snake, and Praying Mantis.

The next stage is to relax the muscles as much as possible. The more the muscles relax, the more the *Qi* can be used, allowing the tendons to take over control of the motion and keep it flowing smoothly. In order to emit power without relying on the muscles, the force is used in a pulse-like fashion. When this fluid, tendon-oriented *Jin* is the main source of power instead of the muscles, it is called *Ruan Jin* (soft *Jin*, 軟勁). It is considered the highest type of *Jin*, in regards to both theory and technique.

Taijiquan and Liu He Ba Fa are styles which use this kind of *Jin*.

However, the *Jin* just described is still of a low level if the supporting *Qi* is generated from the local area. For higher levels of *Jin* the *Qi* must be generated from the *Dan Tian*. When the *Qi* comes from the local area, the *Jin* is called *Wai Jin* (external *Jin*), and when the *Qi* is generated from the *Dan Tian*, it is called *Nei Jin* (internal *Jin*).

Some martial artists use a kind of "jerking power" and believe that it is *Jin*. This jerking power is only a part of *Jin*. It is considered *Wai Jin* because it relies upon locally generated *Qi* to reinforce its power. Even with external *Jin*, in order to develop maximum power you must still build the root in the feet, generate *Jin* from the legs, use the waist to control the *Jin*, and store power in the postures.

When a person trained in *Qi* development has achieved Small Circulation and Grand Circulation, he can use the *Qi* generated at the *Dan Tian*. The energy passes through the Sea Bottom cavity and is led to the feet, and it is also led up the spine and out to the hands. When *Qi* from the *Dan Tian* is used to support the tendons, the *Jin* can reach a high level. Naturally, the root, legs, waist, and postures must also be considered. This kind of *Jin* is called *Nei Jin* (internal *Jin*) and is the goal most *Taiji* martial artists aim for.

The final level of *Taiji* power is not *Jin*, but is using pure *Qi* to affect the enemy. This is the highest level of *Taijiquan* and is rarely seen today. When you train *Taiji* correctly for thirty years or more, your *Qi* will grow stronger and stronger. One day you may reach the point where you are able to pass your *Qi* out of your body or take in *Qi* from the enemy by touch. This is the highest level of *Dian Xue* (cavity press, 點穴). At this level, with a touch to an enemy's vital cavity you will be able to upset his body's energy balance or shock the organ which corresponds to the cavity.

We have seen that *Jin* can range from external to internal. In the spectrum of energy, one end is *Li* and the other is *Qi*. *Jin* is in the middle, using both *Li* and *Qi*. The *Jin* used by beginning *Shaolin* is generally the external variety which relies mostly on *Li* and local *Qi*. However, when a *Shaolin* martial artist reaches a high level of achievement, his *Jin* will tend to be softer and *Dan Tian Qi* will take the place of local *Qi*.

Taijiquan stresses the internal *Jin* first. The muscles are relaxed so that *Qi* from the *Dan Tian* can circulate and support the muscles. However, when a *Taiji* martial artist has reached a high level of internal *Jin*, he should also master external *Jin* to cover the entire range of *Jin* training. In Chinese martial society there is a saying: "*Shaolin* from hard to soft, *Taiji* from soft to hard — the approaches are different, but the goal is the same." For this reason section 6 of this chapter will include both hard and soft *Jins*.

3-3. General Theory of Taiji Jin

The last few sections have given you a general idea of *Jin*. In this section we will discuss the theory and important points of the soft *Taiji Jins*. The theory and emphasis of hard *Jins* and soft-hard *Jins* are somewhat different. If you are interested in these subjects, please refer to the book, ***The Essence of Shaolin White Crane***, by YMAA.

Categories of Jin

There are many ways to categorize *Jin*. To help you understand the *Jins* discussed in this volume, the author has organized them in the way shown in Table 3-1. The types of energy can be divided into two groups: sensing *Jin* (*Jue Jin*, 覺勁) and manifested *Jin* (*Xing Jin*, 形勁).

Sensing *Jin* can be divided into active sensing *Jin* and passive sensing *Jin*. Active sensing *Jin* is the ability to generate a strong *Qi* flow which, in coordination with your *Yi* and breath, can be led in a wave into the opponent's body. This pulsing *Qi* flow is usually used to support hand forms (see section 2-3) for either attacking or healing. In external styles, this *Qi* flow is coordinated with techniques such as grabbing or poking, in which case they are more properly classified as manifested *Jins*. In internal styles the *Qi* flow is harder to see since it is not combined with *Li*, and can usually only be felt. An example of this internal *Jin* is Graze Skin False Critical *Jin* (see next section).

Passive sensing *Jin* is the capability of perceiving the opponent's energy. For example, one of the passive sensing *Jins* is called "Listening *Jin*," in which you use your skin and Spirit to sense the opponent's energy. The advanced stage of this is called "Understanding *Jin*" where, upon listening to the opponent's energy, you understand his intention. It is confusing to Westerners to call the ability to listen to the opponent's *Jin* a form of *Jin*. It becomes clearer when you understand that listening to *Jin* is not entirely passive. You have to stick with the opponent and move with him, almost matching his moves. When he emits *Jin* you must be able to deal with it easily and comfortably, which demands a degree of skill, sensitivity, *Qi* flow, and the ability to use *Jin* in your own movements.

Manifested *Jin* can be broken down into active *Jin* which is called *Gong Jin* (Offensive *Jin*, 攻勁) or *Fa Jin* (Emitting *Jin*, 發勁), and passive *Jin* which is called *Shou Jin* (Defensive *Jin*, 守勁) or *Hua Jin* (Neutralizing *Jin*, 化勁).

Active *Jin* is considered *Yang*, and is the emitting of power from the body, usually for attack. *Yang Jin* can also be discriminated into pure *Yang Jin* (*Chun Yang Jin*, 純陽勁) or pure offense *Jin* (*Chun Gong Jin*, 純攻勁), and *Yang* with some *Yin Jin* (*Yang Zhong Dai Yin Jin*, 陽中帶陰勁) or offense with some defense (*Gong Zhong Dai Shou Jin*, 攻中帶守勁).

Passive *Jin* is considered *Yin* and deals with the ability to yield to, lead, and neutralize the opponent's *Jin*. *Yin Jin* is usually used for defense and is in turn divided into pure *Yin Jin* (*Chun Yin Jin*, 純陰勁) or pure defense *Jin* (*Chun Shou Jin*, 純守勁), and *Yin* with some *Yang Jin* (*Yin Zhong Dai Yang Jin*, 陰中帶陽勁) or defense with some offense *Jin* (*Shou Zhong Dai Gong Jin*, 守中帶攻勁). In addition, there is a type of *Jin* which is neither *Yin* nor *Yang* (*Fei Gong Fei Shou Jin*, 非攻非守勁), and is normally used for *Jin* training and raising the Spirit of Vitality.

Table 3-1.

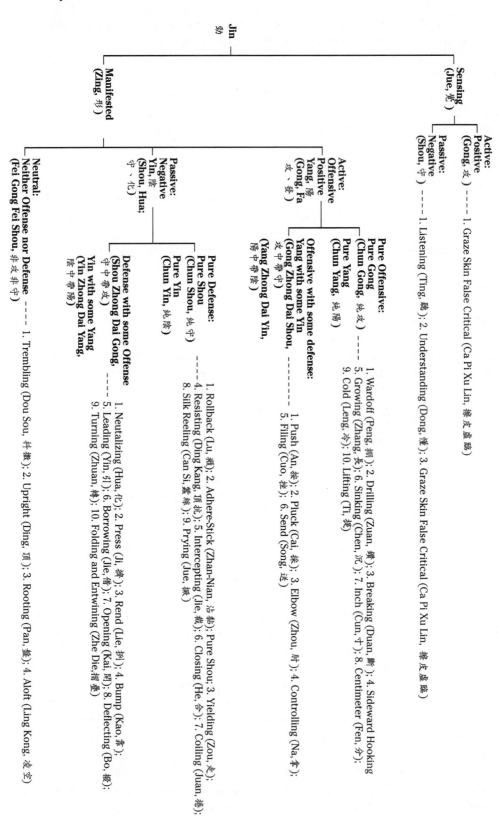

Jin
勁

Sensing
(Jue, 覺)

    Active:
    Positive
    (Gong, 攻) ---- 1. Listening (Ting, 聽); 2. Understanding (Dong, 懂); 3. Graze Skin False Critical (Ca Pi Xu Lin, 擦皮虛臨)

    Passive:
    Negative
    (Shou, 守) ---- 1. Graze Skin False Critical (Ca Pi Xu Lin, 擦皮虛臨)

Manifested
(Xing, 形)

    Active:
    Offensive
    Positive
    Yang, 陽
    (Gong, Fa
    攻、發)

        Pure Offensive:
        Pure Gong
        (Chun Gong, 純攻) ---- 1. Wardoff (Peng, 掤); 2. Drilling (Zuan, 鑽); 3. Breaking (Duan, 斷); 4. Sideward Hooking
        5. Growing (Zhang, 長); 6. Sinking (Chen, 沉); 7. Inch (Cun, 寸); 8. Centimeter (Fen, 分);
        9. Cold (Leng, 冷); 10. Lifting (Ti, 提)

        Pure Yang
        (Chun Yang, 純陽)

        Offensive with some defense:
        Yang with some Yin
        (Gong Zhong Dai Shou,
        攻中帶守,
        Yang Zhong Dai Yin,
        陽中帶陰)** ---- 1. Push (An, 按); 2. Pluck (Cai, 採); 3. Elbow (Zhou, 肘); 4. Controlling (Na, 拿);
        5. Filing (Cuo, 挫); 6. Send (Song, 送)

    Passive:
    Negative
    Yin, 陰
    (Shou, Hua;
    守、化)

        Pure Defense:
        Pure Shou
        (Chun Shou, 純守) ---- 1. Rollback (Lu, 捋); 2. Adhere-Stick (Zhan-Nian, 沾黏); Pure Shou: 3. Yielding (Zou, 走);
        4. Resisting (Ding Kang, 頂抗); 5. Intercepting (Jie, 截); 6. Closing (He, 合); 7. Coiling (Juan, 捲);
        8. Silk Reeling (Can Si, 纏絲); 9. Prying (Jue, 撅)

        Pure Yin
        (Chun Yin, 純陰)

        Defense with some Offense
        (Shou Zhong Dai Gong,
        守中帶攻)
        Yin with some Yang
        (Yin Zhong Dai Yang,
        陰中帶陽)** ---- 1. Neutralizing (Hua, 化); 2. Press (Ji, 擠); 3. Rend (Lie, 挒); 4. Bump (Kao, 靠);
        5. Leading (Yin, 引); 6. Borrowing (Jie, 借); 7. Opening (Kai, 開); 8. Deflecting (Bo, 撥);
        9. Turning (Zhuan, 轉); 10. Folding and Entwining (Zhe Die, 摺疊)

    Neutral:
    Neither Offense nor Defense
    (Fei Gong Fei Shou, 非攻非守) ---- 1. Trembling (Dou Sou, 抖擻); 2. Upright (Ding, 頂); 3. Rooting (Pan, 盤); 4. Aloft (Ling Kong, 凌空)

Almost every *Jin* classified above can again be divided into near (*Jin*, 近) or far (*Yuan*, 遠) *Jin*, and long (*Chang*, 長) or short (*Duan*, 短) *Jin*. Near or far refers to the distance from your body that the technique is done. Long and short refers to the distance that your hands travel while actually emitting energy. Long *Jin* normally requires more time to emit and is used to bounce the opponent away without hurting him. Short *Jin* is normally sharp and fast and is usually used to injure or kill the enemy. Both long and short *Jin* can be done either near to the body or at a distance.

Jin and Yi

Jin and *Yi* (mind, will) are probably the most important keys to success in *Taiji*. You should understand that if there is no *Yi*, the *Qi* will be stagnant, and if the *Qi* is stagnant, then it cannot be applied to *Jin*. Therefore, **wherever the *Jin* is to go, the *Yi* must go first, and the *Qi* will naturally follow**. When you use your *Yi* to lead *Qi* in support of *Jin*, the *Yi* should always be further than the *Jin*, otherwise the *Jin* will be restrained and not completely expressed. This is best done by maintaining a sense of having an enemy in front of you. Imagination is the key here. If you only put your attention on your hands, the energy will have difficulty reaching them. When you put your mind on an imaginary opponent in front of you, the *Qi* will more easily reach your hands and pass through them. Therefore, it is said: "*Jin* (can be) broken, mind not broken" (Appendix A-3).

Jin, Muscles, and Qi

As mentioned in the previous sections, almost all *Jins* require using the muscles. Muscles play the major role in hard *Jins*, a lesser role in soft-hard *Jins*, and a relatively small role in the soft, pulsing *Jins* used in *Taiji*. As the role of the muscles decreases, the role of the tendons gradually increases, and the expression of *Jin* changes from the slower muscular version to a fast pulse strike.

In Chinese martial arts, all of these *Jins* require *Qi* support. How does this *Qi* support work? Let us digress for a moment and consider several factors affecting muscular strength. Most people know that we use only a portion of the capacity of our brains. The same situation prevails with our muscles, for we use only about forty percent of their capacity. There are several ways to increase this percentage. The will (*Yi*) is important, sometimes to an astounding degree. When people are confronted with emergencies, they can sometimes do things far beyond their normal, everyday ability. When you decide you MUST do something, your body follows your will. Another factor which increases muscular strength is concentration. You have probably already observed that concentration increases the effectiveness of your exertion. When all of your mind is on what you are doing, and none of your attention is distracted by extraneous matters, all of your efforts and energy can be focused on one target.

Wherever your mind is, your *Qi* is. Once you have developed Grand Circulation, you should be able to move your *Qi* from your *Dan Tian* to any part of your body. When you put your mind (*Yi*) on a particular technique, for example a push, your *Qi* will go to the muscles being used. The stronger your imagination is, and the greater your concentration, the more the *Qi* will flow and fill the active muscles. This energizes them the way a surge of electricity brings an electric motor to life. It will also increase the flexibility and elasticity of the muscles and make them feel inflated and capable of resisting a punch or generating a lot of power. The more disciplined your will and concentration are, the more effectively you can move your *Qi*. Western science reports that concentration generates a chemical reaction in your muscles that increases the power much more than usual. I do not doubt that this is caused by the *Qi* that this concentration of the mind brings.

When you have trained your *Qi* and muscles, you will find that you can generate the same power with less muscle tissue. You will be able to relax your muscles, which will let the *Qi* flow even more easily. The main bulk of the muscle fiber, which is in the middle of the muscle, will relax, and you will rely more on the ends of the muscles near the tendons. It is said that *Taiji Jin* comes from the tendons. This demands great skill and control on your part. To move in the loose, fluid, almost boneless fashion of *Taiji*, you have to be able to place every part of your body in the correct relationship to each other part, the ground, and the target. The force generated by your legs is bounced off the floor and coiled through your body. The force cannot pass through any kinks or around any corners. Tension in any muscle will hinder the flow of force and *Qi*. The tendons, which are the connectors of the parts of the body, transmit the force from each part to the next. The ends of the muscles use the minimum amount of effort to keep the flow going and direct it.

Most people have parts or patches of their bodies that they are not really aware of. This may show up as, for example, a place on your thigh where you are not as sensitive as elsewhere. This means that your Spirit (*Shen*) doesn't normally reach everywhere in your body, and consequently, your Mind and *Qi* don't go there either. You must train your Spirit, Mind, and *Qi* to fill your body like a thread passing through every part of the pearl with the nine-curved passage. Only when your consciousness and *Qi* suffuse your muscles can you really control them and your movement.

There are several ways you can fill your body with Spirit and *Qi* after you have completed Grand Circulation. You can visualize that you are a balloon being inflated with energy and awareness. However, the main way that *Taiji* uses is doing the sequence slowly. When the form is done at a slow, steady pace you have a chance to pay attention to the movement of *Qi* without sacrificing anything else. Accumulate *Qi* in your *Dan Tian* and coordinate it with your movements through your breathing.

You will always use some muscular energy (*Li*) when you move. It is impossible to move without it. Similarly, there is always *Qi* moving in your body. It only stops when you die, or a part of your body dies. An external stylist can develop *Qi* to strengthen his movements, but it is local *Qi*, developed in the arms and shoulders. Since this kind of movement uses tensed muscles, the *Qi* from the *Dan Tian* cannot reach the arms. An external style of *Gongfu* like Tiger style uses this kind of local *Qi* to greatly strengthen the hands and arms. A soft-hard style like White Crane uses this local *Qi* to strengthen the arms, and balances it with attention to the waist and *Dan Tian*. Most of the time, however, the *Qi* in the *Dan Tian* is not circulated up the back and into the arms. External styles exhale to get the air out, and coordinate it with the energy, but it is stiff energy, not the soft energy of *Taiji*.

Jin and the Feet

One of the most important factors in expressing *Jin* through the palms and fingers is the root. Your root is like the root of a tree: without it, the tree will fall. If you do not have a good root when you apply techniques, they will float and have no power. It is like trying to push a heavy object while wearing roller skates. The root of *Jin* and all techniques comes from the feet. The feet must be stable. To develop this stability **you must visualize your root a few inches beneath your feet**. If your thought is only on your feet, the connection between your feet and the ground is broken and the root will not grow deep into the ground. Almost all Chinese martial styles train root at the very beginning of the martial training. Without a good root, all the techniques are weak and ineffective. Thus, it is said: "The root is in the feet" (Appendix A-1); and also: "The foot and sole are the third chancellor" (Appendix A-5A). The classics also mention: "(If) the Bubbling Well (*Yongquan* cavity) has no root, the waist has no master, (then) you can try hard to learn until you almost die, you will still not succeed" (Appendix A-14).

Jin and the Legs

Once a martial artist has his root, the next step is to look to the legs. The legs are the main source of *Jin*, so investigate carefully how they bend and straighten to generate energy. When emitting *Jin*, you must balance force and counterforce with your legs. The rear leg usually generates the force and transmits the counterforce back into the ground. Without balancing the force. through your legs in this way, it is difficult to generate power. This should be apparent to anyone who has ever tried to push a car or other heavy object. Therefore, it is said: "(power is) generated from the legs" (Appendix A-l).

Jin, the Waist, and the Spine

Once you have a firm root and can generate *Jin*, the next step is to control and direct it. The most important factor in the application of *Jin* is probably the waist and spine. It is said: "The waist and the spine are the first master" (Appendix A-5A). Also: "(*Jin*) controlled by the waist" (Appendix A-1). It is also said: "The mind is the order, the *Qi* is the message flag, and the waist is the banner....The *Qi* is like a cartwheel, the

Figure 3-2

waist is like an axle" (Appendix A-3). All of these sayings emphasize that it is the movement of the waist which directs the force being emitted by the whole body.

The Song of the Thirteen Postures says: "The tailbone is central and upright" (Appendix A-15). To have the tailbone central means that the body is balanced above it, not leaning to either side or to the front or rear. To have the tailbone upright means that most people must pull their buttocks in. When this is done, the lower spine loses its usual curve and straightens out. Most people do this when they sit down. When this is done properly, the bowl that is the pelvis is even, instead of tilting forward (Figure 3-2). This lets the organs in the abdomen rest comfortably within and on top of the pelvis instead of hang out the front. Proper posture eases strain on the organs, and allows the motion of your breathing to gently massage them. Also, when the lower spine is straight it is easier to transmit force through it, and you have a better chance of avoiding strain.

For a number of *Jins*, a jerking movement of the waist is needed to lead the *Jin* from the legs to the hands. In order for the *Jin* to be integrated and strong, there should not be any stagnation in the waist area. When *Jin* is stagnant, its strength will be broken or reduced. Therefore, the timing must be right and, above all, the waist must be relaxed. It is said: "Relax your waist and relax your thighs" (Appendix A-10).

Another important reason for the emphasis on the waist is that it is the location of the *Dan Tian*, which is the original source of the *Qi* used in *Taijiquan*. The *Qi* generated there is led to the legs, as well as up the spine, out the arms, and to the palms and fingers to support *Jin*. Without this *Qi*, the *Jin* will remain at a low level, perhaps supported only by local *Qi*. The spine acts not only as a conduit for the *Qi*, but also as a storage area. After long and correct training, *Qi* will accumulate in the marrow of the spine. Thus, it is said: "Power is emitted from the spine" and "(The mind) leads the *Qi* flowing back and forth, adhering to the back, then condensing into the spine" (Appendix A-3); "In every movement the heart (mind) remains on the waist, the abdomen is relaxed and clear, and *Qi* rises up" (Appendix A-15).

Jin and the Hands

In *Taiji* fighting, the palms and fingers are extremely important. These are the parts which most often touch the enemy. From this touch, a *Taiji* martial artist will sense or feel the enemy's power, understand his intention, neutralize his power, and finally counterattack with *Jin*. Therefore it is said: "The root is in the feet, (power is) generated from the legs, controlled by the waist and expressed by the fingers" (Appendix A-1). It is also said: "The fingers and palms are the second chancellor" (Appendix A-5A).

Jin and Sound

Almost all martial styles use different sounds in practice and fighting. There are two sounds, Hen and Ha, which are especially important in *Taijiquan*. These sounds serve several purposes. During a fight, a loud sound can scare the enemy and disturb his concentration. Yelling can raise your fighting spirit and help increase your concentration. **A yell can raise the Spirit of Vitality to the maximum, and help the *Qi* move quickly and smoothly**. The Hen sound, when made on the inhale, is *Yin* and can help to store *Qi* and condense it in the bone marrow. When the Hen sound is made on the exhale it is a mixture of *Yin* and *Yang*, and will help you emit energy while still conserving some to support the defense. The exhaled Ha sound is extremely *Yang*, and can be used to raise the *Jin* to its maximum. It is said: "Grasp and hold the *Dan Tian* to train internal *Gongfu*. Hen, Ha, two *Qi*'s are marvelous and infinite" (Appendix A-13). It is also said: "The throat is the second master" (Appendix A-5A).

Balancing Jin

Balancing your *Jin* includes balancing your *Yi*, *Qi*, and posture. When *Yi* is balanced, the mind is centered and able to handle all directions. Upward and downward must also be balanced or you will lose your root. It is said: "Up and down, forward and backward, left and right, it's all the same. All of this is done with the mind, not externally. If there is a top, there is a bottom; if there is a front, there is a back; if there is a left, there is a right..." (Appendix A-1). Furthermore, *Yi* is the leader of *Qi*, and if the *Qi* is not balanced, then the force and counterforce relationships in the body are not balanced. Finally, you should use the balanced *Qi* to support the tendons and muscles when expressing *Jin* externally. With this balance and support the *Jin* can reach its maximum. It is like when you push a heavy object - you need to mobilize your *Yi*, and to direct power backward in order to push the object forward. It is said: "(When you) wish the foot to go forward, you must push off from the rear (foot)" (Appendix A-14). Thus, it is understood that **first you must have backward, then you can have forward. You must have downward first, then you can have upward**.

Lastly, balancing your posture is extremely important. In regards to *Jin*, this means balancing the forces inside your body: If you want to push forward with a certain amount of force, you must push backwards with exactly the same amount of force in order to counterbalance it. You also need to balance the upward and downward forces, otherwise you will lose your root and push yourself up and away from your opponent.

It is also necessary to balance forces in your two hands. When your posture is balanced the body is centered and stable, and the root is firm. This allows the power from the legs to be fully transmitted to the hands. Thus it is said: "When standing, the body must be centered, calm and comfortable, so you can handle the eight directions" (Appendix A-3). It is also said: "Postures should not be too little or too much (i.e., insufficient or excessive). They (the postures) should seek to be centered and upright" (Appendix A-10). **If you can grasp the key of balancing your Yi, Qi, and posture, you will have gained the secret of pushing hands and Taiji fighting**.

Jin's Substantial and Insubstantial

A very important part of *Taiji* fighting strategy is the principle of substantial and insubstantial. It applies to *Jin*, postures, and techniques. In the *Taiji* diagram, where one side is heavy the other side is light, and where one side is light the other side is heavy. In *Taijiquan*, this means that where your opponent attacks (is substantial), you yield and neutralize (are insubstantial). The other side of this is that you attack (are substantial) where the opponent is weak (insubstantial). To attack where the opponent is strong is called "mutual resistance." This is inefficient, and contrary to *Taiji* principles. You must train so that you automatically meet the opponent's substantial (attacking) *Jin* with an insubstantial (defensive) *Jin*. As you defend, you may simultaneously counterattack, or set yourself and your opponent up for your counterattack.

Offensively, attack where the opponent is weak. This does not mean where he is insubstantial, because you would be falling into a trap. Instead, attack when he is switching from a substantial *Jin* to an insubstantial, or vice versa. If you catch him just before he emits an offensive *Jin*, or just after he has emitted *Jin* and before he can switch to a defensive *Jin*, you will be certain to succeed.

Substantial and insubstantial *Jins* are determined by your *Yi* (mind). When you sense the opponent's intention, your *Yi* can change your actions from substantial to insubstantial, and vice versa. To facilitate this, **do not emit all your energy. Rather, conserve some so that you can easily switch from one technique to another**.

If you can switch easily and quickly between attack and defense, you will be able to conceal your techniques so that the opponent cannot understand what you are doing. When you look like you are attacking, you should not necessarily be attacking, and when you look like you are withdrawing, you should not necessarily be withdrawing. Your opponent should not be able to sense your intention from how you express your *Jin*. This is called skillfully exchanging substantial and insubstantial. After a great deal of practice with many partners, your opponent will not be able to understand what you are doing, whether you are attacking or feinting, resisting or neutralizing, and he will not perceive how you are going to attack. This is reflected in the saying: "false-false, real-real, real-false, and false-real."

When you fight against an opponent who has mastered Listening,

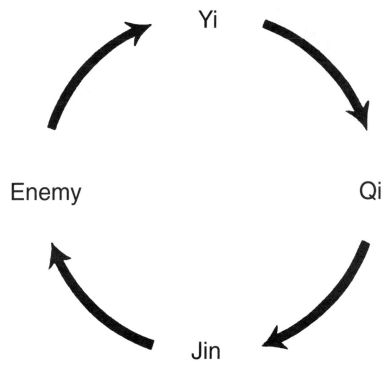

Figure 3-3

Understanding, and Neutralizing *Jins*, it is very hard to apply your *Jin* to his body. This is because when you store your *Jin* for an attack, your opponent has already sensed your intention. Therefore, you must **shorten the time of *Jin* storage**. If you can store *Jin* in a very short time, and can skillfully exchange substantial and insubstantial, you will be hard to beat. Therefore, the classics say: "Suddenly disappear, suddenly appear. When there is pressure on the left, the left becomes insubstantial; when there is pressure on the right, the right becomes insubstantial. Looking upward it seems to get higher and higher; looking downward it seems to get deeper and deeper. When (the opponent) advances, it seems longer and longer; when (the opponent) retreats, it becomes more and more urgent. A feather cannot be added and a fly cannot land. The opponent does not know me, but I know the opponent. A hero has no equal because of all of this" (Appendix A-2).

3-4. Accumulating Jin in the Postures

Before you can emit *Jin* you must first generate or accumulate it. This is done through your *Yi*, *Qi*, and posture. *Yi* must lead the way. *Jin* is generated through understanding the enemy's intention and neutralizing his power. When you neutralize the opponent's attack you may see an opportunity or the possibility of an opportunity to counterattack. As you sense the opponent's intention, your *Yi* is stored and raised. As shown in Figure 3-3, your *Yi* will then lead you to store *Qi* in your *Dan Tian*. This perception of the opponent's attack will help you to coil your

Figure 3-4

body as you evade in such a way as to accumulate power in the posture. Therefore, as you neutralize the opponent's attack your mind draws in to accumulate energy, and your *Qi* and body follow. Remember: **the mind leads, the *Qi* follows the mind, and the body follows the *Qi*.** *Jin* accumulation is facilitated by inhaling. If you inhale with the Hen sound it will help the *Qi* condense deep into the bones. **When you know how to store *Yi*, *Qi*, and postural energy, you have built the foundation of *Jin*.**

Many people know how to store *Yi* and *Qi*, but don't know how to use their posture correctly. Everything must be done correctly and coordinated properly at the right time; a lapse in any area will cut down the effect of the whole effort. *Jin* can be stored in the bend of a joint, a twist of the body, the arcing of the chest, and even in the sinking of the body. In this section we will discuss the ways in which *Jin* is stored in the body. Once you understand this, you should be able to discover the best ways to store energy for the different *Jins* discussed in the next section.

Legs

The legs are the major source of manifested *Jin*, and control how much *Jin* is emitted. In order to function effectively, the feet must be firmly rooted; the posture of the legs, especially the knees, must be correct; and the thighs must be relaxed. *Jin* can be stored in either the front or the rear leg. When the front leg is used to store *Jin*, it is bent (Figure 3-4), and when the *Jin* is expressed, the leg pushes forward to generate the backward *Jin* (Figure 3-5). When *Jin* is stored for this backward *Jin*, the front knee should not pass over the toes. Backward *Jin* is usually used to pull the opponent or to neutralize his attacking *Jin*.

When *Jin* is stored in the rear leg, the knee is also bent (Figure 3-6). When *Jin* is emitted, the knee straightens out, though not completely (Figure 3-7), as the leg pushes downward. When the *Jin* is emitted to its maximum, the front knee may pass the toes for an instant. In order to prevent your opponent from using this over extension, your knee must

Figure 3-5

Figure 3-6

Figure 3-7

immediately bounce back to restore the body's stability and equilibrium. It is just like a spring which stretches out to emit force, but immediately moves back to its equilibrium position. Similarly, the rear leg may straighten out at the final moment of expressing your *Jin* but it must move back to its bent and relaxed state right after the *Jin* reaches its maximum. Naturally, most of the time you won't be making an all-out attack, and so the front knee will not pass over the front toes and the rear leg will remain slightly bent.

Figure 3-8

Figure 3-9

Figure 3-10

The push by the front leg or rear leg builds the root from which the *Jin* is bounced backward or forward. The *Jin* passes through the thigh and hip, joins the *Jin* from the waist, and reaches the final target.

The legs can also generate sideward *Jin*. In this case the legs generate a twisting force (Figure 3-8) which is enhanced by the twisting force of the waist before it is expressed through the hands.

Hips

The hips do not usually play an important role in generating *Jin* in *Taiji*. However, in some styles such as wrestling and *Judo*, where the body or hips are generally in contact with the opponent, they take most of the credit for the techniques. A twist or bounce of the hips, in coordination with *Jin* from the legs, can pull up the opponent's root or bounce him away (Figures 3-9 and 3-10). In *Taijiquan*, the hips are sometimes used to absorb the opponent's force and then rebound it. In all of these, the hips move in one direction to accumulate *Jin*, and in the opposite direction to emit it.

Figure 3-11   Figure 3-12

A sitting down motion of the hips can be very useful in coordinating your upper body and legs when emitting *Jin*. When you shift your weight from the rear foot to the front foot, sit down slightly as you sink into the front foot (Figures 3-11 and 3-12). This sitting and sinking motion is precisely coordinated with the emitting of *Jin* through the hands. It may feel as if you are shifting weight or force from the rear leg, and bouncing it off your front foot into your hands. The hips are also used in a sinking motion to prevent the opponent from pulling you up. Remember, the *Jin* generated in the legs passes through the hips, so they must be relaxed and flexible.

Waist

The waist is the most important part of the body in the expression of *Jin*. The success of almost every *Jin* depends upon the right movement and timing of the waist. It directs *Jin* to the right place at the right time, and controls the degree of force used and the way that *Jin* is expressed. The waist can also generate *Jin* and add it to the force which has been generated by the legs. Your posture must be correct so that the waist can move freely to transmit both the *Jin* of the legs as well as its own. Usually this is done with a jerking motion - a sudden pulse which transmits force from the legs to the shoulders and on to the hands. Every part of the body moves together, with the waist in the center coordinating it all. The waist usually moves first in one direction to accumulate the *Jin* (Figure 3-13), and then in the other to emit it (Figure 3-14). The accumulation phase can be done very subtly, so that it is part of the motion of neutralization or of stepping toward the opponent. The waist can also fold in to store *Jin* (Figure 3-15) and straighten out to emit

Figure 3-13

Figure 3-14

Figure 3-15

Jin in coordination with the *Jin* of the legs (Figure 3-16). Usually this is done when both hands are used simultaneously for attack. The emitting motion is done suddenly, in exact coordination with your shoulders, as you match the force of action toward the opponent with the reaction into your root. You can experiment with generating *Jin* from the waist by jerking your waist while standing on roller skates. This will give you a feel for generating force only with the waist, and also demonstrates how necessary a firm root is.

Figure 3-16

Figure 3-17

Figure 3-18

Torso

The torso is also an important place to store *Jin*, and once you catch the knack of it your *Jin* will gain in strength. You store *Jin* by hollowing the chest as if embracing someone, and by arcing the back slightly (Figure 3-17). The body acts like a bent bow, ready to shoot an arrow. When emitting *Jin*, the body straightens and the chest opens up (Figure 3-18). The classics refer to this, saying "Hold the chest in, arc the back" (Appendix A-10). This arcing of the back and hollowing of the chest, along with condensing *Qi* in the spine is referred to as closing. Straightening the body and emitting energy is known as opening (See Appendix A-12, Fifth saying). There may also be some rotation of the body, which acts like an axle in that it rotates to neutralize the opponent's *Jin* or to emit *Jin* sidewards or forward. When this is done, the chest is held in as the waist rotates the body to accumulate *Jin* (Figure 3-19), and then the chest opens up as the *Jin* is expressed (Figure 3-20).

Figure 3-19

Figure 3-20

Figure 3-21

Figure 3-22

Shoulders

The shoulders can move in a number of ways to accumulate and emit *Jin*. Sometimes a shoulder moves back first to store *Jin* (Figure 3-21), and then jerks forward with the waist as the root to emit the *Jin* (Figure 3-22). Sometimes the shoulder curves inward toward the chest to store *Jin* (Figure 3-23), and then opens outward to emit *Jin* (Figure 3-24). To get a feel for the role of the shoulders, sit on a table so your feet are off the ground, and then move your shoulder back and jerk it forward. Experiment with different techniques. Then try curving your

Figure 3-23

Figure 3-24

Figure 3-25

shoulders in and arcing your chest to accumulate *Jin*, and then suddenly opening as you emit the force. Also try rolling your shoulder outward to accumulate force, then closing your shoulders in to compress this force, and then expanding your shoulders as you emit the force directly forward. This last movement is used in Press and in Brush Knee and Step Forward. If you experiment this way, you should be able to easily understand the principle of using the shoulder to store and emit *Jin*.

When you do not have a good root or cannot use the waist, you can still generate some *Jin* and express it with the arms and shoulders alone. Naturally, this *Jin* generation is local and will not be as strong as the *Jin* generated from the legs and controlled by the waist. When the *Jin* is generated locally, the shoulder acts like the legs and generates the *Jin*, and the elbow acts like the waist and directs and controls the expression of the *Jin*. In this case the root is in the waist.

Some *Jins* are used to lift the opponent and destroy his root, such as in Embrace Tiger, Return to the Mountain. In this case the shoulders are lowered to store *Jin* (Figure 3-25) and raised slightly as you lift the opponent (Figure 3-26).

Figure 3-26

Figure 3-27

Elbows

The elbow usually bends to store *Jin* in the arm (Figure 3-27), and straightens to direct its *Jin* and the *Jin* of the whole body out to the hand (Figure 3-28). Thus it is said: "Find the straight in the curved; accumulate, then emit" (Appendix A-3). When you emit *Jin*, the elbow must remain sunken. This not only seals several vital areas but also increases your stability and your control of the *Jin*. This is analogous to sinking the waist when it is being used to direct the *Jin*. Since your elbow directs the *Jin*, its movement and position will strongly influence a number of *Jins*, especially Adhere-Stick, Coiling, Silk Reeling, and Rotation. When you know how to store *Jin* in your elbow and how to use your elbow to lead the *Jin* effectively, you have learned the important knack of expressing local *Jin*.

Figure 3-28

Figure 3-29

In some cases, the elbow will accumulate *Jin* when straight, and bend to emit. This occurs when pulling the opponent, or when pulling your hand out of his grasp.

Wrists

The wrist has three ways of storing *Jin*. The first posture is used to store *Jin* when it is going to be expressed forward, the second when you are going to pull your hand back, and the third is for when the *Jin* is going to be expressed in coiling, drilling, rotating, and silk reeling. In the first case the hand is curved slightly while the wrist may be either straight or bent slightly (Figure 3-29). When *Jin* is expressed forward, the bottom of the palm will snap forward as the fingers straighten and rise (Figure 3-30). This is what is meant by "Settle the wrists, extend the fingers" (Appendix A-10). The second *Jin* is commonly used to withdraw from the opponent's hooking or grabbing. The hand form in this case is just the reverse of the last one. When storing, the wrist is settled (Figure 3-31), and when *Jin* is expressed the hand and fingers are curved in and the wrist is straightened. In order to escape from the opponent's grasp, the wrist must be jerked back quickly. The rotation of the wrist is important (Figures 3-32 and 3-33). Experience will show the best direction and timing for various situations.

Figure 3-30

Figure 3-31

Figure 3-32

Figure 3-33

In coiling, drilling, rotating, and silk reeling, the whole arm is generally turning, including the wrist. It may move in a short, sharp motion as
you pull out of the opponent's grasp or drill forward in a strike, or it may
be a longer motion with no particular focus point as you coil around
your opponent. In either case the storing and emitting of *Jin* is
expressed not by the bending, but rather by the rotating of the wrist.
This turning of the wrist is also involved when the focus of energy is
moved to various parts of the arm, or when energy is stored in the body
and brought out as needed.

Hands

The fingers are the furthest point to which your *Jin* travels inside your body. From them the *Qi* can flow to a weapon or to the opponent's body. With your hands you can sense the opponent's *Jin* and even his intention, or you can grasp and control him. If your finger position is wrong, you may not be able to store *Jin* and *Qi* effectively.

Taijiquan's most common hand form is called *Wa Shou* (Tile hand)(see section 2-4), in which the fingers and palm are curved in the shape of a Chinese roof tile. The hand flattens and the fingers straighten out when *Jin* is expressed, and the hand curves in to store *Jin* or to grasp something. When the fingers are extended while emitting *Jin*, the muscles of the hand are tensed somewhat to hold the *Qi* in the hand so that it may be coordinated with the *Jin*. When grabbing, the muscles are also tensed slightly to keep the *Qi* in. When accumulating energy, the hand is curved in slightly and relaxed so that the *Qi* can move back to the body.

From the above discussion you can see that there are three major places where you can generate *Jin* — the legs, waist, and shoulders. A number of other places, such as the torso, elbows, hands, wrists, and hips can store *Jin*, however it is difficult to generate *Jin* by using these places alone. Although the legs, waist, and shoulders can generate *Jin* independently, their *Jins* will still be weak unless they are coordinated with each other. To express *Jin* strongly and effectively, you must first generate *Jin* in your rooted legs, combine it with the *Jin* of the waist, where the combined flow is controlled, and route this flow through the shoulder. The shoulder adds its own *Jin*, and makes any adjustments necessary to express the total *Jin* out the arm.

The most common difficulty beginners have in coordinating these three places is the timing. When emitting *Jin*, the legs, waist, and shoulder move right after each other, without a break. When there is a lag between two parts, the *Jin* is broken, and the technique will be weak. In order to connect these three *Jins*, you need to use other places such as the chest and elbows, where *Jin* can be stored in the postures. For example, when you pass your *Jin* from your leg to your waist, your hips must be loose and relaxed, and they must be in the best position to store and emit their own *Jin*, as well as lead the leg *Jin* to the waist. In the same way, to connect the waist *Jin* to the shoulders, your chest and back must be in the correct posture, otherwise, the *Jin* will be weak or even broken. It is said: "The root is in the feet, (power is) generated from the legs, controlled by the waist and expressed by the fingers. From the feet to the legs to the waist must be integrated, and one unified *Qi*" (Appendix A-1). It also discussed in the Five Key Words: "Fourth saying: *Jin* is integrated. The entire body's *Jin*, (when) trained, becomes one family (one unit). Distinguish clearly insubstantial and substantial. Emitting *Jin* must have root and origin. *Jin* begins at the foot's root, is controlled by the waist, expressed by the fingers, emitted by the spine and back..." (Appendix A-12).

3-5. The Key Points of Taiji Jin

First, Jin is integrated.

It is said: "*Jin* is integrated; The entire body's *Jin*, (when) trained, becomes one family. (one unit)...Emitting *Jin* must have root and origin. *Jin* begins at the foot's root, is controlled by the waist, expressed by the fingers, emitted by the spine and back" (Appendix A-12). It is also said: "From the feet to the legs to the waist must be integrated, and one unified *Qi*. When moving forward or backward, you can then catch the opportunity and gain the superior position" (Appendix A-1).

Second, Qi supports Jin.

In order to use *Jin*, you must be able to circulate *Qi* at will throughout your body. With *Qi* suffusing your muscles, they will be more efficient and responsive to your will. You must learn to move so as not to interfere with the flow of your *Qi*. As your mind leads the *Qi*, so your *Qi* leads the body. After a great deal of training, your *Qi* will come from the *Dan Tian* naturally, and flow deeply within your bones.

Third, the Spirit of Vitality enlivens the Jin.

When the Spirit of Vitality is raised, the *Qi* will be highly stimulated and able to move faster, stronger, and more naturally to support the *Jin*. The Hen and Ha sounds can condense the *Qi* deep into the bones and help to raise the Spirit of Vitality. "(If) the Spirit of Vitality (*Jing-Shen*) can be raised, then (there is) no delay or heaviness (clumsiness). That means the head is suspended" (Appendix A-3).

Fourth, Jin is balanced.

Every action has a reaction. When you emit force in one direction, there is a counterforce in the opposite direction. These must be carefully balanced not only in your posture, but also in your mind (*Yi*) and *Qi* flow. This will keep your body centered and stable, and your root firm.

Fifth, Jin must be accumulated before it can be emitted.

Emitting *Jin* is like shooting an arrow from a bow - you must draw the bow first. This is done in your posture by coiling your body, hollowing your chest, and slightly arcing your back. You must vividly visualize yourself drawing your body's total energy inward, compressing and coiling it like a spring.

Sixth, when Jin is used, the body is relaxed.

To enable *Qi* to circulate smoothly and support *Jin*, the muscles must be relaxed. This allows *Qi* from the *Dan Tian* to reach and support them. The tendons should be used to transmit force so that it springs through the limbs. It is said: "When emitting *Jin*, be calm and relaxed, concentrated in one direction" (Appendix A-3).

Seventh, soft Taiji Jin is emitted in a pulse.

The ends of the muscles connected to the tendons play the major role in generating soft *Jin*, and the tendons transmit it through the body. This power is best expressed in a pulsed, whip-like motion, rather than in a long, sustained motion.

Eighth, your Jin should be mysterious to the opponent.

Insubstantial and substantial strategy should be used skillfully in order to confuse the opponent. The time used to accumulate *Jin* should be as short as possible, so that you don't telegraph your intention.

Ninth, Jin is not a form or technique, it is a way of expressing power.

Each *Jin* is a different manner of expressing power, and can be used in many different techniques. Also, most techniques use several different *Jins*.

3-6. The Different Jins and Their Applications

Jin can be expressed by the hands, elbows, shoulders, hips, knees, legs, or even the body itself. *Taijiquan* emphasizes the upper limbs and the body, and uses the legs and feet as secondary weapons. In this section we will discuss the major areas first, and then the secondary areas.

As mentioned before, excluding leg and foot *Jins*, there are more than forty different kinds of *Jin*. They can be distinguished into sensing *Jins* and manifested *Jins*. Sensing *Jins* include passive sensing *Jins*, which are the ability to sense the opponent's power, and active sensing *Jins*, which are the ability to move *Qi* into or out of another person's body. Manifested *Jins* visibly exhibit the use of force and can also be divided into *Yang Jins* or offensive *Jins* (*Gong Jin*, 攻勁), *Yin Jins* or defensive *Jins* (*Shou Jin*, 守勁), and Neutral *Jins* or neither *Yin* nor *Yang Jins* (*Fei Gong Fei Shou Jin*, 非攻非守勁)(Table 3-1). Because offensive *Jins* usually emit force onto the opponent's body, they are also called Emitting *Jins* (*Fa Jin*). Defensive *Jins* usually neutralize the opponent's power, and thus are generally called Neutralizing *Jins* (*Hua Jin*, 化勁).

Offensive *Jins* can be subdivided into pure offensive *Jins* and attack with some defense *Jins* (*Gong Zhong Dai Shou Jin*, 攻中帶守勁). The first is strongly *Yang* and can be represented by three solid lines ($\equiv$). The second is also *Yang*, but with some *Yin*, and can be represented by two solid lines and one broken line ($\equiv$, $\equiv$, or $\equiv$).

Defensive *Jins* can also be subdivided. First there are purely defensive *Jins* which are extremely *Yin* and are characterized by three broken lines ($\equiv$). Then there is defense with some attack *Jins* (*Shou Zhong Dai Gong Jin*, 守中帶攻勁). These are *Yin* but have some *Yang* and can be represented by two broken lines and one solid line ($\equiv$, $\equiv$, or $\equiv$). Almost every *Jin*, both offensive and defensive, can be used as a hard or soft *Jin*, long or short *Jin*.

In this next section we will list some important precautions which the beginner to *Jin* training should observe, and then list and explain all the different *Jins*. Sensing *Jins* will be discussed first, and then manifested *Jins*. Manifested *Jins* will be divided into active *Jins*, passive *Jins*, and neutral *Jins*. Active *Jins* will be subdivided into pure offensive *Jins*, and offense with some defense *Jins*. Similarly, passive *Jins* will be divided into purely defensive *Jins* and defense with some offense *Jins*.

In the discussions, the basic theory of each *Jin* will be explained and training methods will be given, along with examples drawn from the *Taijiquan* sequence and pushing hands. Many of the concepts are advanced, so if you are a beginner and are having difficulty understanding them, don't give up hope. Select a few basic techniques and keep working on them, slowly adding new ones when you are ready. Remember: the most important key to learning is perseverance.

Before you start to study, you should know that many *Jins* are mixtures of two or more other *Jins*. For example, Growing *Jin* is a mixture of Controlling, Neutralizing, Resisting, Drilling, and Coiling *Jins*. Before you can understand a complex *Jin* like this you must first learn the simpler ones. Second, you should understand that when most *Jins* are used they are usually coordinated with other *Jins*, either to set up the opponent or to enhance the *Jin* being applied. For example, in pushing hands, you must use Yielding, Neutralizing, and Leading *Jins* first before you can apply Controlling *Jin*. Third, some of the *Jins* are very similar to others, and you may find it difficult to differentiate between them. However, if you persevere in your practice and pondering, and continue to humbly seek the answer, you will eventually come to understand them.

Precautions for Beginners to Jin Training

1. When you generate Jin, do not hold it in the body.

If you hold your energy in, and restrict its passage through your body, you can injure yourself. Knowing how to generate *Jin* is like knowing how to start a car. If you do not know how to control the car or the generated power, it can be very dangerous for you. With a car you must know how to use the steering wheel, and with *Jin* you must know how to use your waist. It is very common for beginners to get strains and injuries, especially in the waist, or in joints, particularly the shoulders, elbows, and wrists. This is most likely to happen when you haven't learned how to use your waist to control and transmit the *Jin* to your hands or legs, or when some part of your body is tight and is restricting the smooth passage of the *Jin*. *Jin* is usually emitted in a sudden, but smooth, jerking motion. If your stomach muscles are tight, this jerking motion will stress them, and sometimes cause strains or pulls. More seriously, if the generated *Jin* is strong it can damage the internal organs. It is for this reason that most Chinese martial arts masters will not teach *Jin* to beginning students until they know that their martial knowledge, in addition to their morality and personality, have reached a certain level.

It is sometimes desirable when emitting *Jin* to hold some of the energy in the body, and not emit all of it. This should not be encouraged in beginners. If energy stagnates in the body, the internal organs can be damaged. If *Jin* is held in a joint, the joint muscles, ligaments, and tissue can be damaged. Only when you understand *Jin* well, and can control it skillfully, should you start to hold part of it in. At that time you will find that it is often desirable to retain part of your *Jin* for tactical reasons, e.g., to counterattack, or to defend against a counterattack.

It is not uncommon for people to injure their joints when they can generate a great deal of *Jin* but do not know how to tense the muscles when the *Jin* reaches the hand or foot. When *Jin* reaches the end of the limb, it keeps on going and continues to exert a pull on the joints. At this time the muscles must be tensed slightly for a second to prevent injury to the joints.

In external styles, it is very common to use a belt to hold the stomach in and prevent injury. This is seldom seen in *Taiji*, because the abdomen must be completely relaxed in order to generate *Qi* in the *Dan Tian* and circulate it around the body. If this area is held tightly, the *Qi* will not be generated naturally and may stagnate. Therefore, in the first few years of *Taiji* training, soft *Jins* are practiced in which none of the energy is restrained. Soft and long range training is emphasized, and the *Jin* is transmitted completely out. Only after you have mastered this should you learn to hold in *Jin* for fast and short range *Jins*.

In external styles, the approach is different. Usually hard *Jins* are trained first, and short *Jin* is emphasized at the same time as long *Jin*. Local *Qi* is used to support the *Jin*, and *Dan Tian Qi* is not absolutely necessary. A belt is usually necessary to prevent waist injury. Once you have approached a high level of *Jin*, you will then turn to the soft *Jin* training and a belt will not be necessary. Naturally, *Dan Tian Qi* also becomes important at this stage. Thus it is said: **internal styles from soft to hard, and external styles hard to soft. The approaches are different but the principles and goal are the same.**

2. From Soft to Hard, Easy to Difficult, and Slow to Fast.

It is very common for a beginner to look high and walk low. That is, he has high expectations and looks to the highest goal, but he is lazy in his training. This frequently causes injury and deviation from the right path. Before you put too much time and effort into the more difficult techniques, you should understand the easier ones. Therefore, you should start with the soft, easy, and slow. Only after you have mastered these should you go on to the harder techniques. If you follow this general rule, you will avoid most injuries.

3. If you have stopped training for a while, go slow.

If you stop training for a while, and then start again, you should take it slow and easy. Experienced martial artists sometimes injure themselves when they forget this. When you take a long break from practice, the muscles which you built up in coordination with the *Jin* weaken. However, your knowledge of how to generate *Jin* does not decrease. When you do a hard technique, the muscles will still be able to generate a lot of force, but they may have lost just enough of their edge so that they cannot fully control the force. This puts a lot of strain on the joints and ligaments, particularly the elbows, shoulders, and knees. Therefore, after a break you should take it easy and let your muscles rebuild their strength.

4. Do not practice just before or after a meal.

You should not practice *Jin* when you are hungry or right after a meal. Hunger will make your mind scattered and a full stomach will cause pain in the waist when you jerk.

5. Do not practice when you are in a bad temper.

When you are in a bad mood, your *Yi* is stimulated, and the *Qi* will not be condensed and controlled. When this *Qi* is used in *Jin*, it can go astray and harm you. As a matter of fact, whenever you are in a bad temper you should not build up or circulate your *Qi*.

6. Do not practice right after drinking alcohol.

As with meditation, you should not practice after drinking. When you drink, your *Qi* is floating and your mind is not clear. Under these circumstances, *Qi* circulation may be harmful.

Table 3-2: Taiji Jins (太極勁)

I. Sensing Jins (Jue Jin, 覺勁): 108
    1. Ting Jin (Listening Jin) 聽勁, 108
    2. Dong Jin (Understanding Jin) 懂勁, 109
    3. Ca Pi Xu Lin Jin (Graze Skin False Critical Jin) 擦皮虛臨勁, 110

II. Manifested Jins (Xian Jin, 顯勁): 111
A. Offensive (Yang) Jins (Gong Jin, Yang Jin, 攻勁、陽勁): 111
    a. Purely Offensive (Yang) Jins (Chun Gong, Chun Yang Jins, 純攻、純陽勁): 111
        1. Peng Jin (Wardoff Jin) 掤勁, 111
        2. Zuan Jin (Drilling Jin) 鑽勁, 115
        3. Duan Jin (Breaking Jin) 斷勁, 118
        4. Heng. Jin (Sideward Hooking Jin) 橫勁, 119
        5. Zhang Jin (Growing Jin) 長勁, 120
        6. Chen Jin (Sinking Jin) 沉勁, 121
        7. Cun Jin (Inch Jin) 寸勁, 122
        8. Fen Jin (Centimeter Jin) 分勁, 124
        9. Leng Jin (Cold Jin) 冷勁, 124
        10. Ti Jin (Lifting Jin) 提勁, 125

I. Sensing Jins (Jue Jin, 覺勁):

1. Ting Jin (Listening Jin) 聽勁

Listening *Jin* is not done with the ears, but rather with the skin. You use your sense of touch to pay very close attention to the opponent's motion and energy. This skin listening capability is generally obtained from training Adhere-Stick (*Zhan Nian*, 沾黏) *Jin*, and from paying careful attention during Pushing Hands. After much practice you develop a sense for precisely what it feels like to have the opponent try each particular technique, and what it feels like when you do a technique on him.

Listening is done with the skin of the entire body. Any part of your body may be touched or attacked during a fight, and almost any part may be used for an attack. For example, if your chest is pressed by your opponent, you must be able to listen to this press, understand it, and react with yielding, neutralizing, or other defensive strategy. Offensively, many parts of the body can be used for attack when the fight opportunity occurs. For example, your hip can be a very powerful weapon for hitting or bouncing the enemy away. However, regardless which technique you use, success is largely determined by how well you can sense the opponent's energy and choose the right timing for offense or defense.

There are three places where listening is particularly important. The first place is the forearm, the second is the palm, and the third is the soles of the feet. The forearm is usually the first part of the body to come in contact with the enemy when you are attacked. It is very important to build up the capability of listening on the forearm. If you can accurately sense the opponent's *Jin* from the first touch, you can neutralize it, and then continue your control of the situation by using Adhere-Stick and other *Jins*.

When Adhere-Stick *Jin* is applied, the palm and the forearm are equally important. They are not used only for defensive sensing (listening), but also for offensive sensing. When you attack your enemy, he will generally react with a block, neutralization, or yielding in any one of a number of ways. When this happens, you must keep listening alertly to understand his further intention. Without this listening, your attack is blind, and it is likely to be nullified or countered. Good Listening *Jin* can help you to direct your offensive *Jin* in the right direction and apply it at the right time. The better your listening *Jin* is, the better you can understand your opponent's *Jin*. If you can sense the enemy's intention before his *Jin* is emitted, you will be able to defend with certainty. The highest Listening *Jin* is demonstrated when Borrowing *Jin* (*Jie Jin*, 借勁)is used by a master. In Borrowing *Jin*, Listening *Jin* is the key to success. The reader can refer to the Borrowing *Jin* section for details.

The third place which is considered important in Listening *Jin* is the soles of the feet. The feet are your root, without which all your techniques would float and be useless. You should always listen to the exchange of energy between your feet and the ground. To build up Listening *Jin* in your feet is to build up your root and develop your balance. The more you can feel your root, the more stable you will be.

The best way to train Listening *Jin* is through pushing hands practice. In pushing hands, you first learn Adhere-Stick *Jin*. Practice following the opponent, not letting go and not separating from him. The more automatically you can do this, the more easily you can pay attention to the opponent instead of yourself. The *Taiji* ball is sometimes used for building up Listening *Jin*. The reader should refer to Chapter 3 of the second volume for pushing hands and *Taiji* ball training.

2. Dong Jin (Understanding Jin) 懂勁

Dong Jin comes from practicing Adhere-Stick (*Zhan Nian*, 沾黏) *Jin* and Listening (*Ting*, 聽) *Jin*. As a matter of fact, Listening *Jin* and Understanding *Jin* cannot be separated in practice, because you must listen before you can understand. If you cannot listen to and understand the opponent, you are blind to him. When you listen, your *Yi* must be wholly concentrated on listening and understanding. If your mind is scattered, you will not be able to understand your opponent's intention and you will miss the purpose of listening. As is the case with Listening *Jin*, *Dong Jin* has two aspects, one for defense and the other for offense. Defensive Understanding *Jin* is the capability of understanding the opponent's offensive intention. Offensive Understanding *Jin* is just the reverse. It is the capability of understanding the opponent's defensive ability and intention when you are attacking him. If you lack this double-sided understanding, you will not be able to skillfully change your strategy and *Jin* from substantial to insubstantial and vice versa.

When you practice adhering, sticking, and listening for a long time, you will gradually be able to understand with just a light touch what the opponent is going to do. The greater your understanding, the less of a hint you will need in order to know where, when, and how the attack is coming, and the more easily you will be able to defend yourself. But it takes a long time. Wang, Zong-Yue said: "After you have mastered techniques, then you can gradually grasp what 'Understanding *Jin* (*Dong Jin*)' means. From 'Understanding *Jin*' you gradually approach enlightenment (spiritual understanding) of your opponent's intention. However, without a great deal of study over a long time, you cannot suddenly grasp this spiritual understanding of your opponent." He also said: "To adhere means to yield. To yield means to adhere. *Yin* not separate from *Yang*. *Yang* not separate from *Yin*. *Yin* and *Yang* mutually cooperate, (understanding this) is 'Understanding *Jin*.' After Understanding *Jin*, the more practice, the more refinement. Silently learn, then ponder; gradually you will approach your heart's desire" (Appendix A-2).

Before you achieve *Dong Jin*, it is easy to resist, to lose balance, to lose contact with the enemy, or to use force against force. When you almost have *Dong Jin* you will still have trouble with broken *Qi*, tightness, and with leaning forward or backward. Practice until you can listen accurately, then you will know when to use power and when not to, when to be *Yin* (insubstantial) or *Yang* (substantial). The highest level of *Dong Jin* is when you understand the opponent's intentions before he moves. Thus, it is said: "Light, agile, and alive, seek *Dong Jin* (to understand *Jin*); *Yin* and *Yang* cooperate mutually without the fault of stagnation" (Appendix A-11).

Understanding *Jin* is best trained through pushing hands. Pay very close attention to what your skin feels. The more you practice, the more you will be able to tell by feel what the opponent is doing or even what he is planning.

3. Ca Pi Xu Lin Jin (Graze Skin False Critical Jin) 擦皮虛臨勁

This *Jin* is probably the hardest *Jin* to understand and practice. *Ca Pi* in Chinese means to lightly rub the skin or to graze the skin. Xu means false and not real. *Lin* means critical. *Xu Lin* refers to the feeling of standing precariously on the edge of a cliff. In *Taijiquan* and some other internal Chinese martial arts, this *Jin* is the highest art and skill. *Ca Pi Xu Lin Jin* is the capability of sensing and understanding the opponent's energy (*Qi*) pattern with only a touch or even with just being near him. When two skillful internal martial artists are fighting, *Qi* in the bodies of both fighters is stimulated to the highest level. *Qi* is vital in the application of *Jin*. Usually, *Yi* leads *Qi* to support *Jin*. If you can sense the opponent's *Qi* flow before it is shown in *Jin*, you should be able to recognize the opponent's *Yi* and intention. Therefore, by sensing the opponent's *Qi*, you know his intentions even before his *Jin* is emitted. The two master fighters will seem to the average observer to be doing very little. However, they may in fact be maneuvering through repeated attacks and counterattacks on a very subtle level which seldom reaches visibility.

The highest level of Graze Skin False Critical *Jin* can be both active and passive. Usually, if you are able to sense the opponent's *Qi*, you should be able to pass *Qi* into him or drain it out in order to shock his internal organs. To do this you must be able to understand his *Qi* pattern with a touch, or even without touching. The passive aspect of this *Jin* is the ability to sense the opponent's intention, and resist his *Qi* attacks. When this kind of battle is occurring, the participants are probably not even aware of their bodies, but instead are putting their whole attention into the flow and exchange of energy. It is unlikely that anyone in today's martial society has reached this level, and so unfortunately the training methods are probably lost.

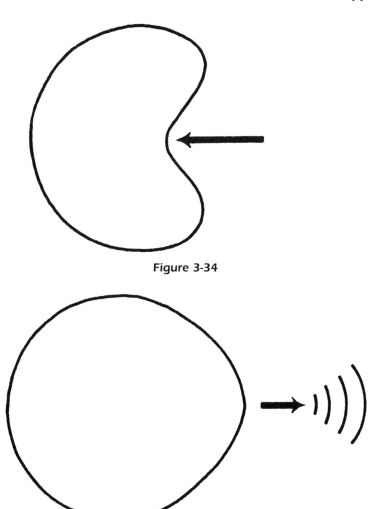

Figure 3-34

Figure 3-35

II. Manifested Jins (Xian Jin, 顯勁):

A. Offensive (Yang) Jins (Gong Jin, Yang Jin, 攻勁、陽勁):

a. Purely Offensive (Yang) Jins (Chun Gong, Chun Yang Jins, 純攻、純陽勁):

1. Peng Jin (Wardoff Jin) 掤勁

Wardoff *Jin* is a strong *Yang Jin* that is used offensively even in defense. In principle, it behaves like a large rubber ball—when pressure is applied it compresses (Figure 3-34), and when a certain point is reached it bounces the outside force away (Figure 3-35). The opponent's force is often directed upward, as you lift his attack the way water lifts a boat. This *Jin* is often emitted at maximum strength in coordination with the sound Ha. It may be done at all ranges, and is often

Figure 3-36

Figure 3-37

Figure 3-38

used to bounce the opponent away. This application is forceful, but not directly destructive.

Defensively, this *Jin* absorbs the opponent's attack and then bounces him away. In this application, your forearm does not generally come into contact with the opponent's body, but instead functions through his attacking arm. Specifically, you absorb some of the opponent's force either at the very beginning or at the end of his attack, and give the force back to him through his stiff arms (also read Borrowing *Jin*).

Wardoff is commonly used against a punch, in which case it directs the attack upward and seals the arm (Figure 3-36).

Offensively, Wardoff is used as a strike, most often to the opponent's chest or arm. When this *Jin* is used to attack the chest, some other neutralization is usually used first in order to set up the attack. For example, if the opponent attacks with a right punch, you may deflect with your left hand (Figure 3-37) and strike his chest with your right forearm (Figure 3-38).

Figure 3-39

Figure 3-40

Figure 3-41

When this *Jin* is used to attack the opponent's arm, his attack must be neutralized downward and sealed first. For example, when the opponent attacks with a right punch, deflect his attack to the right and down with your right arm (Figure 3-39). Then step behind his right leg with your left, while your left arm covers his right arm and then attacks forward (Figure 3-40).

In order to bounce the opponent away, you must first destroy his root to upset his stability and balance. This is done by directing the force of your Wardoff slightly upward (Figure 3-41) or sideward (Figure 3-42). Your body must be sunken in order to build up your own root, stability, and upward power. Wardoff is sometimes done as a sort of double technique. First, apply a small push to the opponent, or deflect his attack and lead him to an unbalanced position. If he

| Figure 3-42 | Figure 3-43 |

rises up a little and his root becomes unstable you should immediately apply a second, stronger push to knock him away. If, on the other hand, he resists and pushes forward, withdraw slightly and lead his momentum upward. As soon as you succeed in leading him, immediately emit your force to knock him away.

As with most of these techniques, muscular force will predominate in the beginning, but as you gain skill the reliance on muscles will lessen and you will do these techniques with arms that are more and more relaxed. Indeed, you will find that you cannot really do these techniques well with tensed muscles because this interferes with accurate sensing and precise control.

There are several ways to train Wardoff *Jin*. A good way is to use a bag, first a light one, and later heavier ones. You can practice striking with the Wardoff, and you can practice pushing. To do the latter, you can place your forearm against the bag and push it slightly to get it moving. "Catch" the bag on your forearm as soon as it starts to move toward you, and immediately bounce it away: You can swing the bag and "catch" it near the end of its swing and bounce it, or move the bag around in circles and use Wardoff to redirect it sharply away from you.

You can also practice Wardoff on a partner. When you do this, it is best for the person being pushed to protect his chest with his forearms to prevent injury (Figure 3-43). Another exercise is for one person to stand in the Wardoff position, and the other to push the extended forearm with both hands in a somewhat stiff-armed fashion (Figure 3-44). The first person either absorbs some of the force, directs it into his root, and

Figure 3-44

Figure 3-45

Figure 3-46

then bounces it back, or else emits force just as the other person is about to push.

When doing Wardoff, the body must be centered and stable, and your *Yi* of attacking must be further than the target. *Yi*, *Qi*, and *Jin* must be balanced between the attacking arm, the other arm, and the rear foot.

2. Zuan Jin (Drilling Jin) 鑽勁

Drilling *Jin* is an offensive *Jin* which twists as it penetrates. When your hand touches the opponent's body, your arm and hand rotate clockwise (Figures 3-45 and 3-46) or counterclockwise (Figures 3-47 and 3-48) in a screwing motion, which makes the power penetrate more deeply than with a regular attack. The power, which is generated by turning the waist and shoulder, is usually directed forward, although it can also be used sideward. The fist, finger, or knuckle are usually used for attack, frequently against vital cavities. The muscles must be tensed somewhat to direct the *Jin* and to insure

Figure 3-47

Figure 3-48

Figure 3-49

that it penetrates, and also to protect the hand against injury. Also, your *Yi* must be concentrated inside his body in the organ or cavity being attacked. Drilling *Jin* is also occasionally used to pull your arm out of the opponent's grasp. Here too the shoulder and waist are the source of the *Jin*.

Because Drilling *Jin* is used in both external and internal styles, many training methods have been developed. One of the common ways used in external styles is to drill your fist or knuckle into a bucket of *mung* beans. (*Mung* beans are used because of their medicinal properties.) With practice you will be able to drill deeper and deeper. Later, sand can be used in place of beans. Punching bags are also popularly used for drilling training. Start with your fist or knuckles touching the bag lightly (Figure 3-49). Suddenly generate the *Jin* from the waist and shoulder and drill your hand forward to bounce the

Figure 3-50

Figure 3-51

Figure 3-52

bag away (Figure 3-50). *Taiji* uses less muscle than external styles, so the training approach is different. One method uses a thick layer of soft material, for example tissue paper, on a table (Figure 3-51). The fist is pushed down with a screwing motion (Figure 3-52). The muscles should be relaxed as the *Yi* strives to extend the *Jin* to the surface of the table. When you can bounce the *Jin* off the table, increase the thickness of the material. The thicker the material is, the greater the drilling power required. It is important to also do this exercise horizontally.

Figure 3-53

3. Duan Jin (Breaking Jin) 斷勁

Breaking *Jin* is used for breaking the opponent's bones or joints. Forward Breaking *Jin* is commonly used to break ribs, and sideward or downward Breaking *Jin* is used to break limbs. The *Yi* is concentrated slightly beyond the target (see Figure 3-53). This is different from the penetrating Drilling *Jin*, where the *Yi* is concentrated deep in the organ being attacked. If you have ever chopped wood you should understand how to use this *Jin*. When you are chopping a branch, if you concentrate and aim a bit beyond the branch you should have little trouble chopping through it. Also, if just before the axe reaches the wood you suddenly increase your speed and jerk the power out, you will find that you can cut the branch without using much power.

In breaking, when the *Qi* and *Jin* reach the target the muscles must be tensed so that all the power is expended in the target. In *Taijiquan*, the time that you are tensed is kept as short as possible. This allows you to remain relaxed and make your breaking *Jin* sharper and more concentrated. A great deal of speed must be developed. Once the target is hit, the speed stops, but the *Yi* continues on through. It is important that the *Yi* be focused only slightly beyond the target. If you focus too far beyond the target, your *Jin* will pass uselessly through it. There is also a danger of injuring yourself. Because you normally tense your muscles only a short distance before the focus point, if the focus is too far beyond the target you will be relaxed when you hit. This will allow the power to bounce back to you and injure your arm or fist.

Many training methods are used both in the external and the internal styles. The most common way to train sideward Breaking *Jin* for use on the opponent's elbow is with a wooden rod about an inch and a half in diameter. Hold one end in one hand, fix the other end so that it cannot move, and hit it with your hand or forearm (Figure 3-54). Some people train with branches on trees. In the beginning, wrap the rod or branch with cloth to avoid injuring your arm. When applying

Figure 3-54

Jin, the root must be firm. The power is generated from the legs, and guided by the waist onto the target. (See also the section on Sideward Hooking *Jin*.) Punching bags are also used, especially for training forward breaking *Jin*. To break ribs your *Yi* must be centered a little past the ribs, so aim your techniques a few inches inside the bag. Remember, *Yi* is the most important factor in breaking.

4. Heng Jin (Sideward Hooking Jin) 橫勁

Heng Jin, which is called *Gua Jin* (挂勁) in external styles, is a hooking strike. A typical example in the *Taiji* sequence is Strike the Tiger. The *Jin* which is generated in the leg goes up the spine and coils outward, swinging the fist or elbow to strike the enemy from the side. This *Jin* is similar to Turning *Jin (Zhuan Jin,* 轉勁). Both use the same principles of coiling and *Qi* generation, but Hooking *Jin* is used for striking, whereas Turning *Jin* is used for defense. Also, Sideward Hooking *Jin* is done in a more explosive and destructive fashion, with your fist snapping back after striking. Your body is relaxed while you approach the target, and then suddenly all of your force penetrates the opponent's body. Turning *Jin* is used to turn the opponent's offensive *Jin*, therefore its motion is extended and continuous. A typical example of Turning *Jin* in the *Taiji* sequence is Wave Hands in Clouds. To train *Heng Jin*, first work on the coordination of your whole body, using a minimum of force and no target. Generate *Jin* in your legs, direct it with your waist, and express it through your fist or elbow (Figure 3-55). Stay very relaxed until just before the end of the swing, then tense your body and arm slightly and drop your weight into your feet, mentally balancing the force and counterforce in your fist and feet. Right after you strike, the fist should be snapped back so that all the energy goes into the opponent. When you can swing or coil your *Jin* out naturally, you should then start training on a punching bag (Figure 3-56). *Heng Jin* is a soft-hard *Jin*. It is first relaxed, and then sharp and penetrating. Its focus point is inside the opponent's body,

Figure 3-55

Figure 3-56

so your arm and body stay relaxed until the surface of your target, or just before it. Once you hit the target, your body tenses slightly- just enough to put all your force into the target and prevent any force from bouncing back to you. Remember, the motion comes from the legs and the rotation of the body, not from the arms.

5. Zhang Jin (Growing Jin) 長勁

Growing *Jin* is a soft, slow, and extended offensive *Jin*. It is actually a mixture of many *Jins* - Controlling, Neutralizing, Resisting, Drilling, and Coiling. Even though it is a mixture of many *Jins*, both *Yin* and *Yang*, Growing *Jin* is considered pure-ly *Yang* because your *Yi* is concentrated on approaching and attacking the opponent. Once you have control of your opponent with Controlling *Jin*, but cannot yet attack because his defense is still strong, you can use Growing *Jin* to work your way through his defense. You should "grow" continually toward your opponent, evading his defenses, moving around resistance, inexorably overcoming all obstacles. Any offensive move he attempts must be immediately neutralized to the side to open him up, or else turned back on itself. When you encounter Resisting or Neutralizing *Jins* you must change your growing path until you reach your target. It is like passing a thread through a pearl whose hole has nine curves. Once your growing has reached your opponent's body, then you can attack suddenly with a fast, short *Jin* like Inch *Jin* or Centimeter *Jin*.

It should be clear from the discussion that Growing *Jin* is not completely soft. The muscles are tensed and relaxed repeatedly as you shift from one *Jin* to another. Because you are doing many techniques in a row, the *Yi* and *Qi* are long and extended. For Growing *Jin* to be effective, you must be skilled at Listening and Understanding. You must understand the opponent's *Jin* in order to control, neutralize, and overcome it.

Since this *Jin* is a mixture of several other *Jins*, the best way to master it is through pushing hands. When you do Growing *Jin*, your hands relentlessly and insidiously keep approaching the opponent. If you are thwarted, don't try to force your way in. Evade and coil around obstacles, and immediately neutralize any forward motion of the opponent. Keep your *Yi* on the opponent, adapt to circumstances, and keep moving toward him so that "when (the opponent) retreats, it becomes more and more urgent" (Appendix A-2).

6. Chen Jin (Sinking Jin) 沉勁

In Sinking *Jin* you sink the body to escape from a grab, or to exert downward force in a pull or attack. When you strike downward, you cannot balance the force upward, so you must carefully drop your weight to direct the counterforce into the ground. As with other *Jins*, the mind must lead the motion. First the *Yi* sinks, then the *Qi* sinks, and the body will naturally follow. Sinking should be alive and responsive. Many people think that Sinking *Jin* uses the muscles to pull or hold down the opponent. As matter of fact, this is called "weighting." You should understand that sinking and weighting are different. Weighting has shape and is slow like *Li*, while sinking is shapeless and can be fast. Weighting power is clumsy and stagnant, while sinking is agile and alive. When Sinking *Jin* is used it looks relaxed but it is not relaxed, it seems tight and restricted but is not.

Sinking *Jin* can be used for either a direct or strategic attack. When a direct attack is used, the *Jin* is downward and forward, usually toward the opponent's stomach area (Figure 3-57). When the muscles on the stomach area are struck or pressed downward, they tense immediately. Some of these muscles extend upward and surround the lungs. When they

Figure 3-57

are struck, they constrict the lung, causing difficulty breathing and sometimes unconsciousness. This is called Sealing the Breath (*Bi Qi*, 閉氣). Sinking *Jin* is also used to provide power when you use Rollback to attack the opponent's arm.

To use Sinking *Jin* for a strategic attack, your hand first adheres and sticks to the opponent's arm. If you sink downward and apply this force to his arm, you can immobilize it and restrict further action. Usually, in order to prevent you from attacking after you have restricted his arm, your enemy will automatically raise his arm to resist your sinking. When this happens, you should then follow his upward power and use Lifting *Jin* to increase his upward motion. You may be able to unbalance and push him, or else raise his arm and attack underneath.

Sinking *Jin* is also involved in other *Jins*, such as Prying *Jin*, or downward Pluck *Jin*. When Sinking *Jin* is used to coordinate with Prying *Jin*, the body and elbow are dropped to escape from the opponent's Controlling *Jin* (see Prying *Jin*). When Sinking *Jin* is applied in downward Pluck *Jin*, it is used to thwart the opponent's kick or to trick the opponent into resisting you. When he starts to pull away, immediately add your forward *Jin* to his backward *Jin* and bounce him away. An example of this from the *Taiji* sequence is Pick Up the Needle from Sea Bottom followed immediately by Fan Back.

Sinking *Jin* can be practiced as a downward punch or palm strike on the bag (Figures 3-58 and 3-59). The other applications need to be practiced with a partner.

7. Cun Jin (Inch Jin) 寸勁

Inch *Jin* is the generation and emission of *Jin* in a short distance. Most of the offensive *Jins* can be done this way. This *Jin* is hard to learn, but once learned, it gives a great advantage in a fight. When your attack takes place in a very short space and time, it is very hard for your opponent to sense it, understand it, and react. Drilling *Jin* is commonly done this way. However, unless your *Qi* is strong and you are very skilled, this short range attack will not be as powerful as the longer range attacks.

Figure 3-58

Figure 3-59

There are many possible applications for Inch *Jin*. It is often used after you have approached the enemy by using Growing *Jin*. When you have worked your way through the opponent's defenses and see an opening, you can strike effectively with no warning. Inch *Jin* is also often used for a second attack. When the opponent neutralizes your first attack, he will try to lead and control you, and then counterattack. When your opponent has neutralized your attack and thinks you can do nothing more, he will shift from Leading *Jin* to Controlling *Jin*. If you attack right at this time, you may be able to catch his *Jin* just as it is about to be emitted, and use it to knock him a great distance.

Inch *Jin* is also used when you have neutralized the opponent's attack and have led him into an unbalanced position. A sudden short attack will knock him down before he has a chance to recover his balance. Another common use of Inch *Jin* is when you control one of the opponent's joints through Controlling *Jin*. For example, if you control his elbow with Rollback, you can suddenly apply Inch *Jin* and break or dislocate the joint.

To practice emitting *Jin* in a short distance, start with your fist one inch away from a punching bag. While the accumulation phase of the technique should be as short as the emission, you may want to start training with a longer accumulation phase. In this case, move your body as you normally would for a full sized punch, but have your fist move only a few inches. Once you get the motion, make the wind-up shorter and shorter, until there is no visible preparation for the punch. Keep your whole body relaxed when you throw the punch, and put all your power into the arm, but only bring the energy into the fist at the very end of the technique. The goal is to have the body and fist both move only a very short distance. It is desirable to also practice extending your *Qi*, for example by punching at a candle. Remember, the longer you practice, the stronger your power, and the more natural and smooth your power generation will be.

8. Fen Jin (Centimeter Jin) 分勁

Compared with Inch *Jin*, Centimeter *Jin* is even shorter in both time and distance. Naturally, very strong *Qi* is required to make this *Jin* effective. This *Jin* can be used with the fingers, palm, fist, elbow, or shoulder. It is usually used right after the enemy's body is touched. For example, when your fingers touch the opponent's elbow, Centimeter *Jin* is used to grasp cavities to paralyze the elbow. If your fist or knuckle touches a vital cavity, for example the temple, Centimeter *Jin* can be applied suddenly to strike and rupture the artery.

The training methods of Centimeter *Jin* are the same as Inch *Jin* except that you often start the technique touching the target. This *Jin* takes even longer to train since *Qi* is needed more than muscle to make it effective.

9. Leng Jin (Cold Jin) 冷勁

Cold *Jin* is used for surprise attacks. The imagery of the name is that of a shiver from a cold wind which suddenly blows over you. It is a sudden attack from a "cold start," and there should be no visible preparation or other indication that you are going to attack. Cold *Jin* can be any technique - what characterizes it is the suddenness of its execution. This is one of the hardest *Jins* to learn and understand. It is said that *Yang, Ban-Hou* specialized in Cold *Jin* and never met his match.

Since Cold *Jin* is a surprise attack, it is essential that the *Jin* storage time be as short as possible. If your opponent can sense that you are storing *Jin*, he can prepare for your attack. It is very important to psych out your opponent so that he doesn't suspect your attack. He attacks and you seem to retreat, but all of a sudden you attack him. Cold *Jin* is used while Yielding, Neutralizing, Controlling, or Adhere-Stick *Jins* are being used. For example, when you are neutralizing your opponent's *Jin*, he might sense it and prepare a strategy against your neutralization. When his *Yi* is on his new strategy and he is about to begin it, you suddenly change your strategy and attack. This sudden attack is called Cold *Jin*.

When you are about to use Cold *Jin*, you must be careful

not to expose your intentions. You must be cool, calm, and steady. It seems like nothing is going to happen, then out of nowhere you attack.

Cold *Jin* depends upon faking out the opponent, and so you need a partner to practice it. You must first practice accumulating *Jin* as subtly as possible. Sometimes this may mean doing it in as short a time as possible. At other times it may mean accumulating *Jin* as inconspicuously as possible during your normal movement. The second part of Cold *Jin* is learning how to emit *Jin* instantly. This means that your body must be in the ideal position to do the particular technique, and when you attack your whole body moves as one unit. The third part of Cold *Jin* is patience. You must wait until you have your opponent in the right position before you do the technique. For example, if you want to push him, you must wait until he is unbalanced or almost unbalanced, and you must be in a position to instantly move his mass in an effective direction. If you wish to lock or break his arm, you must wait until his arm is in an exposed position and can be instantly incapacitated. If you pick the wrong time you may be countered, and if you try repeatedly to do a technique without being in a good position, the opponent will figure out what you are trying to do and will be on guard.

10. Ti Jin (Lifting Jin) 提勁

Lifting *Jin* is the exertion of an upward force. It can be a pull or a push, and it is used to uproot the opponent. One example in the *Taiji* sequence is Embrace the Tiger and Return to the Mountain (Figures 3-60 and 3-61). Many techniques use some Lifting *Jin*. Wardoff has some lifting, and Push is often done upward. Sometimes a small lifting move is used to upset the opponent's root just before a major technique. Often a lifting technique is done right after a sinking move; a good example of this in the sequence is Fan Back (Figure 3-62). Sometimes you may lift before doing a sinking technique. For example, you may deflect an attack upward with Wardoff before using Rollback to lock the opponent's arm downward.

When you use Lifting *Jin*, you must have your root firmly grounded. The more *Jin* you apply downward, the more upward Lifting *Jin* can be generated from the legs. This *Jin* is not very fast but also not very slow. If you do it too fast, your own root will be affected, and if you do it too slowly, your opponent may sense your intention and change his strategy to thwart you.

Lifting *Jin* can be practiced both on a bag and on a partner. A trick of lifting is, when you are in the right position and have found the center of mass of the bag or person, to think of sinking. This will help you to break his root. This works both when you are moving forward to a stationary opponent, as perhaps with Diagonal Flying, and when you are receiving an attack, as in Fair Lady Weaves Shuttle. With some techniques you may

Figure 3-60

Figure 3-61

Figure 3-62

shift your weight forward and use the upward force that comes from sinking your weight into the front foot. Do this smoothly so that you "bounce" off the front foot.

b. Offense With Some Defense Jin (Yang Zhong Dai Yin Jin, 陽中帶陰勁):

1. An Jin (Push Jin) 按勁

Push *Jin* is applied by using one (Figures 3-63 and 3-64) or both hands (Figures 3-65 and 3-66) to push downward, forward or to strike the opponent's chest, arms, shoulders, or back. Frequently both hands will be on the opponent, but only one hand will do the actual pushing. Sometimes one hand will

Figure 3-63

Figure 3-64

Figure 3-65

Figure 3-66

set the opponent up, and the other will push. Sometimes the opponent will react to your hands and evade you. In this case your two hands are alternately substantial and insubstantial as you follow his body. When you finally have him set up, one hand emits *Jin*.

The direction of the push can be forward, downward, or upward, and the attack can be long or short. Long Push *Jin* is used to push the opponent away, while short Push *Jin* is used to strike. Forward push is generally used to attack the chest or the shoulder blade. Downward Push *Jin* is often used to immobilize the opponent's arms and give you an opportunity for further attack. Upward Push can destroy the opponent's stability and balance. A major use of Push *Jin* occurs when you have neutralized an attack and have led the opponent into a bad position. If the opponent's balance is broken, or if he is in a position where it can be easily broken, you can send him flying if you push him from the correct angle.

The key to effective Push *Jin* is the legs. Your footwork adjusts the distance and sets up an advantageous angle of attack. *Jin* must be emitted from the legs and guided by the waist. Timing is also a decisive factor. The best time to use Push *Jin* is when the opponent is about to emit his *Jin*, but has not yet emitted it. When Push *Jin* is applied at this moment, the opponent can be bounced away with his own power. Remember, when using Push *Jin*, your body should not lean excessively in the direction of the push, otherwise your *Jin* may be used against you. Also, when pushing you should withhold some of your *Jin*. This will make it harder for your opponent to use your push against you.

Push *Jin* can be trained in a number of ways. For sandbag training, you must stand at the right distance, then use your leg to generate *Jin* and use your waist to guide the *Jin* to the bag. When the bag swings back to you at a different angle, adjust your position and push again, using either one hand or both hands. Treat the bag like a real opponent. If you continue the practice, you should be able to grasp the trick and the right timing of the push.

Of course you can also train Push *Jin* with a partner. Have the partner cross his arms on his chest to provide some cushioning (Figures 3-67 and 3-68). His hands should be flat on his chest so that you can feel his mass. Place your hand (hands) lightly on his forearms and try to feel any motion of his body. You may push him slightly to get him to move. A small push may also bring his center up so that you can push it. It is important to push his center of mass, because if you push anywhere else he will be able to yield and deflect you. Don't use a very hard *Jin* on your partner, as this may injure him. When you push him, try to catch his motion. If you catch him when he is moving slightly backward, you can add to his motion and send him flying. You can push him slightly and then withdraw a little bit. If he starts to resist your push he will move forward as you withdraw. Emit your *Jin* just as he is about to come forward, or else let him come forward a little bit and lift him slightly as he does so, and then continue his motion upward and away from you.

Figure 3-67

Figure 3-68

2. Cai Jin (Pluck Jin) 採勁

Pluck *Jin* is a pull used to upset the opponent's stability and set him up for an attack. It can be used to immobilize him, upset his balance, or stop his attack. To use *Cai Jin*, you usually have to first use Controlling *Jin* on one of the opponent's joints such as the wrist, elbow, or shoulder, and then pull his arm downward or sideward. In principle, when your opponent transmits *Jin* to his hand, the force must go through the shoulder, elbow, and wrist. If one of these joints is controlled and pulled, the *Jin* will be cut off and his root broken. The opponent will usually tense his muscles and use his *Li* to resist by pulling in the opposite direction. Once you sense his power, immediately follow the direction of his power and use your Press or Push *Jin* to attack. Once you grasp the trick of this, you will usually win.

When Pluck *Jin* is used to pull sideward, you usually pull the opponent's arm across his chest and downward. This prevents any further attack with his legs or other hand. Sideward Pluck is often used to set the opponent up for an attack, which may be Press, Push, Elbow Stroke (Figures 3-69 and 3-70), or Shoulder-Stroke. When your opponent loses his balance you may also immediately kick his lower body (Figure 3-71) or sweep his leg to make him fall (Figure 3-72).

Pluck is also often used to pull downward. An example of downward Pluck in the *Taijiquan* sequence is Pick Up the Needle from the Sea Bottom. One of the applications of this form is to grasp the enemy's wrist and pull it down (Figure 3-

Figure 3-69

Figure 3-70

Figure 3-71

Figure 3-72

73). When the opponent resists and pulls back and up, follow his motion and accelerate it with Fan Back (Figure 3-74). This is an example of "If there is a top, there is a bottom" and also of "To consider going upward implies considering downward" (Appendix A-1).

The sinking of the body in a downward Pluck is similar to Sinking *Jin*, but the application is different. Both *Jins* use a similar sinking movement of the body, but in Pluck *Jin* you are

Figure 3-73   Figure 3-74

holding the opponent and pulling him downward. When you use downward Pluck *Jin*, you must be aware of your top. Your enemy might use the opportunity to strike your head or upper body.

In order for Pluck *Jin* to be effective, it must be strong and fast. If your pull is not strong enough to force your opponent into the defense, he might be able to use your power against you. If your pull is too slow, your opponent will have the opportunity to sense your intention and reset himself in a new position to your disadvantage. Most importantly, Pluck is an all-or-nothing technique. If you give up on it halfway through, you set yourself up to be countered, because your opponent's stability is still intact.

Learning to use Pluck is fairly easy, though it is harder to learn how to use it well. Be patient and wait for the right opportunity. If you have to struggle, you're doing it wrong. Work on correct timing, and be careful to avoid using *Li*. Since Pluck *Jin* must be used together with many other *Jins* such as Controlling *Jin*, Listening *Jin*, Understanding *Jin*, and Press *Jin* in order to be effective, a partner is necessary for the training. Experiment with different ways of using Pluck *Jin* to unbalance your partner, set him up for attacks, and stop his attacks.

3. Zhou Jin (Elbow Jin): 肘勁

Elbow *Jin* uses the elbow to strike or sometimes push the opponent. This is a short range attack, used when the opponent is too close for a hand technique. When an elbow attack is done properly with the correct timing it is very difficult to block, and can be more damaging than the hand. However, when used improperly it is easily defended against. Since the

Figure 3-75

Figure 3-76

elbow is close to the center of your body, if your opponent can control your upper arm or shoulder he can easily use your *Jin* against you. It is important therefore to keep part of your force in reserve and not commit it all. Remember, *Jin* comes from your legs. Keep your stance stable and balanced, wait for the right opportunity, and control your technique through your waist.

Generally, there are two ways to Elbow. The first is called Forward Elbow (*Zheng Zhou Kao*, 正肘靠), and uses the elbow or forearm to strike forward (Figure 3-75) to attack the solar plexus or nipple area (Figure 3-76). Occasionally it is also used to attack the shoulder blade to numb the opponent's arm

Figure 3-77

Figure 3-78

(Figure 3-77). When Forward Elbow is used, it is destructive, powerful, and dangerous. The other Elbow is called Sideward Elbow (*Ce Zhou Kao*, 側肘靠) and uses the upper arm near the elbow to push or strike (Figure 3-78). This technique is not as powerful and destructive as Forward Elbow. A common way to use this technique is to first raise the opponent's arm to expose his underarm area (Figure 3-79). Next, step behind his front leg to keep him from withdrawing, and use your elbow to hit him or push him down (Figure 3-80).

In practice, you can use a bag to train both Forward and Sideward Elbow. Treat the bag like your opponent's body for striking and pushing. Use your elbows as you would your fists, with the same relaxation and fluidity of application. You can also practice Elbow on a partner if you do it as a push. The

Figure 3-79

Figure 3-80

Figure 3-81

Figure 3-82

person being pushed should hold his arms on his chest to avoid injury (Figures 3-81 and 3-82). However, the best way to train Elbow with a partner is to use a kicking pad (Figures 3-83 and 3-84). This allows you to train striking and pushing techniques realistically without worrying about hurting your partner.

Figure 3-83   Figure 3-84

4. Na Jin (Controlling Jin, literally to grasp, seize, capture) 拿勁

Controlling *Jin* is the controlling of a joint of the opponent. *Na Jin* is very important in *Taijiquan* because it is necessary to control the opponent before you can attack him. When you neutralize an opponent he is in a state of confusion and imbalance because he has lost his power. At this time you are already guiding him. If you can control him through his wrist, elbow, or shoulder you can attack with certainty.

When controlling the opponent, your movements and your touch must be light and agile. If your movements are heavy your opponent can easily sense them, and he will try to escape. If you wait for the right opportunity, when you do grasp him he will not be able to escape.

When two hands are used to control, one hand controls the elbow while the other controls either the wrist or the shoulder (Figures 3-85 and 3-86). When you use both hands to control, it is like using a balance scale to weigh something. When the opponent becomes heavy at one point, you don't resist there, but instead maintain your control at the other point. Technically, your two hands alternate being substantial and insubstantial as they adapt to the opponent's movements. When using Controlling *Jin*, it is not only the hands but also the waist which controls the action. Do not use *Li*, but use your mind and *Qi*.

There are two kinds of *Na*. In the first kind, commonly called *Qin Na*, you actually grasp the opponent. The most basic *Qin Na* techniques are "dividing the muscle" and "misplacing the bone." In dividing the muscle techniques, the opponent's muscles in the joint area are twisted and overextended, tearing

135

Figure 3-85

Figure 3-86

Figure 3-87

the muscle fiber and causing pain. Figures 3-87 and 3-88 show two examples in which the muscles in the wrist area are twisted and extended. In misplacing the bone techniques, the joint is twisted and bent in an abnormal direction to tear the ligament or dislocate the joint. Figure 3-89 shows an example in which the opponent's elbow is locked and overextended, and

Figure 3-88

Figure 3-89

Figure 3-90

Figure 3-90 shows an example in which the thumb is locked and bent.

There is another type of *Qin Na* technique called muscle and cavity grasp in which the opponent's muscles are grasped and pinched to cause pain and numbness. A typical example is shown in Figure 3-91 in which the shoulder muscles are controlled. Alternatively, the grasp can be used on acupuncture

137

Figure 3-91

Figure 3-92

cavities to cause pain and numbness and immobilize the affected area. An example is shown in Figure 3-92 in which the cavities *Quchi* (Figure 3-93) and either *Shaohai* or *Xiaohai* (Figure 3-94) are pinched.

The second *Na Jin* controls the opponent without grasping or using any particular form. The techniques and theory of this *Na Jin* are higher than those of the *Qin Na* discussed above. In this *Na Jin*, you use your adhering and sticking ability on your opponent's joints to lead him and neutralize his slightest movement. When he attacks, you neutralize, when he withdraws you stick and follow. You do not actually grasp your opponent but you make him feel that he cannot attack you and he cannot get away from you, as if you were a sheet of flypaper that he can't shake off. When he tries to withdraw you follow him, maneuvering him subtly into a bad position. When he attacks, you evade and lead his attack further or in a different direction than he intended, and then apply subtle pressure to hold him in an exposed position.

In order to make *Na Jin* effective, you must have good Listening, Understanding, Neutralizing, and Leading *Jins*. You have to listen to and understand his slightest motion, and

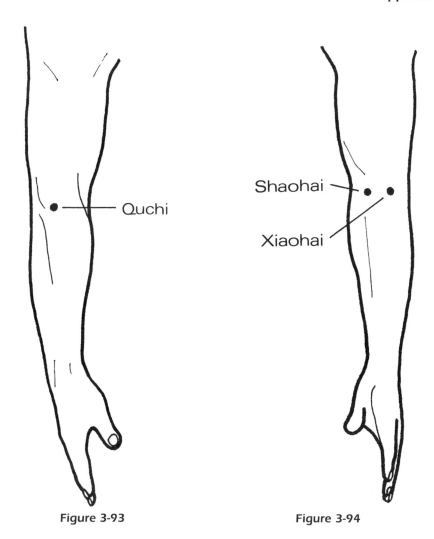

| Figure 3-93 | Figure 3-94 |

then lead and neutralize it so that he cannot free himself. Since there are so many *Jins* involved, it is impossible to practice without a partner. After several years of practice, you should be able to coordinate your steps with your *Na Jin* and maneuver your opponent into a completely passive situation.

5. Cuo Jin (Filing Jin) 挫勁

Cuo in Chinese means to rub or file. When Filing *Jin* is used, you generally use the outside edge of your hand and forearm to "file" forward, sideward, upward, or downward. This *Jin* can be used either as a strike or as a pressing/rubbing action. It can be used against the opponent's arm to stop a technique, or to either lock the arm for *Qin Na* control or clear it out of your way just before you attack. When Filing *Jin* is used against the body, the front or back of the waist is the usual target (Figures 3-95 and 3-96). If the front side of the waist is filed correctly, the muscle will contract and cause the lung to seal the breath (prevent breathing). If the back of

Figure 3-95

Figure 3-96

Figure 3-97

Figure 3-98

the waist is filed, a direct or indirect injury to the kidney will result. It is also commonly used to attack the neck (Figure 3-97).

Filing *Jin* is commonly used to press or rub the arm down to seal and lock the opponent's attack. A typical example of filing down is shown in Figures 3-98 and 3-99 in which the opponent's attack is first intercepted and then filed down to open the neck for a filing attack (Figure 3-97). Upward filing is usually used to set up for striking or *Qin Na* control. An example

Figure 3-99

Figure 3-100

Figure 3-101

of filing up is when you use your right hand to grasp the opponent's right wrist, and then file upward with your left arm on his upper arm (Figure 3-100). This lifts and twists his arm. You can then file downward, circling him down into a *Qin Na* control (Figure 3-101). Both the bag and pushing hands can be used for Filing *Jin* practice. Figure 3-102 shows the direction in which the *Jin* is filed when a bag is used. When you file, keep your muscles relaxed, but suddenly tense them once the edge of the hand and forearm touch the target. The *Jin* is directed into the bag and sideward. When Filing *Jin* is practiced in pushing hands, you must neutralize your opponent's attack first. Once you are in the most advantageous position, apply your Filing *Jin* immediately. Figures 3-103 and 3-104 show the upward and downward filing training using a staff. You can also practice Filing *Jin* by yourself. Figures 3-105 and 3-106 show ways to practice filing up and down.

Figure 3-102

Figure 3-103

Figure 3-104

6. Song Jin (Send Jin) 送勁

To use Send *Jin*, follow the opponent's withdrawing motion, add to it, and "send" him flying away. This is a long *Jin*, but it is shorter than Growing *Jin*. When the opponent is using Yielding or Neutralizing *Jin*, you use the *Jins* of Adhere and Stick to take control of the situation, and then use Push. When it is used properly, the opponent will lose his root and be bounced away.

When the opponent is withdrawing, his *Yi* is on backing up. While this is happening, you should follow his *Jin* and enhance it with your forward motion and your own *Jin* to keep him passive. Take the initiative and keep him withdrawing until you can attack and "send" him flying away. When this *Jin* is used against Yielding *Jin*, keep your footwork alive as you adhere and stick. Keep close to the opponent so that his yield-

| Figure 3-105 | Figure 3-106 |

ing strategy is useless, then when you have an opportunity, add your attacking *Jin*. When this *Jin* is used against Neutralizing *Jin*, you must step skillfully to reorient your position and redirect your opponent's Neutralizing *Jin* toward his body so you can control him. This is what is meant in the *Taijiquan* Classic: "when (the opponent) retreats, it becomes more and more urgent," (Appendix A-2).

This *Jin* is normally trained during Pushing Hands. Send *Jin* can be considered a strategic way of using other *Jins*. When pushing hands, be alert to opportunities for following the opponent as he withdraws. This *Jin* can also be trained with a sandbag. First push the bag and start it swinging. When the bag comes within range, adhere lightly to it, and when it swings away follow and add your push. Remember that your push should be a sudden pulse so that the bag bounces away.

B. Defensive (Yin) Jin (Shou Jin, Yin Jin, 守勁、陰勁):

a. Purely Defensive (Yin) Jin (Chun Shou, Chun Yin Jins, 純守、純陰勁):

1. Lu Jin (Rollback Jin) 攦

Rollback *Jin* leads the opponent's attack past you after you have neutralized it. It is considered purely negative, or *Yin*, although in practice you will usually add a small amount of force. To understand the *Yin* nature of Rollback, consider what happens when you push a bag which is tethered top and bottom. If you do not push the bag directly in the center, it moves back just enough to avoid your force, and turns out of the way (Figures 3-107 and 3-108).

Figure 3-107

Figure 3-108

When you do Rollback, your hands are usually on the opponent's wrist and elbow. When he attacks, withdraw and turn your body to evade his attack, at the same time pulling him slightly to lead him past you. Rollback causes only a small change in the course of the opponent's attack - you let him go pretty much where he wants to go, but make sure that you aren't there. Pulling him slightly will lead him further than he intended so that he overextends himself and loses his root, or else it will guide him slightly off his intended course so that he loses his stability and becomes vulnerable to attack. Your *Jin* must **lead** him. This means that your force must be applied in about the same direction as the direction of his attack. If you apply force at too great an angle to his direction of attack, or try to change his course too radically, you are meeting force with force, and that is not Rollback.

In practice, it is sometimes necessary to wardoff the opponent's attack before doing Rollback. If the attack is fast and from short range, you may not be able to get control of his arm fast enough. In such a case, first deflect him with Wardoff, and if his attack continues or if he tries to force his way through your defense, execute Rollback in the direction he is moving.

Rollback is occasionally used offensively. Since you con-

Figure 3-109

Figure 3-110

Figure 3-111

trol the opponent's arm, it is often possible when you draw back to lock the elbow or break it with a quick turn. This application is very similar to Split *Jin*. You can also use Sinking *Jin* with this technique to apply sudden pressure downward.

There are two kinds of Rollback - large and small. In large Rollback (*Da Lu*, 大攦) you step back as you lead him past you; in small Rollback (*Xiao Lu*, 小攦) you do not step, although you may adjust your feet. In small Rollback, for example, if he throws a right punch you ward it off upward and to your right (Figure 3-109). You then circle your right hand around his arm, and draw him to your left rear (Figure 3-110). This will open the right side of his body for a moment, allowing you to attack (Figure 3-111). Similarly, if he throws a left punch, ward it off upward (Figure 3-112). Curl your right hand clockwise around his arm so that you can control his arm at the elbow (Figure 3-113), and pull him off balance to your left rear. His left arm will probably be locked, allowing you to counter effectively with a press (Figure 3-114).

Figure 3-112

Figure 3-113

Figure 3-114

Figure 3-115

In large Rollback, step either directly backward or else turn 270 degrees and place your foot behind you. For example, if the opponent punches with his right, Stick and connect to his arm with your right arm (Figure 3-115). Follow his force and step back with your right leg. At the same time, control his arm at the wrist and above the elbow, and draw him to your right rear (Figure 3-116). The opponent should fall or lose his stability, giving you the opportunity to attack. The trick to

Figure 3-116

Figure 3-117

Figure 3-118

making your opponent lose his stability is that right after you neutralize the attack, you suddenly add your Rollback *Jin* in a sharp pulse. If your neutralization is subtle and doesn't alarm him, a quick Rollback should catch him before he can resist.

Alternatively, instead of stepping directly back, step all the way around to your rear (Figures 3-117 and 3-118). This is done when the opponent is close and there is danger of his counterattacking with Shoulder-Stroke if you don't get him completely past you. This application is a mixture of the motion of Rollback and Rend *Jin*.

Rollback is done in response to the opponent's attack, but in some cases you can provoke the attack. If you can push the opponent and cause him to push back, you may be able to extend his push enough to use Rollback, causing him to fall past you. However, if your Adhere-Stick *Jin* is not very good, this may be dangerous. Also, if you don't know how to use Leading *Jin* your Rollback will be ineffective because you will not be able to really control him. In this regard, when a begin-

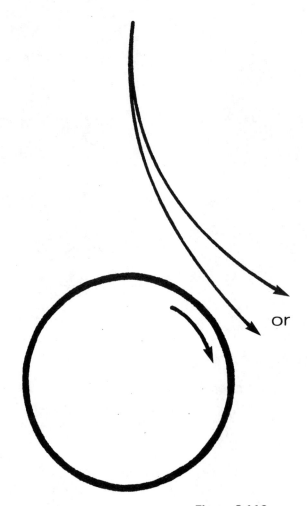

Figure 3-119

ner does Rollback, he should not draw the opponent in too close, but should curve the opponent away from him to avoid the chance of counterattack (Figure 3-119).

The key to Rollback is the waist and legs, not the arms. When using Rollback, first lead the opponent slightly upward, then sit back and sink, keeping the legs. relaxed, and twist the waist to get the Rollback *Jin* out. In Pushing Hands you use Rollback continually to deflect and neutralize attacks. However, be careful not to try to use Rollback to lock or control the opponent when you cannot unbalance him, because he will counter or neutralize you.

Rollback must be trained with a partner. Any exercise which allows you to practice sticking, following, and yielding is preparing you for Rollback.

2. Zhan Nian Jin (Adhere-Stick Jin) 沾黏勁

This is the most fundamental and important *Jin* in *Taijiquan. Zhan* means adhere and *Nian* means stick. These are two different *Jins*, but they are always considered together because they cannot be separated. When you moisten your finger to pick up powder it is called *Zhan*. *Nian* means to stick and not come off. Basically, to adhere means to connect - you move to lightly attach your arm or hand to your opponent. Once attached, you stick with him and follow his movements, moving your body to evade his attacks, and following him as he retreats. Your opponent should feel that he can't get rid of you or shake you off. It is said: "When the opponent is hard, I am soft; this is called yielding. When I follow the opponent, this is called sticking. When the opponent moves fast, I move fast; when the opponent moves slowly, then I follow slowly. Although the variations are infinite, the principle remains the same" (Appendix A-2).

Adhere-Stick is the *Jin* of not losing the opponent. When you learn it properly the enemy is under your control. He cannot reach you because you are always in contact with him and can feel his attacks and avoid them, and he can't get away because you are right there ready to attack at his slightest error. It is said: "Guide (his power) to enter into emptiness, then immediately attack; Adhere-Connect, Stick-Follow, do not lose him" (Appendix A-7).

Zhan Nian Jin is developed initially on the hands and forearms, but once you develop a feeling for it, you can develop the same sensitivity and responsiveness in every part of your body. After a long period of training, if any part of your body is attacked, that part will automatically move just enough to avoid the attack, but not enough to break contact. Just as you move away to evade the attack, you will tend to move forward as he withdraws. There is flexibility in *Zhan Nian Jin* - you don't have to keep the same part of your body in contact with the opponent. You may meet his attack with a forearm, transfer the attack to the other arm, and then switch to a shoulder as you counter with Diagonal Flying.

It is said that this *Jin* is very subtle and has to be taught personally by a master. The master lets the student feel what *Zhan Nian Jin* is like, in a sense "charging his battery" with an understanding of the technique so that he can practice on his own and develop this *Jin*.

After a long period of study a layer of *Qi* is developed on the surface of the body. This is like a cloud on the skin, or like glue covering the whole body. The better the master, the thicker this layer is. It cannot be seen, but it can be felt by those who understand it. It is possible for two experts to evaluate each other just by sensing this layer of *Qi*.

This is the most important and basic *Jin*, and it is developed mainly through pushing hands, where you gradually build up a feeling for what it is. Relax and "listen" to your partner with all your attention. Keep your hands on your partner and concentrate on following him wherever he moves. Move your body to evade him as he attacks or advances, follow him when he withdraws, always keeping your hands lightly attached to him. Even when you move forward offensively or attack, emphasize listening so that you can adapt to whatever he does. If you get pushed or lose your balance, still stay attached to him if possible. Another way to train this *Jin* is through *Taiji* ball practice.

3. Zou Jin (Yielding Jin, literally "walking away Jin") 走勁

This is the *Jin* of no resistance. It is an insubstantial *Jin*, pure *Yin* in character. *Zou Jin* comes from Understanding *Jin*, for if you don't understand the opponent's *Jin*, how can you walk away from it? In its purest form, Yielding *Jin* is simply moving away from the opponent's pressure. In Pushing Hands, when the opponent pushes against your arm, you become insubstantial where he is pushing. You may simply move directly away in the direction of his push, or you may empty the side of the body he is pushing against, turning your body to let his attack go past you. If you don't resist, the enemy will feel only emptiness wherever he advances. His power will also feel empty because it has nothing to push against. Beginners usually need a relatively heavy pressure applied to them before they yield, and if a light pressure is applied they tend to resist. This is because their sensitivity is still low, and they don't feel or understand the energy.

The key to Yielding *Jin* is the waist and legs. The footwork must be correct, and the waist must coordinate the body and legs when you move and turn to get out of the way. You must also understand Adhere-Connect and Stick-Follow, for if you cannot stay in contact with the opponent you cannot clearly know his motion.

In *Taiji* fighting strategy, Yielding and Adhere-Stick *Jins* are used to connect to the opponent when you are separate. When the opponent attacks, adhere to the attacking arm and yield completely without resisting or losing contact. In Figure 3-120, the enemy's attack is shown as a solid line, while your defensive action is shown as a dash line. Follow the opponent's direction and adhere to him without losing him. This is done through the skillful use of your legs, waist, and steps. Thus, it is said: "When the opponent is hard, I am soft; this is called yielding." Also," When there is pressure on the left, the left becomes insubstantial; when there is pressure on the right, the right becomes insubstantial. Looking upward it seems to get higher and higher; looking downward it seems to get deeper and deeper. When (the opponent) advances, it seems longer and longer" (Appendix A-2).

The best way to practice Yielding *Jin* is through pushing hands. Listen to the opponent's attack carefully, readjusting your position smoothly and swiftly so that the attack meets only emptiness. This *Jin* can also be practiced with a bag. Start the bag swinging, and stay lightly attached to it. As the bag swings toward you, readjust your position to evade it.

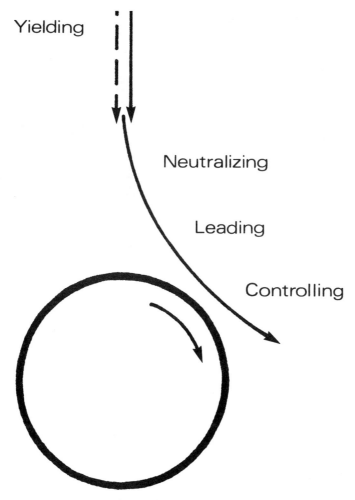

Figure 3-120

A good exercise to train yielding is to have someone push you as you practice not resisting. Start in a bow and arrow stance with 60% of your weight on your front foot, and imagine that you are a molded rubber figure, glued to the floor. Wherever you are pushed — yield. Stick to the hand pushing you, and don't separate from it. This means when you are pushed you move back only as far as the hand moves, and no farther. When he pulls his hand back, adhere and follow it so that you come back to your starting position. This following back keeps your actions spring-like, and not just wet noodle-like. It also keeps you thinking offensively — you evade his attack and follow it back to attack him. Try to keep your stance as much as possible. Sometimes you will have to adjust your feet to keep your balance, but always come right back to your starting position. If you are pushed off balance, don't stop the exercise, just correct your stance.

There are three ways to yield. The first way is turning (Figures 3-121 and 3-122). This is the best way because you stay close to the opponent where you can attack him. As a

Figure 3-121

Figure 3-122

Figure 3-123

general rule, when your right side is attacked, shift your weight to the left leg, and vice versa. You should generally move as little as possible, and only where you are pushed, i.e., when he pushes a shoulder you empty that shoulder and move it back while the rest of your body stays still. Remember to always follow his hand back until you reach your starting position.

The second way to yield is to simply move away from the attack. This is not quite as good as turning, because you lose the ability to counterattack. The third way to yield is to bend the body (Figure 3-123). There are times when you will have to do this to avoid resisting, especially in the beginning, but bending should always be the last choice. When you bend your lower body back you tend to expose your upper body, and vice versa. Yielding is just half of this exercise, the other half is the active side. Move your partner as if you are trying to loosen him up, for in fact you are. Don't use much *Jin*, especially with beginners, just move him around in ways he can usually deal with. Push mostly with one hand at a time, using single pushes and combinations as if you were boxing. Be rhythmic, but don't be like a machine. Do not try to knock your partner over too often, since this may prevent him from finding his root. This exercise is for helping him learn how to yield, so if you make him too tense or keep him off balance too much, he may start resisting and overreacting. Push and pull in every direction, all over his body, including legs, neck, and head. Alternate long and short pushes, straight and curved ones; vary the speed, and throw in some fakes to make sure he doesn't anticipate the push.

Pushing your partner around like this gives you an excellent opportunity to look at your body dynamics. Balance the force of your push with the counterforce going into your supporting foot. Make sure you move from the waist, coiling to accumulate energy, expanding slightly to emit energy. Don't throw your body forward when you push because you can be easily countered.

4. Ding Kang Jin (Resisting Jin) 頂抗勁

This is the *Jin* of resistance. Even though you use force, this *Jin* is considered purely *Yin* because you do not initiate the action - you respond only when the opponent emits force onto you. Many people misunderstand *Taiji* and believe that only soft *Jins* are used, and that all resistance and hard *Jins* are avoided. This is an incomplete view of the art. Like any other Chinese martial art, *Taiji* uses a wide range of *Jins*. Soft *Jins* are emphasized, but the hard *Jins* are not given up.

There are three main uses for Resisting *Jin*. The first is as a training exercise to build up root and *Qi* support. Skilled *Taiji* practitioners who have trained their *Qi* to fully support their muscles will often train extending the duration of their *Jin* so that they will be able to resist long, powerful muscular attacks. *Taiji* masters will frequently demonstrate their Resisting *Jin* by standing in the Wardoff position and having people push them. Sometimes *Nei Kong* masters will compare their Resisting *Jins* by pushing each other. As you extend the duration and increase the strength of Resisting *Jin*, the local *Qi* support must initially play a major role. Since the muscles tend to be tensed, *Dan Tian Qi* has difficulty reaching them. However, with sufficient training you will be able to relax and let the *Dan Tian Qi* circulate.

The second use of Resisting *Jin* is for Borrowing *Jin*. In this case you use Resisting *Jin* as the opponent starts his push so that he pushes himself away from you (see Borrowing *Jin*).

The third use is as a last resort when there is no other way to neutralize the opponent's attack. For example, if your wrist or arm is held tightly by a fighter from another style, you may have to use Resisting *Jin* to prevent him from doing anything more to control or hurt you. This is *Jin* against *Jin*, but it is not stiff or stagnant. You emit a pulse of force only when your opponent's *Jin* is applied onto you. Prevent him from continuing his action, and once his *Jin* is gone, immediately relax.

| Figure 3-124 | Figure 3-125 |

The easiest and most basic method of training Resisting *Jin* is to ask your partner to push your forearm (Figure 3-124). You can also train forearm against forearm with both side exerting force (Figure 3-125). A third way is to use either of the above two postures and have one person suddenly exert Push *Jin*, while the other uses Resisting *Jin* to resist the pulse of energy. Stay relaxed until the other person pushes, then use only enough force to stop his push, and then relax again.

When practicing, relax and transport *Qi* from your *Dan Tian* to your forearm, then lightly tense the forearm muscle to keep the *Dan Tian Qi* there. This tensing will also generate local *Qi*, but if only local *Qi* is used, your *Jin* will be of a low level. Relax all the shoulder muscles as much as possible - the more you relax, the more your *Dan Tian Qi* can support the *Jin*. Remember, it is your *Yi* which leads and controls the *Qi*.

When doing these exercises, both practitioners must pay attention to their stability and central equilibrium. You can test each other occasionally by suddenly pulling your arm away. If the other person falls or loses his balance forward, it is because he has lost his center and is using his body's strength to push instead of *Jin*. When pushing or resisting, your *Yi*, *Qi*, and posture must be balanced, and your body should be upright.

5. Jie Jin (Intercepting Jin) 截勁

Intercepting *Jin* is used to intercept and control the opponent's attack. It is a mixture of visual "listening" with Understanding, Neutralizing, Yielding, Wardoff, and Adhere-Stick *Jins*. Normally during a fight your hands are not sticking

Figure 3-126

to the opponent. When he attacks with a punch or kick, you use this *Jin* to meet his attack halfway. You must first direct some force into the side of his attacking arm so that you can adhere to it. You can then move the attack back toward him so that any further action is hindered, or use some other *Jin* such as Opening, Deflecting, or Rollback.

Intercepting *Jin* is usually the first *Jin* to be used when dealing with an attack. Both external and internal martial styles train it, however they use different approaches. Most external styles will intercept the opponent's attack first and counterattack as soon as possible. They will often use this *Jin* to block and bounce the attack away. The *Taiji* practitioner will make contact with the attacking arm and adhere to it, attempting to control the attacker through it. This is a refined technique which is much harder to do than the intercepting used by other styles. Unfortunately, the average person in *Taiji* nowadays emphasizes pushing hands and only trains the *Jins* which can be obtained from pushing hands. Consequently, when he encounters a punch, he does not know how to intercept it, and cannot apply the *Jins* he has learned.

To train Intercepting *Jin* you must first train your eyes to "listen" and then learn proper timing. Use your eyes to mentally "touch" the opponent. As with physical touching during pushing hands, your mind will eventually be able to understand the opponent's intentions. When your eyes listen and your mind understands, you will be able to effectively intercept attacks. Eye reaction training is the most important part of the training. This is best done with a partner, practicing with different types of attacks.

In addition to visual listening, and the technique of directing some force into the side of the attacking limb so that you can adhere to it, you must also learn how to use the fingers to connect to the attacking arm so that it cannot separate from you. When someone punches at you, first adhere to his forearm with your forearm (Figure 3-126). Neutralize his attack by leading it to the side, at the same time transferring contact

Figure 3-127

Figure 3-128

from your forearm to your hand (Figure 3-127). Hook your hand lightly around his arm so that you can stick to it as it advances or withdraws. This is best learned with a partner. Start with slow punches, and gradually increase the speed. Initially use arranged routines, and gradually introduce variations.

6. He Jin (Closing Jin) 合勁

Closing *Jin* is a defense against a sudden attack to the chest. Your hands follow the opponent's arm or arms in and "smother" his attack. Your chest arcs in and rotates sideways slightly to avoid the attack as well as to accumulate energy for a counterattack (Figure 3-128). You may also find it necessary to step back. As you smother the attack, draw his hands together and control them, creating the opportunity for a counterattack. Typical examples in the sequence are the first parts of Lift Hands and Lean Forward, and Crane Opens Wings.

This *Jin* is developed in Pushing Hands. As you withdraw your chest from a sudden attack, if your hands are following the opponent you will find after a while that you start smothering the attack. With further practice, you will start accumulating energy while doing the motion, and eventually counterattacking.

Figure 3-129

Figure 3-130

7. Juan Jin (Coiling Jin or Curling Jin) 捲勁

Juan in Chinese means to roll up, curl, or wrap. It also has the sense of a snake curling around a branch. Because it can mean curling inward or curling outward, and also coiling like a spring, it is also translated coiling. In *Taijiquan*, *Juan Jin* refers to the clockwise or counterclockwise coiling of your arm around the opponent's arm. The body can also coil up and down to evade and neutralize the opponent. In addition to this coiling movement, the entire body, from lead hand to rear foot, also compresses and expands like a coiled spring. This springy, snakelike coiling accumulates energy in the posture, rather than in tensed muscles.

To train the hands and arms for Coiling *Jin*, practice wrapping and coiling your hands around a stick the way a snake coils around a branch (Figures 3-129 to 3-131). When you can wrap your hand and forearm back and forth, clockwise and counterclockwise around the stick without breaking contact, you will be able to control an opponent's arms.

8. Can Si Jin (Silk Reeling Jin) 蠶絲勁

Silk Reeling *Jin* is like Coiling *Jin*, except that it involves the whole body in the smooth back and forth coiling movements

157

Figure 3-131

which are characteristic of *Taiji*. Whereas Coiling *Jin* is generally one direction at a time, Silk Reeling *Jin* can be an involved, continuous movement as you lead and follow the opponent, and adapt to his changes. It is a mixture *Jin* which contains Coiling, Prying, Drilling, Growing, Neutralizing, and Adhere-Stick *Jins*. When a silkworm spins its cocoon, the motion must be smooth and continuous, for any hitch in the movement will break the thread. When doing *Taiji*, your motion must be smooth and continuous so that you don't break the flow of energy, and so your whole body is behind every movement. When you pull thread from the cocoon, the cocoon spins. *Can Si Jin* also refers to this combination of linear and circular motion.

Silk Reeling *Jin* trains the body and hands in coiling, drilling, and growing, with both moving and fixed steps. More than this, it teaches the basic feeling of *Jin* - how the motion begins in the legs, and coils through the whole body and out the arms to the hands. The motion of each part of the body comes from the motion of the part before it, e.g., the motion of the arms comes from the movement of the shoulders. *Can Si Jin* is also an excellent way to train listening, understanding, sticking and adhering, and not losing the opponent.

When using this *Jin*, follow the opponent's motion smoothly, whether you are evading and leading his forward motion, following his withdrawal, or controlling him as you move into an attack. While this *Jin* feels soft and smooth, it can be very aggressive strategically. When it is mixed with Growing, Coiling, and Drilling *Jins* it can be used to approach the opponent's body for further attack. When it is mixed with Neutralizing and Coiling *Jins* it can neutralize and control the opponent's attack and make his *Jin* seem to disappear into thin air. However, you must be skilled with the other *Jins* in order to use this *Jin* effectively.

To practice Silk Reeling *Jin*, follow the pattern of the *Taiji* symbol. There are several ways to do it, and once you learn one you can easily learn others and experiment on your own.

One Person

Figure 3-132

Figure 3-133

Figure 3-134

For single person practice, as shown in Figure 3-132, start at 1 in the Bow and Arrow stance with your right palm facing out (Figure 3-133). Move your hand down to 2, rotating your hand to the right so the palm faces left (Figure 3-134). From 2 to 3,

Figure 3-135

Figure 3-136

Figure 3-137

Figure 3-138

continue to rotate your hand until the palm faces up (Figure 3-135). From 3 to 4, sit back into the Four-Six stance and turn your body to the right, with the palm still facing up (Figure 3-136). From 4 to 5, turn your body to face forward, rotating your palm to face downward (Figure 3-137). From 5 to 6, turn your body again to the right and continue rotating your palm counterclockwise (Figure 3-138). From 6 to 7, turn your body forward and at the same time rotate your palm clockwise to

Figure 3-139

Figure 3-140

Figure 3-141

face down (Figure 3-139). From 7 to 8, rotate your palm clockwise until it is facing up (Figure 3-140). Finally, from 8 to 9, change into the Bow and Arrow stance again and continue on to 1 (Figure 3-141), rotating your palm until it faces out. This pattern should be repeated continuously. The above description is only an example for the *Taiji* beginner. Once you are familiar with the above movements you can vary your stance or add stepping to coordinate the direction of the coiling with your strategy.

For two person Silk Reeling *Jin* training, the *Taiji* pattern is still used. However, you will complete only half of the cycle, and your partner will do the other half. As shown in Figure 3-142, one person is active and completes 1 to 4, then his partner becomes active and finishes from 4 to 7. When you are

Two Person

Figure 3-142

Figure 3-143

Figure 3-144

active, you neutralize, coil, drill, and grow. When you are passive, you listen, understand, stick and adhere. While practicing, your right forearm and wrist maintain contact with your partner's forearm and wrist (Figure 3-143). Starting at 1, circle down to 2 in the Bow and Arrow stance (Figure 3-144). Then

Figure 3-145

Figure 3-146

Figure 3-147

Figure 3-148

shift your weight back into a Four-Six stance, turn your body to the right and at the same time rotate your palm until it faces up (Figure 3-145). At 4, your partner will take the active role, starting in the Bow and Arrow stance, repeating the same motions you made (Figures 3-146 to 3-149). First practice this exercise standing stationary, and when you are familiar with the techniques, practice coordinating stepping with the movements as you circle both to the right and to the left.

Figure 3-149

Figure 3-150

Figure 3-151

Figure 3-152

Two person Silk Reeling *Jin* training can also be done while you and your partner are stepping forward and backward. This allows you to switch from right hand to left hand practice and back. When you reach 1 during continuous practice you should neutralize your partner's power to the right. You can then use this opportunity to step forward and attack your partner's chest (Figures 3-150 and 3-151) or throat with your left hand (Figure 3-152). In order to prevent your attack, your partner must step back and use his left hand to intercept your

Figure 3-153

Figure 3-154

Figure 3-155

attack (Figure 3-153). Once connected, he should continue the moving pattern. Alternately, you can attack your partner while your hand is up at 1. You can then step your left leg forward and attack your partner's chest under his right arm. Your partner should step backward and connect his left arm with yours.

9. Jue Jin (Prying Jin or Lever Jin) 撅勁

Prying *Jin* is used when you twist your arm to escape from an opponent's grasp, or to free yourself from his sticking control. It is usually used when your techniques have been locked or sealed by your opponent's Controlling *Jin*, and you are in a bad position, or when you are held (Figure 3-154). When this happens, drop your elbow suddenly to reverse the situation (Figure 3-155). Do not try to move his hand, since this would be force against force. Instead use one part of his hand as a fulcrum, and lever your hand out of his grasp. Drop your body so that your whole

Figure 3-156

weight is behind your arm motion, and adjust your stance as appropriate. As your hand is escaping, immediately rotate your hand and arm so that you now control him (Figure 3-156). This technique can be used even when the opponent is holding your arm with both his hands. Escapes such as this are usually done with Cold *Jin* so that the opponent has no warning or chance to change his technique.

To practice Prying *Jin*, have your partner grab your wrist or stick to and control your arm. Experiment with different ways to lever your arm free. Remember — don't fight his grasp. Use your weight to put all your force against one or two of his fingers.

b. Defense With Some Offense (Some Yang in Yin) Jin (Yin Zhong Dai Yang Jin, 陰中帶陽勁):

1. Hua Jin (Neutralizing Jin. Literally, to smelt, change, influence.) 化勁

Neutralizing *Jin* is using four ounces to repel one thousand pounds. It is an insubstantial *Jin*, but it is not purely *Yin* - there is also some *Yang* in it. This means that when you understand your opponent's *Jin*, you use a little power to neutralize and lead it to the side, upward, or downward. Figure 3-157 shows the direction of the opponent's *Jin* and your *Jin* as you neutralize the attack. This is different from Yielding *Jin*, which is purely yielding without any pressure on your part. Neutralizing *Jin* is a combination of Sticking, Yielding, and Leading *Jins*. It is somewhat active, whereas Yielding *Jin* is purely passive. Usually, as you are using Neutralizing *Jin* you are also storing part of your energy for a counterattack. It is said that: "*Hua* has some *Peng Jin* (Wardoff)," because you sometimes bounce the opponent away as you neutralize his attack. This saying also implies that you often have to put a little force into the opponent's arm in order to connect to it (see Intercepting *Jin*).

The key to Neutralizing *Jin* is timing. This is the *Jin* of using the enemy's power against him, so when the enemy's *Yi* (mind) has already started to attack and he is about to emit *Jin*, you must immediately seize this opportunity to neutralize.

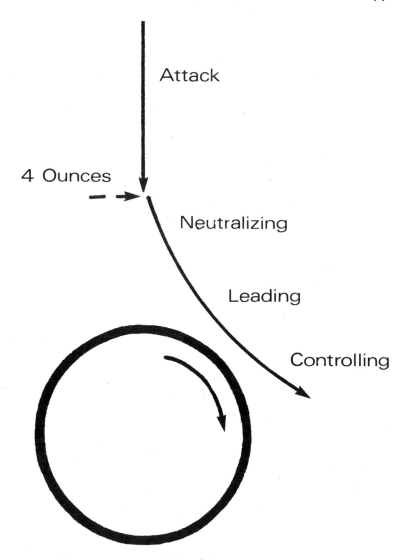

Figure 3-157

If you wait until your opponent's *Jin* is almost all emitted, unless you are an expert, it will be too late to use four ounces to neutralize his one thousand pounds. Thus, it is said: "The opponent does not move, I do not move; the opponent moves slightly, I move first" (Appendix A-3).

Wherever you feel pressure, neutralize. Do not use the arms and shoulders, because that would be *Li* (muscular strength) and not good *Taiji*. You must rely totally on the waist and legs to neutralize the attack. Stick to the opponent and follow his posture, speed and height. As his attack comes in straight, your neutralization should be curved. Neutralization is a circle. When you are a beginner, your circle will be large, but as your skill increases the circle will get smaller and smaller. A large circle gives you more time to listen, understand, and then neutralize. However, when the circle is large your opponent has time to sense your intention and change his strategy. A *Taiji* expert whose circle is small will wait until the opponent's *Jin* is almost all out and his *Yi* is fully on the attack. Then, when he reacts, the opponent will not be able to change his motion. Of course, this small circle defense is dangerous because it lets the opponent's attack almost reach your body. You must be very quick and good at listening, understanding, and neutralizing, otherwise you will not succeed. This is why it is said: "First look to expanding, then look to compacting, then you approach perfection" (Appendix A-3).

Some beginners believe that yielding is neutralization, but this is not the case. Neutralization must use some force, because an attack may be very strong. It is wrong to believe that *Taijiquan* relies only on softness. The best *Taiji* masters look very soft on the outside, but on the inside they are as hard as steel. It is not only that their *Yi* (Mind) is strong, but their internal *Jin* is also strong. This strength does not show on the outside. It is also wrong to believe that the mind directly guides the *Jin*. If you use your mind to directly control the muscles, *Qi* support will be limited and muscular strength will predominate. Rather the mind should guide the *Qi*, which in turn guides the *Jin*. This is how to use the truly internal energy called *Jin*. If you use this *Jin* to neutralize, using the correct timing and a correct understanding of the opponent, then you can truly neutralize a force of one thousand pounds with four ounces.

Neutralization begins with Adhere-Connect and Stick-Follow. Once these are developed, you will begin to understand *Jin*, which means that you will be able to understand the opponent's intentions. Once you understand his intentions you will be able to neutralize effectively, and then you will be light and agile.

You must neutralize correctly before you can counterattack effectively. If you cannot neutralize effectively to gain an advantage, how can your own attack succeed? If a martial artist's skill is high, he may move forward as he neutralizes, perhaps counterattacking at the same time. In this case the upper body looks like it is withdrawing, but the legs are already moving forward. The best way to learn Neutralizing *Jin* is through pushing hands practice. You can also stand with your arm in the Wardoff position, and have your partner apply Push *Jin*. The moment you feel his energy, withdraw slightly and turn your body. Adhere to his arm. Do not push his arm away, instead lead it to the side. This is done by turning your body, not by moving your arm independently of your body. In the beginning you may deflect his attack at a 45 degree angle, but as you gain in skill, the angle will get smaller.

2. Ji Jin (Press Jin, literally to squeeze or compress) 擠勁

Press *Jin* is a push which is often applied at an angle to the original line of motion. A hand is held against the forearm or wrist (Figure 3-158) to press against the opponent's arms, shoulder, or body in order to knock him down or push him away. The technique may also be used as a strike.

Figure 3-158

Figure 3-159

Figure 3-160

Figure 3-161

Press is often used to counter the opponent's Rollback *Jin*. For example, if you push and the opponent uses Rollback on your right arm (Figure 3-159), first adjust your waist and legs to put yourself in a good position and the opponent in a bad position. Place your left hand on your right forearm where you intend to apply force, and use Press in the correct direction to make the opponent lose his balance (Figure 3-160). Press *Jin* is also commonly used to counter Shoulder-Stroke (Figure 3-161)

Figure 3-162

Figure 3-163

Figure 3-164

or Elbow-Stroke (Figure 3-162). Again, you must first adjust your position, and then press the opponent either from inside (Figure 3-163) or from the back (Figure 3-164) to make him lose his balance.

When Press is used as a strike, it is sharp and short. The striking zones are usually on the chest or shoulder blade. When certain targets such as the solar plexus or the cavities near the nipples (*Yingchuang, Rugen,* and *Jiuwei*)(Figure 3-165) are struck, the opponent's breath can be sealed. When the center of the shoulder blade (*Tianzong*)(Figure 3-166) is attacked, it can make the opponent's entire arm and shoulder numb. In order to strike the chest, you usually use Small Rollback (see Rollback *Jin*) first to open up the opponent's chest area. Right after the Rollback is applied, immediately use Press *Jin* to strike his solar plexus or nipple area to seal his breath. When you want to attack the shoulder blade, first use Large Rollback to break the opponent's root and expose his shoulder blade (see Rollback *Jin*). You may then use Press *Jin* to strike his shoulder to numb his arm.

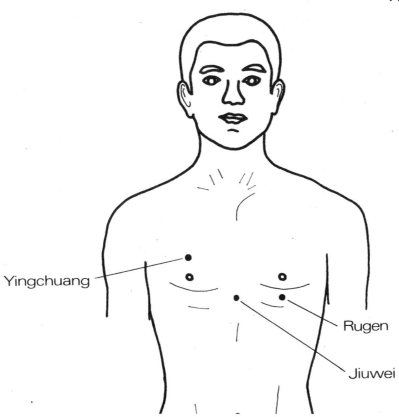

Yingchuang

Rugen

Jiuwei

Figure 3-165

Tianzong

Figure 3-166

171

| Figure 3-167 | Figure 3-168 |

When using Press *Jin*, do not use *Li* from the arm, because the opponent will be able to use his *Li* against it. Use the *Jin* from the legs and control it with your waist. When pressing the opponent, your body should be centered and stable - it should not lean in the direction you are pressing. When you are executing an upward Press, your *Yi* should be on breaking the opponent's root. Sometimes a small amount of Lifting *Jin* is used just before the Press to make the opponent float. Press can also be applied downward. This is used to seal the opponent's arms and open him up for a second attack.

Press can be trained on a bag or partner in the same way Wardoff is trained. It is often practiced on a partner in combination with Rollback.

3. Lie Jin (Rend Jin) 挒勁

When you rend or tear something, you pull it in two directions at once. When you use Rend *Jin*, you use your two hands or your hands and a foot to tear the opponent off his stance. This often has a whirlpool effect, as you twist him down.

When Rend *Jin* is used for attack, it is frequently used right after Rollback *Jin* or Pluck *Jin*. For example, when you use Rollback and have your opponent in an unstable position, twist your body to change the direction of your pull (Figures 3-167 and 3-168). Before your opponent can regain his balance, your Rend *Jin* pulls him off his feet. The same principle applies when Rend *Jin* is used after Pluck *Jin*. If you have pulled your opponent's lead arm to his left and have unbalanced him, you can block his front leg with your left leg and take him down (Figures 3-169 and 3-170). Alternatively, if your Pluck causes

Figure 3-169

Figure 3-170

Figure 3-171

Figure 3-172

the opponent to resist, you may be able to step behind his leg and use Rend in the direction of his movement, taking him down to his rear (Figures 3-171 and 3-172).

When Rend *Jin* is used for defense, first change the direction of your opponent's attack and make him miss his target, then use Rend *Jin* to make him lose his balance. For example, when your opponent uses Rollback *Jin*, do not resist, but instead calm yourself and follow his *Jin*. Change the direction

Figure 3-173

Figure 3-174

Figure 3-175

of his *Jin* by rotating your body, lock one of his legs with your leg, and pull him off his feet (Figures 3-173 to 3-175). In this case you have used your enemy's Rollback *Jin* against him.

To use Rend *Jin* effectively you must have a firm root, otherwise when you try to move your opponent you will lose your own root and be controlled by him. As with any other technique, you must use the correct timing and choose the right opportunity. If you can sense your opponent's intention just before his *Jin* is completely out, you will have the best chance for success. When you are using Rend as a takedown, don't use *Jin* until you have the opponent either unbalanced or overextended, so that he will lose his balance the moment you apply *Jin*.

Rend *Jin* can be trained through pushing hands and by practicing individual applications with a partner.

4. Kao Jin (Bump Jin) 靠勁

Bump *Jin* uses the shoulder, chest, back, thigh, or even head to bump the opponent off balance. Here, we will use the

Figure 3-176

Figure 3-177

Figure 3-178

Shoulder-Bump or Shoulder-Stroke as an example. This *Jin* can be long or short - long to bounce or throw the opponent, short to strike, particularly to the solar plexus or the shoulder blade cavity. The outside of the shoulder is usually used for striking, while the front and back are often used for throwing the opponent. Shoulder techniques can be applied in any direction.

Shoulder-Stroke is frequently used when your opponent uses Rollback against you (Figure 3-176). Follow the direction of his Rollback, then redirect the force toward him and use your shoulder to bounce him away or strike him (Figure 3-177). This *Jin* can be used any time your enemy's chest, shoulder blade, or armpit is exposed. When used as a strike, Shoulder-Stroke is similar to Elbow-Stroke, except that it is done from a shorter range.

Shoulder-Stroke *Jin* is also used in throwing or takedown techniques. The opponent can be thrown with the same motion you use to throw a shovelful of snow over your shoulder (Figure 3-178), or taken down over your leg with a shrug of your shoulder (Figures 3-179 and 3-180).

| Figure 3-179 | Figure 3-180 |

Shoulder-Stroke *Jin* can be practiced on a bag. Be sure to step in close enough so that you don't have to lean. Practice sharp strikes and slower pushes. You can also catch the bag on your arm, roll it toward your shoulder as you withdraw slightly and coil to accumulate energy, and then bounce the bag away.

When you practice with a partner, a kicking bag or other type of padding (Figure 3-181) will let you use full power without hurting him. You can practice pushes and light strikes without cushioning if your partner holds his arms across his body for protection (Figure 3-182). His arms should be touching his chest so that they don't absorb the force of your technique. Diagonal Flying and similar techniques also use the shoulder, and can be practiced with a partner.

5. Yin Jin (Leading Jin) 引勁

Leading *Jin* moves with the opponent's force to lead him into a disadvantageous position. It is usually used between Neutralizing *Jin* and Controlling *Jin*. When the opponent attacks, neutralize his attack until most of his *Jin* has been expended. Lead his remaining *Jin* so that he becomes overextended, unbalanced, or otherwise vulnerable to attack. Leading *Jin* uses the other person's *Jin*, adds to it, and either redirects it or leads it further than he had intended.

This *Jin* is usually easy to apply to beginning *Taiji* students and to people who throw their weight forward when they attack. It is harder to use against the more experienced fighter. When your opponent keeps some of his *Jin* in reserve and is wary of being led, you have to use false Leading *Jins* to confuse him. You may have to lead him high and attack low, or lead him straight and attack laterally.

Figure 3-181

Figure 3-182

Since Leading *Jin* works together with Listening, Understanding, and Neutralizing *Jins*, the only way to learn it is through pushing hands. To learn Leading *Jin*, after you have neutralized your partner's attack, lead it a little further. Only experience can teach you how to lead his *Jin*, and how to put him into positions that allow you to attack. This is a subtle *Jin*, so be careful not to get into the habit of hauling on the other person's arms. If you can't lead him, don't force it. Wait for another opportunity when you can smoothly lead him a little further than he had intended.

6. Jie Jin (Borrowing Jin) 借勁

Borrowing *Jin* is the trick of using the opponent's *Jin* so that he is bounced out by his own power. It is one of the hardest *Jins* to understand and apply, but once you understand it you will have a great advantage in a fight. It is a high art which, when mastered, may even be done without your conscious attention.

Many *Taiji* practitioners misunderstand this *Jin*, thinking it is like Neutralizing *Jin* or Yielding *Jin*. Others may think that to apply Borrowing *Jin* you follow the opponent's *Jin* and add your own *Jin* to his to make him fall. In fact, that would be a combination of yielding and leading - the real Borrowing *Jin* is more aggressive. If the opponent attacks, you bounce him, if he is about to attack but hasn't yet attacked, you still bounce him. With Borrowing *Jin* you give back just what you were given — if the opponent's *Jin* is hard, so is yours; if his is soft, so is yours. Usually you need to use only a small amount of *Jin*, which can be applied through almost any part of your body.

Stability is extremely important, as is the coordination of the waist and legs. However, the most important factor is timing. There are two timings that can be used. The first is when your opponent is just about to emit his *Jin*, but has not yet emitted it. This is the same timing that is used with Neutralizing *Jin*. It is easier than the second timing and is usually learned first. When the opponent is about to emit his *Jin*, his *Yi* is already on moving forward. Use your Resisting *Jin* to catch him just as he emits his *Jin*. Since you prevent his forward motion, he will push himself away. If you add some of your *Jin* to his momentum, you can bounce him far away. The classics say: "The opponent does not move, I do not move; the opponent moves slightly, I move first" (Appendix A-3). We can use an example to explain this. When a person is about to step through a door, and has lifted his foot and started to move forward, if the door is suddenly shut, the person will usually be bounced backward. If the timing is right, you do not need much energy to do this.

The second timing is just before your opponent's *Jin* is completely out. When someone is striking you, his *Yi* is on the striking, and this *Yi* is focusing his *Jin* so that it reaches its maximum at a point inside your body. If you stop his forward motion just before his *Jin* reaches its maximum, his *Yi* will be interrupted, but he will not be able to stop his forward energy. As with the previous timing, since he cannot go forward, his energy will bounce back to him. If his arms have any stiffness he will bounce backward, especially if you add your own energy to the motion. In order to understand this, imagine that someone is punching you, and you are holding a strong, resilient balloon in from of you. If you move the balloon forward into his punch just before the punch reaches the balloon, you will find that his power will not just be stopped, it will be bounced back into him. You can see that this Borrowing *Jin* is higher than the one mentioned above.

In order to use either timing, you must be skilled in Resisting *Jin*, and must have your *Qi* developed throughout your body so that your body is resilient like a balloon, yet strong enough to bounce back the opponent's power. A strong root is also necessary to absorb the other person's power and send it back to him. Your opponent should have the feeling that he is pushing a wall which pushes back at him at the same time, so that he only succeeds in pushing himself away from it. Borrowing *Jin* requires a high level of Understanding *Jin*, and great subtlety. If your opponent sees that you are alert and ready for him, he will be very careful. If he thinks you are vulnerable, then he will attack with a lot of force. There are stories of *Taiji* masters bouncing opponents several yards away. The harder the opponent attacks, the further he bounces.

When you have mastered the basic *Jins* and wish to practice Borrowing *Jin*, have a partner push you and work on the

Figure 3-183

Figure 3-184

first timing. Try to catch him just as he is about to emit his *Jin*. When you perceive his *Jin*, direct it into your root and let it bounce directly back into him. Add a small amount of your own *Jin*, but not too much. Rather than trying to push him as he is pushing you, guide him so that he pushes himself away from you. To practice the second timing, yield before your partner's attack, and when his energy is three quarters expended, direct the rest of it into your root and let him bounce off your root.

7. Kai Jin or Zhan Jin (Opening Jin or Spreading Jin)
開勁、展勁

Opening (or Spreading) *Jin* is one of the most basic *Jins* in the martial arts. When your opponent's *Jin* is coming toward you, connect to his arm and "open" your arms to lead him to the side. This is a long *Jin*, so the muscles are used more than with other *Jins*. When the opponent attacks, connect to his arm and neutralize, then lead him further. Grasp his wrist or other joint as necessary, then "open" or "spread" your arms, pulling him into an exposed position so you can strike him. In the *Taiji* sequence, many forms belong to this *Jin* such as Crane Opens Wings (Figure 3-183) and Seal Tightly (Figure 3-184).

Train this *Jin* during Pushing Hands the way you would train Leading *Jin*. As you neutralize your partner's attack, "close" your body (arc your back and draw in your arms near your body). Then "open" your body to extend his motion.

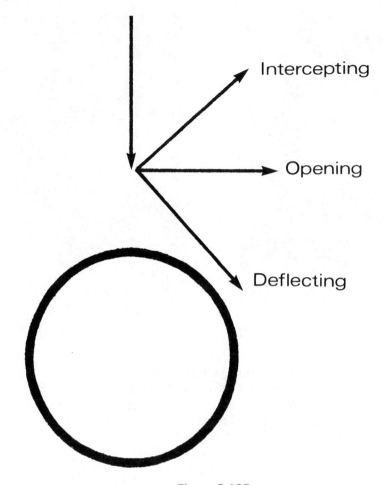

Figure 3-185

8. Bo Jin (Deflecting Jin) 撥勁

Deflecting *Jin* is similar to Opening *Jin*, except that you deflect the attack past you and to your rear. Since you are changing the course of the opponent's attack only slightly, your arms do not extend out very far. Figure 3-185 shows the difference between Deflecting, Opening and Intercepting *Jins*. With Deflecting *Jin* you are only in contact with the opponent's arm for a short time. You do not try to adhere to his arm, rather you deflect it past you so that you can counterattack.

To train this *Jin*, have your partner punch your chest (Figure 3-186), and use your arm to deflect it to the side (Figure 3-187). Your main action is to turn your body so that the waist does the work and not your arm. Your body must withdraw somewhat so that you do not deflect the attack too sharply to the side.

9. Zhuan Jin (Turning Jin or Twisting Jin) 轉勁

Turning *Jin* is a turning movement generated by the waist and expressed through any part of the body. Sometimes when you are grabbed or controlled you can reverse the situation and gain the advantage just by turning or twisting part of your

Figure 3-186

Figure 3-187

Figure 3-188

body such as the wrist, arm, or waist. Many offensive *Qin Na* moves uses this *Jin*. Offensive or defensive, the motion is generated by the waist. This allows you to get your whole body behind the move so that it is strong without needing much force.

When your opponent grabs your right wrist with his right hand and pulls down (Figure 3-188), first use Prying *Jin* to drop

Figure 3-189

Figure 3-190

Figure 3-191

your elbow and loosen his grip. At the same time, use Turning *Jin* to turn your wrist so that your palm faces him and can grasp and control his wrist (Figure 3-189). Another example is Wave Hands in Clouds. Assume your opponent has grasped your right wrist with his right hand (Figure 3-190). Rotate your body to the right and rotate your palm to face out (Figure 3-191), putting the opponent into a defending position. This turning is done with the whole body so that he cannot easily resist it.

Turning *Jin* is also used in *Qin Na* to control the opponent. For example, once you have grasped your opponent's wrist, put your forearm on his elbow (Figure 3-192), and then rotate your whole body downward to control him (Figure 3-193). If you also turn to the side you will spiral the opponent down and pull him off his root. This application is similar to Rend, only longer.

Figure 3-192

Figure 3-193

Figure 3-194

10. Zhe Die Jin (Folding and Entwining Jin) 摺疊勁

Folding and Entwining *Jin* is the use of small turning and leading movements of the hands and arms to evade, redirect, and control the opponent's arms. Folding is when one part of the body bends to escape being controlled. This motion is easily continued into a spiraling movement through which your hands entwine or wrap around the opponent's arms and control them. This *Jin* is a combination of Leading, Controlling, Prying and Coiling *Jins*. It is frequently used in *Qin Na* and pushing hands. For example, when the opponent controls one of your arms, that arm evades or escapes while your other arm leads the opponent's hand away or controls it (Figures 3-194 to 3-198). Although there is relatively little body motion in this *Jin*, the

Figure 3-195

Figure 3-196

Figure 3-197

Figure 3-198

waist must still guide the motion so that the whole body can support it. This *Jin* is very common in southern martial styles such as tiger, snake, and crane, which, like *Taiji*, emphasize close-range fighting.

To practice this *Jin* during Pushing Hands, lead your partner's *Jin* and wrap your hands around his arms. Keep alert for opportunities to continue the spiraling of his arms into *Qin Na* techniques.

C. Neutral (Neither Offense nor Defense) Jin (Fei Gong Fei Shou Jin, 非攻非守勁):

1. Dou Sou Jin (Trembling Jin or Shaking Jin) 抖擻勁

This *Jin* is a sudden trembling or shaking of the body which is used primarily as a training method for generating and transmitting *Jin*. You can also use it when you are held tightly, as in a bear hug, to escape or even cause serious internal injury to your attacker. It is sometimes used to raise the Spirit of Vitality.

To get an idea of this *Jin*, watch a dog or bird shake water off its body. You will notice that the motion is like a shiver in that it is a sudden, almost compulsive explosion of motion and energy. There is a lot of energy expended in a small space, and the water can fly quite a ways. The animal's stance is very stable, and the power is generated from the inside out. These are very important principles in the generation of *Jin*. Chang, San-Feng's **Taiji Treatise** states that: "The root is in the feet, (power is) generated from the legs, controlled by the waist and expressed by the fingers. From the feet to the legs to the waist must be integrated, and one unified *Qi*" (Appendix A-1). The *Taiji* beginner must learn these principles before he can apply his *Jin* to anything else.

To practice this *Jin*, stand in a stable stance and relax. Imagine that you are shaking water off your whole body. First twist your body to one side, then twist back and forth in a quick, shiver-like motion. Generate the *Jin* in your legs, and use your waist to lead it to your shoulders and arms. Do not try to control the movement too much, or you will be stiff and the energy will not reach your limbs.

2. Ding Jin (Upright Jin) 頂勁

Upright *Jin* is a *Jin* which can be felt but not seen. It is the *Jin* which a fighter uses to hold his body upright and centered, and at the same time raise his Spirit of Vitality. It is said: "An insubstantial energy leads the head upward. The *Qi* is sunk to the *Dan Tian*" (Appendix A-2). This is an example of the division of substantial and insubstantial in the body. Let the *Qi* sink to your abdomen so that it becomes substantial, and your upper body and head become insubstantial. As the *Qi* sinks, there is a corresponding rising of energy and a lifting of the head from inside. You can also imagine that you are suspended like a puppet from a string on the top of your head. Since the top of your head is being lifted, the rest of your body sinks and the substantial settles in your abdomen.

In this *Jin*, *Yi* is more important and critical than the form. When your *Yi* is balanced up and down, your body will be upright, the root will be firm, and your spirit will be raised. *Ding Jin* training is closely related to rooting training since the downward Rooting *Jin* will enhance and help to balance the Upright *Jin*.

Figure 3-199

3. Pan Jin (Rooting Jin) 盤勁

Rooting *Jin* is the energy of sinking your root deep into the ground. A good root is necessary for stability as well as for the generation and transmission of energy. Rooting *Jin* can also be used defensively when your opponent tries to move you or knock you down. This *Jin* training is very popular among Chinese martial styles. It is commonly called *Qian Jin Zhui* (Thousand Pound Sinking, 千斤墜). In this training, your *Yi* is the key to success — you must imagine that you weigh a thousand pounds and your opponent can't move you even slightly. Your entire *Yi* is straight down and the *Qi* is directed a few inches beneath your feet.

A good way to train this *Jin* is by standing in a horse stance on bricks (Figure 3-199). Your *Yi* must be directed straight downward — if your *Yi* is scattered your feet will move sideward and the bricks will fall. This .training can also be done on ice or marbles.

4. Ling Kong Jin (Aloft Jin) 凌空勁

Aloft *Jin* is the energy generated in the waist, legs, and feet for jumping. This *Jin* is used whenever a *Taiji* fighter needs to jump up for kicking or withdrawing. As with the *Jin* in the arms, the use of *Li* is cut to a minimum. In Aloft *Jin*, the waist starts the motion, then the legs contribute their energy, and finally the feet push off the ground. The *Qi* sinks down to support the action. This *Jin* is harder than any of the *Jins* applied through the hands. In ancient times good *Taiji* masters were said to be able to jump several yards into the air. Because this *Jin* is hard to understand and train, it has been gradually ignored.

D. Leg Jin (Tui Jin, 腿勁):

The *Jins* discussed above are expressed primarily through the hands, arms, and shoulders. When *Jin* is expressed through the legs, the principles of generation and expression are somewhat different. The *Jin* which is expressed by the upper body is rooted in the feet, generated by the legs, and controlled by the waist. When you kick you are on only one foot, and so your root and your ability to generate *Jin* are weakened significantly. Since it is more difficult to maintain your center and balance, it is harder for your waist to control and direct the *Jin*. When your body's balance is off, it is also more difficult to balance your *Jin* and *Qi*, and your power is cut down considerably.

Although there are many difficulties in the training, the legs can still be very powerful and effective tools in combat. They are longer than the arms, and can therefore attack sooner and from a greater range. There is a saying in Chinese martial society "One centimeter longer, one centimeter of advantage" (*Yi fen chang, yi fen li*, 一分長一分利). This means that if your weapon is longer than your opponent's, you have an advantage. Furthermore, because the legs are well below eye level, it is harder to sense their attacks. To remedy this, Chinese martial artists train to watch and sense the opponent's shoulder movement. Whenever someone attacks with either hands or legs, his shoulders must move first. If you have enough experience, you should be able to sense your opponent's intention just before his attack starts.

Because the legs have stronger muscles, they can still generate a great deal of power even if *Qi* is not used. If you know how to use your *Qi* to express *Jin* through your legs, your legs will be more powerful than your hands and they will be undefeatable. Some kicks, particularly low kicks, can be done without sacrificing too many of the conditions necessary for the generation of *Jin*.

Chinese martial artists have researched different ways of kicking to minimize the reduction of *Jin*. They have divided the kicks into four categories: Low Kicks, Middle Kicks, High Kicks, and Spinning Kicks. Each of these four groups has advantages and disadvantages. There are at least 40 different kicking techniques trained in the different styles of Chinese martial arts. *Taijiquan* uses only a few kicking techniques, most of them low, to assist the hand techniques. The hands remain the main weapons in *Taijiquan*.

a. Low Kicks (Di Ti, 低踢):

Of all the kicking techniques, low kicks are probably the fastest, safest, and most effective. These kicks specialize in attacking the knee and below. The most common targets are the knee, leg (*Tiaokou* and *Zhongdu* cavities), ankle (*Jiexi* cavity), and foot (*Taichong* cavity)(Figures 3-200 and 3-201). Most of the southern martial styles emphasize low kicks. There is a proverb that says: "*Zu bu guo xi*" (foot not higher than the knee, 足不過膝). This is because whenever you kick higher than the knee, you start losing your center and stability. Not only that, you open the door to the groin area which your opponent can take advantage of. Furthermore, a kick higher than the knee is easier to block.

When kicking low, it is still usually possible to maintain enough of your center, balance, and stability to generate *Jin*. Even though your waist control is limited, you can train your

Figure 3-200   Figure 3-201

legs to develop a high level of destructive power. The disadvantage of low kicks is that they are short range. In order to use them for middle and long range, it is necessary to hop or jump to approach the opponent. However, whenever you do this, you lose your root, stability, and balance. For this reason, the middle, high, and spinning kicks usually predominate in long range fighting.

Because of these reasons, and because of the adhere-stick principle, *Taiji* emphasizes mostly short range fighting and low kicks. The common kicks in *Taijiquan* are *Cai* (踩), *Chuai* (踹), *Di Qie* (低切), *Di Qiao* (低蹺), and *Di Sao* (低掃). The general principles for generating *Jin* are the same for all of the low kicks, most of the middle kicks, and some of the high kicks. The *Jin* is first generated from the leg on the ground. Before the *Jin* passes out the kicking leg, the waist jerks so that the *Jin* reaches the foot in a powerful, short pulse (Figure 3-202). This is difficult to learn, but if you persevere you will grasp the trick and suddenly understand it.

Figure 3-202

Figure 3-203

Remember that balancing *Yi* and *Qi* is as important with kicks as it is with hand techniques. In order to get the maximum energy out to your kicking leg you must put your *Yi* into your supporting foot.

Next, we will discuss the low kicking *Jins* which are commonly used in *Taijiquan*.

1. Cai Jin (Forward Stepping Jin) 踩勁

Cai Jin uses the bottom of the foot to attack primarily the knees and the top of the feet. It is fast and sharp, concentrated and precisely directed. In short range fighting, you can sometimes use the rear foot to attack the opponent's knee (Figure 3-203). If you use the right angle, the knee can be broken. The front foot is frequently used to attack the opponent's

Figure 3-204

Figure 3-205

front foot by hopping forward (Figure 3-204). If you step on the right spot you will numb the leg and limit his ability to kick and move. To do this kick, lift the foot up to cock the leg, and snap it forward and down. *Jin* is generated by the supporting leg and directed to the target by the waist's jerking motion. The kick is relaxed until just before the target.

2. Chuai Jin (Stamping Jin) 低掃

Chuai Jin uses the heel to stamp on the knee, shin, ankle, and back of the foot. *Chuai Jin* is similar to *Cai Jin*, but it is more penetrating and destructive. With *Cai Jin*, the jerking of the waist matches the *Jin* generated from the leg. With this *Jin* however, the jerking of the waist is a little behind the leg's *Jin*. In other words, the leg first leads the foot to the target, and just before the foot hits, the waist jerks forward to enhance the *Jin*. *Chuai Jin* is usually used to attack the opponent's front leg with your own front leg or rear leg, usually at a downward angle (Figure 3-205). It can also be used to attack the back of the foot (Figure 3-206).

Figure 3-206

Figure 3-207

3. Di Qie Jin (Low Snap Cut Jin) 低切勁

Di Qie Jin is a snap kick which uses the outside of the foot to attack the opponent's leg (Figure 3-207). Common targets are the ankles, shins, and knees. When attacking the ankle, the *Jin* is directed forward and downward. The waist leads the leg's *Jin*, and the body sinks to increase downward power. The sequence of movements is as follows: the waist first leads the knee out as the foot lags behind, the foot then snaps out, and then the body sinks just as the foot is about to strike the target. When *Di Qie* is used to attack the shin, the *Jin* generated from the other leg is directed forward and slightly downward to the target (Figure 3-208). The body does not usually sink in this attack. When this kick is used for a knee attack, the *Jin* is directed forward to the opponent's knee.

Generally speaking, *Qie Jin* is sharper and more penetrating than *Cai Jin* and *Chuai Jin*. However, its power is weaker, and so its breaking capability is less. *Qie Jin* is used in many martial styles. Its shin and knee attacks are fast and can usually forestall the opponent's attack. If the body is not dropped for the ankle attack, it too can be fast, although in this case its power would be reduced.

Figure 3-208

Figure 3-209

4. Di Qiao Jin (Low Lift-Hook Jin) 低蹺勁

Di Qiao Jin specializes in attacking the shin. It is sometimes called *Shang Ding* (Upward Press Kick, 上頂) or *Liu Tui* (Strolling Kick, 溜腿) by other styles. To use this kicking *Jin*, hop forward on the rear leg and kick upward with the ball of the front foot (Figure 3-209). To hop, rock your weight onto the front foot, and let your rear leg come forward. Just before the rear foot touches the ground, start the kick with the front foot. The kicking leg stays relatively straight as it rises to strike the shin (Figure 3-210). Hopping is usually necessary to set up the right range and to generate forward power. This kick is generally not very powerful. However, because it is applied suddenly, and because it attacks the shin, which is a vulnerable target, it may be possible to immobilize the opponent with just one kick.

5. Di Sao Jin (Low Sweep Jin) 低掃勁

Di Sao Jin uses the bottom of the foot (Figure 3-211) to strike the side of the ankle, shin (Figure 3-212), or knee. Though not very destructive, this kick is very useful. It can break your opponent's root and upset his stability, opening

Figure 3-210

Figure 3-211

Figure 3-212

the way for another attack. If done accurately to the side of the shin or knee it can numb your opponent's leg and limit his fighting capacity. When using this *Jin*, the root in the other leg is extremely important. The *Jin* is generated mainly by turning the waist and is directed down to move the kicking leg.

Zhongwan

Zhangmen

Qihai

Shayin

Figure 3-213

b. Middle Kicks (Zhong Ti, 中踢):

Most of the middle kicks are used for mid-range fighting. Common targets are the stomach (*Zhongwan* cavity), waist (*Zhangmen* cavity), abdomen (*Dan Tian* or *Qihai*), groin (*Shayin* cavity)(Figure 3-213), and thigh (*Jimen*, *Xuehai*, and

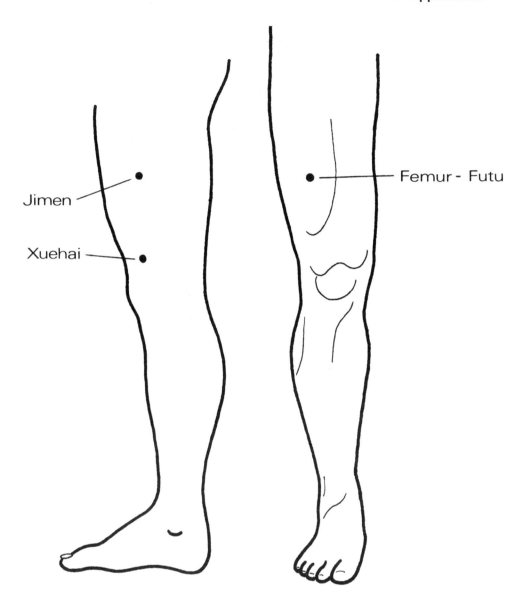

Jimen

Xuehai

Femur - Futu

Figure 3-214   **Figure 3-215**

Futu cavities)(Figures 3-214 and 3-215). Whenever you use the middle kicks you lose a portion of your stability, and weaken your *Qi* and *Jin* balance. You also expose your abdomen and groin to attack. To minimize this vulnerability it is important to kick fast. In addition, because your stability and balance are minimal, it is much harder to generate *Jin* from the supporting leg than it is with the low kicks. However, if you practice perseveringly it is still possible to reach a high level of power.

To generate a more powerful *Jin*, some styles twist the waist and hips. However, this significantly weakens your root. When a person who uses this hip and waist twisting is blocked or misses his target, he frequently is so off balance that he is

Figure 3-216

Figure 3-217

vulnerable to a quick counterattack. The Chinese consider the root supremely important. *Jin* must be generated by the rooted leg and guided by the jerking of the waist. It will take you longer to develop *Jin* this way, but once you have done it, you will be able to kick from a more advantageous position.

The most common middle kicks in *Taiji* are: *Ti* (踢), *Deng* (蹬), *Zhong Qiao* (中蹺), and *Zhong Qie* (中切).

1. Ti Jin (Toe Kick Jin) 踢勁

Ti Jin is a "toe" kick which usually attacks the groin with the top of the foot (Figure 3-216). Either the front or the rear foot can be used. Usually when the front leg is used, the rear leg hops forward to set up the range and increase the forward *Jin* (Figure 3-217). While this hopping is taking place, the waist jerks to enhance the kicking *Jin* and direct it to the target. When the rear leg is used for the kick, the front leg should be rooted firmly first. Then the rear leg pushes back to generate the forward kicking power, your weight shifts to the front foot, and the rear leg kicks forward. As the power is being generated, the waist also jerks and directs the *Jin* to the target. Your kicking leg should be snapped out like a flexible spring. The

Figure 3-218

knee moves out first and then the foot follows. When done accurately, this kick can kill, so you should be very careful when practicing.

2. Deng Jin (Heel Kick Jin) 蹬勁

Deng Jin snaps the heel out to the opponent's midsection (Figure 3-218). Common targets are the groin, solar plexus, and *Dan Tian* (Figure 3-219). The technique is similar to *Ti Jin* except that the heel is used instead of the toe. Again, the knee lifts first and the foot curves in toward you and then snaps out to the opponent. This kick is usually more powerful than the toe kick, and because the heel is used, it is more effective against some targets.

Figure 3-219

3. Zhong Qiao Jin (Middle Lift-Hook Jin) 中蹺勁

This is a straight-leg rising kick. The technique and the principle of *Jin* generation are the same as *Di Qiao Jin*. However, it is a longer range kick than *Di Qiao Jin*, and it is usually used to attack the cavity behind the groin (Figure 3-220). Because the power is hooked and directed upward, it can reach this cavity more easily than most other kicks. When done accurately, this attack will cause death.

4. Zhong Qie Jin (Middle Snap Cut Jin) 中切勁

Like *Di Qie Jin*, *Zhong Qie Jin* uses the outside edge of the

Figure 3-220

Figure 3-221

foot to kick. Common targets are the abdomen, stomach, waist, and the side of the waist (Figure 3-221). *Zhong Qie Jin* can be done either in place or hopping. Hopping is used to shorten the range and generate forward power.

c. High Kicks (Gao Ti, 高踢): Chinese martial artists seldom use single-foot high kicks because they sacrifice root, stability, and balance. Also, in order to avoid counterattack, high kicks must be extremely fast, and recovery time must be short. As with middle kicks, some non-Chinese martial styles use the hip and waist to generate *Jin*, and sacrifice the root entirely.

Because high kicks can be effective in long range fighting, Chinese martial artists will use them, but in a different way. The Chinese martial artist generally uses double kicks — in other words, one leg leaps up and forward, and then pulls back to move the other leg out. This motion generates *Jin*. The waist also jerks to speed up the kick and enhance the kicking power. Therefore, when the high kicks are used, you don't have any root at all — your body is completely in the air. While one leg is attacking, the other leg is curved up to protect vital areas such as the abdomen and groin. When you land, drop immediately into a low stance to regain your stability. This kicking strategy allows you to be mobile and agile. The semi-stable state should be avoided — it is probably the worst situation to be in when you are fighting.

In *Taijiquan*, high kicks are seldom used. The main use for such kicks is to cover the distance to the opponent, and to

| Figure 3-222 | Figure 3-223 |

increase forward *Jin*. Even when double jump kicks are used, it is only to attack the middle and lower body.

d. Spinning Kicks (Bai Tui, 擺腿):

Most of the spinning kicks are classified as high kicks. The difference is that spinning kicks use the waist to spin the whole body and thereby generate *Jin*. There are two kinds of spinning kicks — stable spinning and jump spinning. In stable spinning kicks, one leg stays rooted and supports the waist as it generates jerking power and leads the kicking leg in a circular motion to strike the target. These kicks use the motion of only part of the body to generate power. Typical examples of the stable spinning kick are external sweep (*Wai Bai*, 外擺) and internal sweep (*Nei Bai*, 內擺). The other kind of spinning kick is jump spinning, in which the body completely leaves the ground and moves in a complete circle. The waist generates spinning power and leads it out to the leg. A typical example of this kick is the tornado kick (*Xuan Feng Tui*, 旋風腿). *Taiji* uses only two stable spinning kicks: external sweep and internal sweep.

1. Wai Bai Jin (External Sweep Jin) 外擺勁

Wai Bai Jin uses the outside edge of the foot to attack. Common targets are the kidneys and the back of the head (Figure 3-222). One leg stays firmly rooted while the waist jerks in a curved motion to generate the power and move the attacking foot in a circular motion (Figure 3-223). This kick is also used to kick a weapon out of a person's hand (Figure 3-224). When this *Jin* is used, the circular motion is first generated by a quick, circular jerk of the waist. If you are kicking with your right leg, it starts out moving to the left before it

Figure 3-224

Figure 3-225

Figure 3-226

cuts over to the right. Once the kick reaches the highest point, the waist twists suddenly to pull the leg abruptly down. When the foot hits the target it is just past the highest point in its arc, and moving downward. Striking the target downward this way generates the most force.

2. Nei Bai Jin (Internal Sweep Jin) 内擺勁

Nei Bai Jin is similar to *Wai Bai Jin*, except that it circles in the opposite direction. In *Nei Bai Jin* the bottom of the foot is used to strike. Common targets are the kidneys, stomach, and head (Figures 3-225 and 3-226). It may also be used to strike the opponent's hand to force him to release his weapon. The principle of *Jin* generation is the same as *Wai Bai Jin*, however the timing of the strike is different. With *Nei Bai Jin* you usually strike when the foot reaches the highest point, although on occasion this kick will be used to strike downward to the back of the head. The waist generates power as with *Wai Bai*, although the motion is harder to learn and takes more practice.

3-7. Summary of Jin Training

After reading about *Jin* theory and the different types of *Jin*, you are probably wondering how to start training. As matter of fact, all of the training principles and methods have been discussed in the last section. In this section we would like to review and highlight the important points for the benefit of those who have not had experience in *Jin* training before. Hopefully this section will lead you to the entrance of this secret. Since *Taijiquan* specializes in hand applications, we will discuss only hand *Jins*. Once you have grasped the trick of generating hand *Jins*, you should have no problem in figuring out the leg *Jin* training by yourself.

Sensing Jin

Sensing *Jins* are much harder to train than the manifested *Jins*. They take a lot of patience, and especially a lot of time. This is because the higher levels of Sensing *Jin* require well-developed *Qi* circulation. Even if you do not practice any *Qigong* exercises other than the *Taiji* sequence, you can still train your Sensing *Jins* by using your natural sensing ability.

Since you are developing your sensitivity to another person's motion and intention, it is generally necessary to have a partner to train sensing *Jin*. If no partner is available, the *Taiji* ball can provide some training, but it can only take you to a certain level. Pushing hands is the most important way to train. The more you practice, and the greater the variety of body types and personalities you encounter, the more you will progress. Listening *Jin* is the first step. After much listening, you develop a feel for what is happening, and can tell from a touch or a slight motion what the opponent is doing, or even what he is planning to do. When you have reached this level, you have entered the gate of Understanding *Jin*. How well you progress with these *Jins* depends upon two factors. The first, sensitivity of feeling, depends to a large degree on how well developed the *Qi* circulation to your skin is. The second factor is calmness of the mind. When your mind is calm, you can concentrate to feel and sense. Without a calm and concentrated mind, your attention is scattered and your sensitivity is reduced.

When you have practiced for many years, you may then reach a level where you can sense the opponent's *Jin* even before it is emitted. It is said: "After you have mastered techniques, then you can gradually grasp what 'Understanding *Jin*' (*Dong Jin*) means. From 'Understanding *Jin*' you gradually approach enlightenment (intuitive understanding) of your opponent's intention. However, without a great deal of study over a long time, you cannot suddenly grasp this intuitive understanding of your opponent." It is also said: "After understanding *Jin*, the more practice, the more refinement. Silently learn, then ponder; gradually you will approach your heart's desire" (Appendix A-2).

Yin (Passive) sensing *Jin* is trained in pushing hands practice. *Yang* (Active) sensing *Jin* is trained through your *Yi*. First you build up your

Qi either in the *Dan Tian* or in a particular part of the body, usually the arms. This *Qi* is then passed into the opponent's body, in coordination with your exhalation, to disturb his *Qi* pattern. If you coordinate the technique with an inhalation, you can withdraw *Qi* from his body.

Manifested Jin

Manifested *Jins* are easier to understand and train than sensing *Jins*. *Yin* (Passive) manifested *Jin*, because it is a response to an attack, needs a partner for training. It must be learned and experienced through pushing hands, which will be discussed in a later book (***Tai Chi Chuan Martial Applications***, by YMAA). In this section we will focus on the *Yang* (Active) manifested *Jin* training, since it is the most basic and easiest to approach of all the *Jins*. You can train *Yang* manifested *Jin* without a partner because it is generated within your body. Once you understand the key points you can develop a fair level of skill by training with a punching bag, sand bag, or candle. It is useful to select individual techniques from the sequence and practice them repeatedly, practicing rooting, balancing energy, and getting the *Jin* out to the hand or arm being used. It is also very helpful to do the solo sequence at medium and fast speeds. The most important factor is understanding the theory and principles. Naturally, a good instructor can save you a lot of time and confusion.

Active manifested *Jin* is also called Emitting *Jin* (*Fa Jin*). You must firm your root, generate your preliminary *Jin* with your leg and pass it up to meet the *Jin* generated by the waist. This waist *Jin* is important in directing the leg *Jin* to the right place. The combined *Jin* is then passed to the shoulder to join with the *Jin* generated there, and the total *Jin* is expressed through your hands. These different parts must be coordinated and timed precisely so that the *Jin* is integrated, for only then can it reach a high level. Your *Yi* must lead the *Qi* to flow naturally in support of the relaxed muscles for the *Jin* to be expressed at maximum power. From this point, the stronger your *Qi* support, the stronger your *Jin* will be. The ultimate goal is to cut muscle usage down to a minimum and have the *Qi* predominate.

From this theory review, you can understand that in order for you to emit your *Jin*, you must know: 1. How to generate *Jin* from the rooted legs. 2. How to generate *Jin* from the waist and connect it with the *Jin* from the legs. This also includes knowing how to lead *Jin* to the desired place. 3. How to combine this *Jin* with the *Jin* generated by the shoulders, and express it through the hands. 4. How to refine the unified *Jin* and enhance it through hip and thigh relaxation, arcing the chest, and storing *Jin* in the elbow. We will now discuss these four items in detail.

1. Generation of Jin from the legs:

Generally, there are three ways to generate *Jin* with the legs: forward and backward, sideways, and upward. For all three ways of *Jin* generation, the root is critical - without a firm root it is like trying to push a car while you are standing on ice. In order to generate *Jin*, you must lead your *Yi* and *Qi* down first, and at the same time push down through your bent legs. This pushing down will cause the reaction force, which is the source of the *Jin*, to bounce back from your leg.

When you push backward to generate forward *Jin* (or push forward for backward *Jin*), the direction of the push must be accurate. The leg muscles should be tensed for as short a time as possible. Treat your legs like springs - when you compress them they push in the opposite direction. The push must be done in a short time in order to generate the pulse-like spring power. If the push is done too slowly, your leg muscles will be tensed and the power generated will be *Li* instead of *Jin*. When you want to generate upward *Jin*, follow the same principle as that of forward and backward *Jin* generation except that you push straight down.

For sideways *Jin* generation, twist your legs as if winding a spring, and then twist back with a jerk. The *Jin* is generated from the twisting. You must follow the same key points as described above. Remember to tense the leg muscles for only a very short time, and to keep them loose and relaxed the rest of the time.

2. Generation of Jin from the Waist:

Once you have generated the *Jin* with your legs, your waist plays the major role in its application. As it passes the *Jin* on, it directs, controls, and enhances it with it's own *Jin*. The timing is extremely important - if it is off, the *Jin* from the legs will be broken or weakened, and become useless. The waist should start to generate its *Jin* just before the *Jin* from the legs reaches it. This is like a relay race-the second runner starts running before the first runner reaches him. In this case, the waist *Jin* leads and directs the leg *Jin* to the target.

Generally, there are two ways to generate *Jin* with the waist: laterally and forward. Lateral *Jin* is commonly used to direct the *Jin* to the arm for forward striking if only a single hand is used, or to direct the *Jin* to the side for a sideward strike. In order to generate lateral *Jin*, the waist is twisted and then jerked back. A single forward jerk can direct *Jin* to the hand for a forward strike, and a complete back and forth jerk can generate spinning and rotating *Jin* for a sideward strike. The forward waist *Jin* is usually used for a double hand push or strike. To generate it, the waist (abdomen) is caved in slightly to accumulate *Jin*, and then straightened out suddenly to emit.

Here, the author would like to point out two things. First, since when you generate *Jin* with your legs you push downward in order to project the force away from the legs, the force is actually going toward your head. If you do not direct this leg *Jin* completely into the arms, part of the force will go to your head and make it jerk, which will cause headaches. Second, if you fail to direct the leg and waist *Jin* out to your arms, part of the *Jin* will remain in the waist area and cause the intestines to jerk and vibrate, causing pain or even injury. Beginners frequently have either or both of these problems. When you feel pain you should stop practicing. When the pain goes away, resume practice, but cut down the strength of the *Jin*. The more tense you are, the worse it will be. Remember, relaxation is the medicine.

3. Generation of Jin from the Shoulder:

Like the waist, the shoulder can generate both sideward and lateral *Jin*. Lateral *Jin* is usually used to direct and enhance the *Jin* coming from the waist for a sideward strike, while the forward *Jin* is generally used for striking forward. The trick of timing for the shoulder *Jin* is the same as for the waist, i.e., slightly ahead of the incoming *Jin* from the waist.

4. Other Posture Coordination:

Once you grasp the above keys to *Jin* generation, you have entered the door to *Jin* training. However, your *Jin* may still not reach a high level because the connections from the legs to the waist, the waist to the shoulders, and from the shoulders to the hands may be incomplete. If these places are not connected continuously, the *Jin* will be weakened or even broken. The main culprit is tenseness, which bottlenecks the energy and hinders the smooth flow of your body. Also, in order for these three areas to contribute their *Jin*, your posture must be correct. You must be able to store and emit *Jin* from the various parts of your body. You must be relaxed so that the *Jin* can flow, and you must find your *Jin* storage in curves.

A common way to test your *Jin* is with a candle. Stand in a stable stance so that your extended hand is about a foot away from the candle. Try to put out the flame using either a punch or an open hand strike (Figure 3-227). Use *Jin* in a relaxed, whip-like motion. If your *Jin* is powerful, accurate, and concentrated, you should be able to extinguish the flame with the wind generated from your motion. Once you can extinguish the flame from a distance of one foot, increase the distance. Naturally, your mind and *Qi* must be more concentrated and the *Jin* more powerful in order to do this.

You can reach a fairly high level of *Jin* expression using this method and emphasizing *Yi* and posture. However, you will find that further progress is limited unless you develop your *Qi*. If you strengthen and train your *Qi*, it will eventually become the main factor in your *Jin*, and your level of energy will continue to rise.

Here the author would like to bring up a very important point. Most of this discussion has been based on your being in a stable situation. As matter of fact, in a fight, both you and your opponent are moving. Therefore, even if you can emit very strong *Jin* when you are standing steady, this does not mean that you will be able to generate the same kind of *Jin* while you are moving. This is because when you are moving your root is very weak. You have probably experienced that, although you can hit a bag with a certain amount of power from a stable stance,

Figure 3-227

if you are moving while you are punching you lose at least half your power. If you want to fight effectively, you must train emitting the various *Jins* while moving, and develop fighting strategies and tactics which take this into account. Doing the *Taiji* sequence fast will greatly help to train this. Simply put, the trick to using *Jin* effectively while moving lies in timing. You should emit *Jin* while your feet are rooted. Once the *Jin* is generated and transmitted to your extremities (substantial hand and supporting foot), you can step or change your stance. Naturally, you will still lose part of the *Jin*, since you have lost the root which balances the energy in the hand. However, if you keep practicing, you can learn how to root and emit *Jin* in an instant, and then quickly continue your movement. It is clear then that a large part of strategy consists of setting up your footwork most advantageously, so that you can be mobile, and then, when you strike, be rooted so that your opponent cannot escape from you.

As mentioned in the beginning of this chapter, the author's knowledge of and experience with *Jin* is limited. Because of this, some *Jins* are discussed in only a limited way. Also, because the various *Jins* are explained according to the author's background and understanding, it is possible that the reader may not agree with his ideas completely. It is the author's desire to encourage martial artists to research this side of the art which has been so neglected for so many years.

Chapter 4
Conclusion

結 論

Hopefully this volume has given you a better concept of *Taiji* theory and principles. You no doubt have a number of questions, especially about *Jin*, since it has been kept secret for centuries. This volume is the first major discussion of *Jin* in the English language. You should study and practice, experiment and research. Discuss and share your ideas with others. Most important of all, you should be humble enough to ask others. In China, it is said: "*Man zhao sun, qian shou yi*" (滿招損，謙受益) which means "Satisfaction causes damage and humility gains benefit." You should understand that as long as you are humble, you will continue to learn until one day you become a real *Taijiquan* master. When you feel full, you are satisfied and naturally not humble enough to ask and research. Like most of Chinese culture and the martial arts, *Taiji* is an accomplishment of art, culture, skill, morality, and self-discipline. The more you know the less you feel you know. Every time you reach a higher level of *Taijiquan*, your ability to understand will also increase. Therefore, you should study this volume again and again, especially Appendix A which contains the translation of ancient poetry and songs and commentary. These works are the creations of many experienced masters through hundreds of years of research and study.

Reading this volume and understanding the theory and principles of *Taijiquan* is still not enough to become a proficient *Taiji* martial artist. You must also know the other part of the *Taiji* secret: *Taiji* fighting techniques. *Taiji* was created for fighting, and every form which has been passed down from generation to generation contains many secret fighting techniques concealed inside. Usually, these techniques remain secret unless you have earned the trust of a teacher or have been chosen as the successor of a style. There are more than 250 *Taiji* techniques known today. There are more which are still hidden in the forms and waiting for you to discover them. To help you in this, the author has published a second book on advanced *Yang* Style *Taijiquan* which will specialize in the fighting techniques which are hidden in the forms, pushing hands, and the fighting set — ***Tai Chi Chuan Martial Applications.***

Theory and practical experience are mutually related. The deeper you understand the theory, the better you can put it to work. In the same way, the more experience you have, the greater your ability will be to analyze the theory.

Taiji theory and principles are so deep and profound that it is impossible to cover them completely in a single volume. The author hopes that this volume will lead you to the right path and help you to avoid straying too far off the path. Even if you master the material in this book, you should not be satisfied, but should continue to research the art.

Appendix A
Taiji Poetry and Songs

Introduction

Introduction

In the last seven centuries many songs and poems have been composed about *Taijiquan*. These have played a major role in preserving the knowledge and wisdom of the masters, although in most cases the identity of the authors and the dates of origin have been lost. Since most Chinese of previous centuries were illiterate, the key points of the art were put into poems and songs, which are easier to remember than prose, and passed down orally from teacher to student. The poems were regarded as secret and have only been revealed to the general public in this century. The author has chosen fifteen which are the most popular and are considered the most accurate.

It is very difficult to translate these ancient Chinese writings. Because of the cultural differences, many expressions would not make sense to the Westerner if translated literally. Often a knowledge of the historical context is necessary. Furthermore, since every sound has several possible meanings, when anyone tried to understand a poem or write it down he had to choose from among these meanings. For this reason, many of the poems have several variations. The same problem occurs when the poems are read. Many Chinese characters have several possible meanings, so reading involves interpretation of the text even for the Chinese. Also, the meaning of many words has changed over the course of time. When you add to this the grammatical differences (generally no tenses, articles, singular or plural, or differentiation between parts of speech) you find that it is almost impossible to translate Chinese literally into English. In addition to all this, the translator must have much the same experience and understanding, as well as similar intuitive feelings as the original author, in order to convey the same meaning.

With these difficulties in mind, the author has attempted to convey as much of the original meaning of the Chinese as possible, based on his own *Taiji* experience and understanding. Although it is impossible to totally translate the original meaning, the author feels he has managed to express the majority of the important points. The translation has been made as close to the original Chinese as possible, including such things as double negatives and, sometimes, idiosyncratic sentence structure. Words which are understood but not actually written in the Chinese text have been included in parentheses. Also, some Chinese words are followed by the English in parentheses, e.g. *Shen* (Spirit). To further assist the reader, the author has included commentary with each poem and song. For reference, the original Chinese of each song has been included after the translations.

1. Taijiquan Treatise

by Chang, San-Feng

太極拳論

張三豐

Once in motion, every part of the body is light and agile and must be threaded together.

一舉動，週身俱要輕靈，尤須貫穿。

Qing Ling, the Chinese words which are translated "light and agile," are used to describe the movement of monkeys: responsive, controlled, and able to move quickly. The body should be a coherent whole, with all of its parts connected and unified by the energy (*Qi*) moving within them, like ancient Chinese coins connected by a string.

Qi should be full and stimulated, Shen (Spirit) should be retained internally.

氣宜鼓盪，神宜內斂。

The *Qi* which is generated in the Lower *Dan Tian* should fill the entire body like air fills a balloon or a drum. Doing the *Taijiquan* sequence with a controlled mind circulates the *Qi* and strengthens it, which leads to a healthy body. Although the *Qi* is full and stimulated, your mind is centered so that the *Qi* isn't scattered. Retaining the Spirit of Vitality internally means to be calm and patient, and restrained in your actions. This helps to avoid giving away your intentions to the opponent, and conserves your *Qi*.

No part should be defective, no part should be deficient or excessive, no part should be disconnected.

無使有缺陷處，無使有凸凹處，無使有續斷處。

Taijiquan emphasizes balance, efficiency, and precision. No posture or part of the body should stretch out too far or be pulled in too much. Every motion should be smooth, always just right; every force just enough to do the job. Each posture should be rounded and should involve the whole body in a smooth, continuous, flowing motion.

The root is at the feet, (Jin is) generated from the legs, controlled by the waist and expressed by the fingers. From the feet to the legs to the waist must be integrated, and one unified Qi. When moving forward or backward, you can then catch the opportunity and gain the superior position.

其根在腳，發於腿，主宰於腰，形於手指。由腳而腿而腰，
總須完整一氣。向前退後，乃能得機得勢。

If you are firmly connected to the ground, and if, from the feet to the waist, you move as a coherent unit, then your *Jin* will be strong and you will be agile and responsive enough to gain an advantageous position. The *Qi* of the entire body must be unified in the technique. It is important to balance the force and *Qi* of the substantial (active) hand with the root in the feet, and to balance the insubstantial force suspending the head with the *Qi* sunken to the *Dan Tian*.

If you fail to catch the opportunity and gain the superior position, your mind is scattered and your body is disordered. To solve this problem, you must look to the waist and legs.

有不得機得勢處，身便散亂。其病必於腰腿求之。

If you fail in an attempt to attack your opponent, or defend poorly against an attack, it is probably because your mind and body were unbalanced and disorganized. When this is the case, your mind is scattered and your root is loose. When your root is not firm, you lose the foundation through which the legs generate power, and your waist consequently loses control and its actions become meaningless. To remedy the situation you must readjust your waist and legs into the most advantageous position, enabling you to rebuild your root and stabilize yourself.

Up and down, forward and backward, left and right, it's all the same. All of this is done with the Yi (mind), not externally.

上下前後左右皆然。凡此皆是意，不在外面。

For any direction, with any motion, it always comes down to adjusting the waist and legs. You do not rely on quick, forceful motions of the body or arms. Instead, the mind perceives the situation and the most effective solution, and it directs the body.

If there is a top, there is a bottom; if there is a front, there is a back; if there is a left, there is a right.

有上即有下，有前即有後，有左即有右。

Taijiquan emphasizes completeness and balance. When attacking high, you must defend low. When moving in one direction, you must balance *Jin* and *Qi* in the opposite direction. When attacking or defending on one side, you must be aware of the other side.

If Yi (mind) wants to go upward, this implies considering downward. (This means) if (you) want to lift and defeat an opponent, you

must first consider his root. When the opponent's root is broken, he will inevitably be defeated quickly and certainly.

如意要向上，即寓下意。若將物掀起，而加以挫之之意。斯

其根自斷，乃壞之速而無疑。

Your enemy's root is his foundation. When his root is broken, he will lose his foundation and his *Jin* will not be generated from the legs and controlled by the waist. This will greatly limit his fighting ability. If you wish to knock him down or push him away, you must first break his root so that he is unstable and can be easily defeated.

Substantial and insubstantial must be clearly distinguished. Every part (of the body) has a substantial and an insubstantial aspect. The entire body and all the joints should be threaded together without the slightest break.

虛實宜分頃楚，一處有一處虛實，處處總是如此。周身節節

貫串，無令絲毫間斷耳。

It is very important to distinguish between substantial and insubstantial in your body and in the opponent's. The hand acting upon the opponent is substantial, while the other hand is insubstantial. The leg with more weight on it is usually substantial, but an insubstantial leg (such as the front leg in the false stance) becomes substantial upon kicking. When pushing, the front of the hand is substantial, while the back of the hand is insubstantial. You must also clearly distinguish and respond to the opponent's substantial and insubstantial. When the opponent attacks your right side, that side should become insubstantial, and your left side should become substantial and attack him. In order to do all this effectively, your entire body from the feet, legs and waist to the fingers must work like a unit and move as if threaded together.

Additional Sentences from Chang, San-Feng

What is Long Fist? (It is) like a long river and a large ocean, rolling ceaselessly.

長拳者如長江大海滔滔不絕也。

There are two styles of martial arts called Long Fist (*Chang Quan*) in China. One is *Taijiquan*, in which case *Chang Quan* is translated "Long Sequence." This is because the *Taiji* sequence is long and the movements are performed smoothly and continuously like a flowing river. The other *Chang Quan* is translated as "Long Fist" and refers to a Northern Shaolin style which emphasizes long range fighting strategies.

What are the thirteen postures? Peng (Wardoff), Lu (Rollback), Ji (Press), An (Push), Cai (Pluck), Lie (Split), Zhou (Elbow), Kao (Bump), these are the eight trigrams. Jin Bu (Forward), Tui Bu (Backward), Zuo Gu (Beware of the Left), You Pan (Look to the Right), Zhong Ding (Central Equilibrium), these are the five elements. Wardoff, Rollback, Press, and Push are Qian (Heaven), Kun (Earth), Kan (Water), Li (Fire), the four main sides. Pluck, Spit, Elbow, Bump are Xun (Wind), Zhen (Thunder), Dui (Lake), and Gen (Mountain), the four diagonal corners. Forward, Backward, Beware of the Left, Look to the right, and Central Equilibrium are Jin (Metal), Mu (Wood), Shui (Water), Huo (Fire), and Tu (Earth). All together they are the thirteen postures.

十三勢者，掤、攦、擠、按、採、挒、肘、靠，此八卦也。

進步、退步、左顧、右盼、中定，此五行也。掤、攦、擠、按，即乾、坤、坎、離，四正方也。採、挒、肘、靠，即巽、震、兌、艮，四斜角也。進、退、顧、盼、定，即金、木、水、火、土也。合之則爲十三勢也。

This paragraph lists *Taiji*'s basic posture and their correlates. This is discussed in Chapter 1, section 4.

2. Taijiquan Classic

by Wang, Zong-Yue

太極拳經

王宗岳

What is Taiji? It is generated from Wuji. It is the mother of Yin and Yang. When it moves, it divides. At rest it reunites.

太極者，無極而生，動靜之機，陰陽之母也。動之則分，靜之則合。

Taiji can be translated as "Grand Ultimate," or "Grand Extremity," and *Wuji* is translated as "Without Ultimate," "Without Limit," or "No Extremity." *Wuji* can also mean "No Opposition." That means *Wuji* is uniform and undifferentiated. For example, at the beginning of the universe, there was no differentiation, and this state is called *Wuji*. With the first motion things separated into complimentary opposites, called *Yin* and *Yang*, and this state is called *Taiji*. From the interaction of *Yin* and *Yang*, all things are generated and grow. All objects, ideas, spirits, etc. can be identified as either *Yin* or *Yang*. *Taijiquan* was created according to this theory. In the beginning posture of the *Taiji* sequence, the mind is calm and empty, and the weight is evenly distributed on both feet.

This state is *Wuji*. As soon as your mind leads the body into Grasp Sparrow's Tail, the hands and feet differentiate into substantial and insubstantial. The interaction of substantial (*Yang*) and insubstantial (*Yin*) generates all of *Taijiquan*'s fighting strategy and technique.

No excess, no deficiency. Following the opponent, bend, then extend.

無過不及，隨曲就伸。

No part of your posture should be exaggerated or constricted, nothing should be too concave or too convex. When you stick to and follow the opponent, do only what is appropriate - no more, no less. In pushing hands, when your opponent pushes your arm, yield. Adhere lightly to his arm, following his motion with no separation or resistance. When he attacks, give way elastically, and when he withdraws, extend to follow him. This also implies that when he pushes your right side, the right side withdraws and the left side extends to attack him.

When the opponent is hard, I am soft; this is called yielding. When I follow the opponent, this is called sticking.

人剛我柔謂之走，我順人背謂之黏。

When the opponent attacks you, do not resist him, but instead give way so that his attack misses you. The Chinese term translated as "yielding" literally means "walk away." Sticking to the opponent means to maintain contact with him and follow his motions so that when the right time comes you can make the appropriate move.

When the opponent moves fast, I move fast; when the opponent moves slowly, then I follow slowly. Although the variations are infinite, the principle remains the same.

動急則急應，動緩則緩隨，雖變化萬端，而理爲一貫。

The principle here, as in the previous two sections, is to stick to the opponent and follow his motions. You can then respond appropriately no matter what he does. Although there are many techniques, they are all variations on the one basic principle of stick and follow.

After you have mastered techniques, then you can gradually grasp what "Understanding Jin (Dong Jin)" means. From "Understanding Jin" you gradually approach enlightenment (intuitive understanding) of your opponent's intention. However, without a great deal of study over a long time, you cannot suddenly grasp this intuitive understanding of your opponent.

由著熟而漸悟懂勁，由懂勁而階及神明。然非功力之久，不

能豁然貫通焉。

When you can stick and follow, and have mastered the various techniques, then you will gradually begin to understand the opponent's *Jin* and be able to interpret his intentions. The more you practice, the more sensitive you will become. Only then can you enlighten yourself and interpret the opponent's intentions with just a touch, or even without touching him at all.

An insubstantial energy leads the head upward. The Qi is sunk to the Dan Tian.

虛領頂勁，氣沈丹田。

An insubstantial energy lifts the head upward so that it feels like the head and body are suspended by a string attached to the top of the head. This energy is balanced by the *Qi* sunk to the *Dan Tian* and the bottom of the feet. When the head is upright, the Spirit of Vitality will be raised, alertness will increase, and the body will be straight and erect from the tailbone to the top of the head. When *Qi* is sunk to the *Dan Tian*, the mind is calm, and the root is strengthened.

No tilting, no leaning. Suddenly disappear, suddenly appear.

不偏不倚，忽隱忽現。

The head and body are balanced upright. Do not tilt your body in any direction. If you maintain a relaxed, centered, and balanced posture, and stick and follow, you will be able to respond easily and lightly to your opponent. You will then be able to "disappear" in front of the opponent's attack, and "appear" with your own attack where he doesn't expect you.

When there is pressure on the left, the left becomes insubstantial; when there is pressure on the right, the right becomes insubstantial. Looking upward it seems to get higher and higher; looking downward it seems to get deeper and deeper. When (the opponent) advances, it seems longer and longer; when (the opponent) retreats, it becomes more and more urgent. A feather cannot be added and a fly cannot land. The opponent does not know me, but I know the opponent. A hero has no equal because of all of this.

左重則左虛，右重則右杳。仰之則彌高，俯之則彌深，進之

則愈長，退之則愈促，一羽不能加，蠅蟲不能落，人不知我

，我獨知人，英雄所向無敵，蓋由此而及也。

Wherever the opponent attacks, that part of you withdraws. When he tries to reach you, you fade away, just out of range of his power. When he tries to withdraw, you stick to him like glue. He feels that you are right there pushing him, and he can't get away. No matter what he does, you stick and follow. After much practice you can be so sensitive and accurate in your response that a feather can't touch you without setting you in motion. The opponent can never catch hold of you to figure you out, but you always know him. If you reach this level, no one will be able to match you.

There are many martial art styles. Although the postures are distinguishable from one another, after all, it is nothing more than the strong beating the weak, the slow yielding to the fast. The one with power beats the one without power, the slow hands yield to the fast hands. All this is natural born ability. It is not related to the power that has to be learned.

斯技旁門甚多，雖勢有區別，概不外壯欺弱，慢讓快耳。有力打無力，手慢讓手快。皆是先天自然之能，非關學力而有爲也。

Taijiquan is different from most other *Gongfu* styles in which one uses his natural born abilities of strength and speed to defend himself. *Taiji*'s applications are much deeper than one would expect. It not only takes time, patience, and perseverance to learn the skills and techniques, but also requires talent and a comprehending mind to understand the theory, strategy, and approach.

Consider the saying: "Four ounces repel one thousand pounds." It is apparent that this cannot be accomplished by strength. Look, if an eighty or ninety year old man can still defend himself against multiple opponents, it cannot be a matter of speed.

查四兩撥千金之句，顯非力勝。觀耄耋能禦眾之形，快何能焉。

Taijiquan teaches you to rely on technique and an understanding of the opponent, rather than mere strength or speed. After doing the sequence correctly for many years, your body will be healthy and you will have built up an internal energy which is quite different from external strength. If you understand the principles of neutralization, adhering and sticking, and if you have practiced *Taiji* pushing hands and applications for many years, you will be able to fight effectively even when you are old.

Stand like a balanced scale, (move) lively like a cartwheel.

立如平準，活似車輪。

The body stands upright, centered and in equilibrium, just like a scale balancing two weights. Neutralize incoming forces by moving your whole body as a unit, with the center line of your body acting as the axle.

(When the opponent presses) sideward (or) downward, then follow. (When there is) double heaviness (mutual resistance), then (there is) stagnation. Often after several years of dedicated training, one still cannot apply this neutralization and is controlled by the opponent. (The reason for this is that the) fault of double heaviness is not understood.

偏沈則隨，雙重則滯。每見數年純功，不能運化者，率爲人

制，雙重之病未能悟耳。

Whether the opponent attacks high or low, left or right, you do not resist him. Instead you yield and follow, adhering to him patiently until you have the opportunity to attack. If you struggle against him, the liveliness of the interaction stagnates, and victory will go to the one with the most external strength. In *Taiji*, the attacking hand is considered "heavy" because it is putting weight or pressure on the opponent. The Chinese character *Zhong* can be translated as weight and *Shuang* as pair or double. Therefore, some authors translated *Shuang Zhong* as "double weighting." However, the same character *Zhong* can also be pronounced *Chong* and translated as "repeated overlapping." Therefore, *Shuang Chong* can be translated as "double overlapping." This means "mutual covering and resistance" and has the sense of two forces struggling against each other, each striving for the upper hand. If you study for many years, but never grasp the importance of avoiding this "mutual resistance," then you will never get the knack of neutralizing the opponent's force.

To avoid this fault you must know Yin and Yang. To adhere means to yield. To yield means to adhere. Yin not separate from Yang. Yang not separate from Yin. Yin and Yang mutually cooperate, (understanding this) is "Understanding Jin (Dong Jin)."

欲避此病須知陰陽。粘即是走，走即是粘。陰不離陽，陽不

離陰，陰陽相濟，方爲懂勁。

You must thoroughly internalize the principle of always yielding to the opponent's attack while remaining lightly attached to him. Your *Yin* defense is dependent upon and interrelated with his *Yang* attack. When you have neutralized his attack, your *Yin* becomes *Yang* as you attack. If you always stay in contact with your opponent and carefully pay attention (listen) to his motion and *Jin* (energy), you will gradually develop the ability to understand his intention. Once you learn how extreme *Yin* becomes *Yang* and extreme *Yang* becomes *Yin*, you will learn the knack of timing your attacks and defense, and will gain the ability to "borrow" your opponent's force. When you know these things you know Understanding *Jin*.

After Understanding Jin, the more practice, the more refinement. Silently learn, then ponder; gradually you will approach your heart's desire.

懂勁後愈練愈精，默識揣摩，漸至從心所欲。

Once you understand *Jin*, the more you practice, the more you will progress. Your own study and experience, which you ponder silently in your own mind, is your main source of improvement. If you follow this method you can eventually reach the highest levels of achievement, where whatever you wish is done naturally.

Fundamentally, give up yourself and follow the opponent. Many misunderstand and give up the near for the far. This means a slight error can cause a thousand mile divergence. The learner, therefore, must discriminate precisely.

本是捨己從人，多誤捨近圖遠。斯謂差之毫釐，謬以千里，

學者不可不詳辨焉。

The most important principle is to give up yourself and follow the other person. This does not mean becoming totally passive and just meekly following him, giving up counterattacking in the hope of some-day suddenly beaming a master. When one side of a wheel or the *Taiji* diagram moves backward, the other side moves forward. Attack and counterattack, like *Yin* and *Yang*, are inseparably linked. Pay attention to the enemy in front of you. Stick and follow patiently and conscientiously, and when an opportunity presents itself, attack. If instead you try this and that to attack your enemy, or actively try to get him in a bad position, this is called "giving up the near for the far."

It is important for the student to be very discriminating in determining what is right and wrong, because a small error of principle in the beginning of training will have greater and greater consequences as time goes on.

Every sentence in this thesis is important. Not a single word has been added carelessly, or for decoration. Without a high degree of wisdom you won't be able to understand. The past teachers were not willing to teach indiscriminately, not just because of (the difficulty of) choosing people, but also because they were afraid of wasting their time and energy.

此論句句切要，並無一字敷衍陪襯，非有夙慧不能悟也。先

師不肯妄傳，非獨擇人，亦恐枉費功夫耳。

The *Taiji* classics describe a very high level of awareness and understanding. Each description is an attempt to bring the reader closer to the principles of *Taiji* and to the experiences of the author. No part can be separated from the others, and nothing can be omitted. The author arrived at his understanding through long and arduous effort, and anyone wishing to learn this art must be willing and able to match this effort.

3. Thirteen Postures:
Comprehending External and Internal Training
by Wang, Zong-Yue

十三勢行功心解

王宗岳

Use the Xin (heart, mind) to transport the Qi, (the mind) must be sunk (steady) and calm, then (the Qi) can condense (deep) into the bones. Circulate the Qi throughout the body, it (Qi) must be smooth and fluid, then it can easily follow the mind.

以心行氣，務令沈著，乃能收斂入骨。以氣運身，務令順遂，

乃能便利從心。

When the *Xin* (heart, mind) wants to do something, the *Yi* (will) mobilizes the *Qi*. In *Taijiquan* practice, where the mind goes, the *Qi* goes. When transporting (guiding) the *Qi* through your body, the mind must be clear, steady, and calm. Then, the *Qi* can circulate deep into the bones.

The power used in *Taijiquan* applications is called *Jin*. If the *Jin* is united with and supported by *Qi*, it can reach its highest level. However, if it is not coordinated with and supported by *Qi*, the *Jin* will come only from the posture's dynamic force. The *Jin* which is supported by *Qi* has many variations. It can range from *Jins* which function on the skin such as Listening *Jin* (*Ting Jin*), Understanding *Jin* (*Dong Jin*), and Adhering *Jin* (*Zhan Jin*), to *Jins* which come from deep within the bones, where offensive *Jins* such as Wardoff *Jin* (*Peng Jin*) are generated. If the *Qi* cannot reach deep into the bones, the *Jin* will lose its internal *Qi* support and become merely external dynamic force.

When *Qi* circulates throughout the body in *Taiji* practice and meditation, it must not be stagnant or discontinuous. In time the *Qi* will flow smoothly and quickly to the place where it is required. In the beginning, this will be difficult. After years of correct practice, *Qi* can be used to support *Jin* whenever the mind wishes.

(If) the Spirit of Vitality (Jing-Shen) can be raised, then (there is) no delay or heaviness (clumsiness). That means the head is suspended. Yi (Mind) and Qi must exchange skillfully, then you have gained the marvelous trick of roundness and aliveness. This means the substantial and the insubstantial can vary and exchange.

精神能提得起，則無遲重之虞。所謂頂頭懸也。意氣須換得

靈，乃有圓活之妙。所謂變轉虛實也。

The **Taijiquan Classic** by Wang, Zong-Yue states "An insubstantial energy leads the head upward." If you cultivate this feeling, which is like having the head and body suspended by a thread, and balance this with the Qi sunk deeply into the Dan Tian, then the postures will be erect and straight, and the Spirit of Vitality (Jing-Shen) will be able to rise to the top of the head. The Spirit of Vitality is the basic vital energy of your body. When you lift this energy to the top of your head, your postures will be firmly rooted and you will be alert and responsive; therefore there will be no delay or clumsiness. When the mind and Qi are coordinated, then your skill and techniques can be round, smooth, and alive. Therefore, you can easily move yourself to exchange substantial and insubstantial in response to your opponent's actions.

When emitting Jin, be calm and relaxed, concentrated in one direction. When standing, the body must be centered, calm and comfortable, so you can handle the eight directions.

發勁須沈著鬆淨，專注一方。立身須中正安舒支撐八面。

When using Jin to attack, your mind must be calm and your body relaxed, i.e., your movement and circulation must be unhindered and unrestrained. Your attention and your energy must be concentrated in the direction of attack.

Your body should be erect, centered, and stable, and should not lean to any side. If you are calm and relaxed, and your postures natural and comfortable, you will be able to deal with attacks from any direction without resistance or stagnation.

Transport Qi as though through a pearl with a "nine-curved hole," not even the tiniest place won't be reached. When using Jin, (it is) just like steel refined 100 times, no solid (strong opposition) cannot be destroyed.

行氣如九曲珠，無微不到。運勁如百鍊鋼，無堅不摧。

When you build up your Qi and have achieved "Small Circulation," you must accomplish "Grand Circulation" and fill the entire body with Qi. When you use Jin, it must be supported by Qi. Jin and Qi should not be separated. A Chinese emperor had a large pearl that he wanted to put on a string. However, the hole through the pearl was not straight, but instead had nine curves. It was impossible to push a string through it. A wise man finally tied a very fine thread to an ant, and caused the ant to walk through this nine-curved channel pulling the thread. In the same fashion, your mind must lead the Qi throughout your body from the skin to deep inside the bones until it reaches every last part. When you cultivate your Qi, you can develop an internal (Qi supported) energy called Jin which is far superior to external, or purely muscular, strength. This Jin will enable you to overcome and destroy any opposition, no matter how strong or hard.

The appearance (of the attack) is like an eagle catching a rabbit, the Spirit is like a cat catching a mouse.

形如搏兔之鵑，神似捕鼠之貓。

An eagle circles high in the air, watching for prey. When it sees a rabbit it suddenly plunges down, appearing out of nowhere to snatch its prey. When a cat sees a mouse it doesn't attack at once, but instead stalks it, biding its time till the right opportunity presents itself. While poised and watching, the cat is the very model of Spirit - alert, vital, centered, and controlled.

(Be) calm like a mountain, move like a river.

靜如山岳，動如江河。

Your spirit and posture must be calm and stable like a mountain. Any motion large or small should flow like a river - continuous and fluid.

Accumulate Jin like drawing a bow, emit Jin like (a bow) shooting an arrow.

蓄勁如張弓，發勁如放箭。

You accumulate energy by bending like a bow, and then snap straight, propelling your opponent away. Remember that you must draw the bow before you can shoot the arrow, and you must accumulate energy before you can emit it. Here "accumulate" implies two things: 1. *Qi* is generated and accumulated at the *Dan Tian* and condensed in the spine for supporting the *Jin*. 2. *Jin* is stored in the most advantageous posture to either neutralize or attack.

Find the straight in the curved; accumulate, then emit.

曲中求直，蓄而後發。

Store *Jin* in the curves and coils of your posture, but emit *Jin* in a straight line. When an opponent attacks, move your body to evade him and accumulate energy, and then snap straight to attack. Similarly, you can curve the opponent's attack away from your body, and then emit force to send him off on a tangent or right angle. Your counterattack comes out of the neutralization of his attack. You accumulate energy from his pressure, then release it.

Power is emitted from the spine; steps change following the body.

力由脊發，步隨身換。

"Power" here is *Nei Jin Li*. *Nei Jin* means internal energy and *Li* means muscular strength. Any movement requires *Li*, and this is all that most people ever use. When you train your internal energy through meditation, *Qigong*, and the *Taijiquan* form, you can develop an energy in which the muscles are supported more and more by *Qi*. The spine is the major path of *Qi*. When *Qi* is built up in the *Dan Tian* it will pass through the Sea Bottom (*Haidi*) and tailbone (*Weilu*), follow the spine up to the shoulders, and finally move into the arms and hands for defense and offense. Therefore, the *Dan Tian* is the source of *Qi*, but the spine is the distributor of the *Qi* from where it is extended to the arms.

When *Taijiquan* is to be used for fighting, you should not only acquire *Jin* with strong *Qi* support, but also develop a fighting strategy. This is extremely important, for a good *Taiji* fighter uses footwork to position his body most advantageously for each technique.

To collect is to release; to release is to collect; broken, then reconnected.

收即是放，放即是收。斷而復連。

Just as you bend a bow and then release it, you accumulate energy and then emit it. When you neutralize an attack your counterattack should follow immediately. The one leads to the other as *Yin* leads to *Yang*. Immediately after emitting *Jin*, the *Jin* is said to be "broken." But your *Yi* (concentration) is not broken, and its continuity restores the *Jin*.

Back and forth (with the opponent) must have folding and mutual entwining. Advancing and withdrawing must have rotation and variation.

往復須有摺疊，進退須有轉換。

When you are pushing hands or sparring, you are exchanging techniques back and forth. You must be flexible and adaptable, folding and bending as appropriate. When you attack with the hand and the hand is deflected, you "fold" and attack with the elbow. If the elbow is blocked, you fold again and attack with the shoulder. "Folding" can also refer to the spiraling motion of *Chan Si Jin* (silk reeling energy). "Mutual entwining" refers to when your arms are wrapping around your opponent's arms, and you are twisting and twining around, trying to gain an advantage. This is like the children's game where you put your hand out, palm down, and the other person puts his hand on top of yours. You then put your other hand on top of his, he puts a hand on top of yours, and on and on.

When you advance and withdraw during attack and neutralization, you must be rotating your waist and varying your steps. You move in different directions and change your techniques in infinite variation.

(Fist) extremely soft, then extremely hard. If able to breathe (properly), then (you) can be agile and alive.

極柔軟，然後極堅剛。能呼吸，然後能靈活。

Before you can be hard, you must first cultivate softness. Only through complete relaxation can you develop your *Qi* and become supremely sensitive and responsive to your opponent's actions. Only by learning not to rely on external muscular strength (*Li*) can you develop your internal energy and achieve real strength. It is necessary to learn how to breathe properly, that is, to develop your *Qi*, and then coordinate your actions with your breathing and your *Qi*. Only then can you be truly agile, responsive, and alive.

Cultivate Qi straight (naturally), no harm; Jin can be coiled and accumulated, (and) still have surplus.

氣以直養而無害，勁以曲蓄而有餘。

If you develop your *Qi* naturally, there will be no danger. You must proceed slowly and patiently, step by step. Don't push too hard, or try to do advanced techniques before you have completed all the preceding steps. When you move correctly, your energy is alternately coiling up and expanding. It is possible to accumulate energy, and at the same time have enough to move around and attack.

The Xin (heart, mind) is the order, the Qi is the message flag, and the waist is the banner.

心爲令，氣爲旂，腰爲纛。

In ancient Chinese armies, when the general sent an order to a subordinate, the messenger carried a message flag so that the subordinate commander could be sure that the order came from the general. The banner refers to the flag that this sub-unit followed into battle. In *Taijiquan* the mind is the leader and directs the *Qi*. The waist leads the whole body into action.

First look to expanding, then look to compacting, then you approach perfection.

先求開展，後求緊湊，可臻於縝密矣。

When you begin practicing, first make the movements and postures large and open. As you progress, the movements and postures, and the circles they contain, become smaller and smaller until eventually you function with almost no motion at all. At this time your defense will have no gaps, and your attacks will be certain.

It is also said: the opponent does not move, I do not move; the opponent moves slightly, I move first. Appears relaxed, but not relaxed; seems extended, but not extended. Jin (can be) broken, mind not broken.

又曰：彼不動，己不動，彼微動，己先動。似鬆非鬆，將展

未展，勁斷意不斷。

Your actions are determined entirely by what the opponent does. If he doesn't move, you don't move either. However, all of your attention is concentrated on him, so that when he begins to move you can immediately act with certain effectiveness, because you are aware of his intention. In *Taiji* practice, you first build up Listening and Understanding *Jins*. Once you have mastered them, you will be able to sense and understand your opponent's intention even if he only moves slightly. Once you sense the opponent's intention, you should seize the opportunity, and move fast and first before the opponent's *Jin* is emitted. If you catch him when his mind is intent upon attacking, he will not be able to easily switch to a defensive mode of thought. This is how it is possible to deflect a force of one thousand pounds with a force of four ounces. Both your Spirit and posture may look relaxed, but they are alert. Your *Jin* and postures look extended, but they are restrained. When you emit *Jin*, there is a momentary break until you recover, but the continuity of your attention is not disturbed.

It is also said: first in the Xin (heart, mind), then in the body; the abdomen (is) relaxed and clear (sunken) so the Qi condenses into the bones; the Spirit is comfortable and the body is calm; remember this in the heart at all times. Do remember: one part moves, every part moves; one part still, every part still.

又曰：先在心，後在身，腹鬆淨，氣斂入骨，神舒體靜，刻刻
存心。切記一動無有不動，一靜無有不靜。

The mind leads the body. First you must quiet your mind, then the body can be calm. The abdomen is relaxed and sunken. The imagery of the Chinese is that of water that is clear because it is still and all the impurities have sunk to the bottom. When you do this the *Qi* can circulate throughout the body and penetrate into the bones, making them strong.

Remember, the body always moves as a unit. Don't push with just a hand or arm, push with your entire body, mind, and Spirit. When you are still, be totally still, with no stray motions.

(The mind) leads the Qi flowing back and forth, adhering to the back, then condensing into the spine; strengthen the Spirit of Vitality (Jing-Shen) internally, and express externally peacefully and easily.

牽動往來氣貼背，而練入脊骨，內固精神，外示安逸。

As the mind leads and circulates the *Qi* it accumulates in the back and penetrates into the spine. As mentioned, the spine is the distributor in the application of *Qi* to techniques. As you continue to practice and pay attention carefully, the Spirit of Vitality will be strengthened. Be aware of all that is around you, but keep centered on your *Dan Tian*. When you express your will in an external motion, move efficiently and peacefully.

Step like a cat walks; applying Jin is like drawing silk from a cocoon.

邁步如貓行，運勁如抽絲。

A cat steps carefully and quietly. Touch the ground lightly with your foot before you put your weight forward. When applying *Jin*, your *Yi* and *Qi* should be smooth and continuous, as when you are drawing a thread of silk from a cocoon.

(Throughout your) entire body, your mind is on the Spirit of Vitality (Jing Shen), not on the Qi. (If concentrated) on the Qi, then stagnation. A person who concentrates on Qi has no Li (strength); a person who cultivates Qi (develops) pure hardness (power).

全身意在精神，不在氣。在氣則滯，有氣者無力，養氣者純

剛。

Here "*Qi*" refers to both breath and *Qi* (intrinsic energy) because breathing is used to control the circulation of *Qi*. In the beginning of your training you must consciously coordinate your movement, breath, and *Qi*. However, this coordination must become automatic so that you can concentrate on the Spirit of Vitality. The mind leads the *Qi* which leads the body. If you have to pay attention to breathing or the movement of your body, you will be clumsy and weak. If your Spirit is clear and your mind alert, and if you have cultivated your *Qi*, your movements will be quick and strong.

The Qi is like a cartwheel, the waist is like an axle.

氣如車輪，腰似車軸。

When you move, your waist directs the rolling, flowing *Qi*.

4. Song of Eight Words

八字歌

Wardoff (Peng), Rollback (Lu), Press (Ji), and Push (An) are rare in this world. Ten martial artists, ten don't know. If able to be light and agile, also strong and hard, (then you gain) Adhere-Connect, Stick-Follow with no doubt. Pluck (Cai), Split (Lie), Elbow (Zhou), and Bump (Kao) are even more remarkable. When used, no need to bother your mind. If you gain the secret of the words Adhere-Connect, Stick-Follow, then you will be in the ring and not scattered.

掤攦擠按世界稀，十個藝人十不知。若能輕靈並堅硬，沾連黏隨俱無疑。採挒肘靠更出奇，行之不用費心思。果得沾連黏隨字，得其環中不支離。

Wardoff, Rollback, Press, and Push are the four basic movements of *Taijiquan*. Few people understand them properly. The movements are done with *Qi*-supported *Jin*, which allows the power to be either soft or hard. One must avoid external muscular power, called *Li*, which makes movement stiff, clumsy, and stagnant. You must stay light and agile, avoid meeting force with force, and wait for the right opportunity. If you do the right move at the right time in the proper direction, then your techniques will be powerful. You must also learn "Adhere-Connect, Stick-Follow." This is the technique of remaining lightly attached to the opponent, and following him without break or let up, without resistance or force. This is the only way you can really learn how to take advantage of the opponent's actions. If you master the first four moves, then the second four will come much more easily, and in time you will be able to do them automatically. But again, your actions must be based on the opponent's movements and postures, and this can only come about through "Adhere-Connect, Stick-Follow."

5. Three Important Theses of Taijiquan

太極拳之三要論

A. The Thesis of the Mind Comprehending

心會論

The waist and the spine are the first masters.
The throat is the second master.
The heart (mind) is the third master.
The Dan Tian is the first chancellor.
The fingers and palms are the second chancellors.
The foot and sole are the third chancellors.

腰脊爲第一主宰。

喉頭爲第二主宰。

心地爲第三主宰。

丹田爲第一賓輔。

指掌爲第二賓輔。

足掌爲第三賓輔。

In *Taiji* applications, the waist is the source of all movement. It is like the axle of a wheel, directing and controlling the movement and direction. In addition, the *Qi* from within the spine strengthens the *Jin* and enables it to reach its maximum. Without the waist and *Qi* from the spine, you are missing the major center of control and the major source of power. Therefore, the waist and the spine are the first masters.

Even when you have control, and *Qi* from the spine, if you can't use the *Qi*, then it is in vain. In order to move *Qi* to the extremities, the Spirit of Vitality must be raised by coordinating your breathing (exhale when attacking, inhale when yielding), and making the Hen-Ha sound corresponding to the *Yin* or *Yang* of the force used. When the Spirit of Vitality is raised, the *Qi* is instantly guided to the extremities for application. Therefore, the throat (breathing and sound) is the second master.

In addition to the above two factors, the mind must be calm, steady, and clear. The mind must constantly lead the *Qi* as it is being used, and it must also be able to sense the opponent's intentions. Thus the mind is the third master.

The above three factors are important for *Taijiquan*. However, they are not enough to make the techniques perfect. Unless the *Qi* is generated from the *Dan Tian* it will not be strong. It is said "*Qi* sinks to the *Dan Tian*." This must be done to keep generating *Qi*, as well as to increase downward stability.

In addition, you need sensitive feeling in the fingers and palms to listen to and understand the enemy's *Jin*. This enables you to neutralize and react appropriately.

Finally, if you have mastered all of the above elements but do not have a root, then your postures will not be stable and your *Jin* will lose its foundation. Therefore, the *Dan Tian*, fingers and palms, and feet and soles are the three chancellors of all *Taijiquan* techniques.

B. The Marvelous Application of the Entire Body

週身大用論

(You) want your heart (mind) to be natural, and your Yi (thinking) to be calm, then naturally everywhere will be light and agile.

要心性與意靜，自然無處不輕靈。

The mastery of the mind over the body is emphasized. Your awareness and perception of things around you must be clear and not distorted by emotions or preconceptions. If your judgments and intentions are calmly arrived at, then your body and *Qi* will freely and easily follow your will.

(You) want the entire body's Qi to circulate smoothly, (it) must be continuous and non-stop.

要遍體氣流行，一定繼續不能停。

Good *Qi* circulation throughout the body is necessary for *Taiji* and for health. Since *Qi* is linked with awareness and sensing, good *Qi* circulation is also necessary for the body to be obedient to the mind.

(You) don't ever want to give up your throat (voice); question every talented person in heaven and earth.

要喉頭永不拋，問盡天下眾英豪。

The voice here refers firstly to the Hen and Ha sounds made during practice, which help to raise the Spirit of Vitality and to control and direct energy. Secondly, you must be humble enough to use your voice to ask guidance of those who have achieved the higher levels. There is so much to life and the martial arts that other people's views and experiences are necessary to fill out our own partial understanding.

If (you are) asked: how can one attain this great achievement, (the answer is) outside and inside, fine and coarse, nothing must not be touched upon.

如詢大功因何得，表裡精粗無不到。

You can specialize in one small area of the art and become very good at it, but the only way to achieve real mastery and true understanding is to explore every facet of the art, which includes the postures on the outside and the *Qi* on the inside. Large and small, fine and coarse, all aspects must be explored.

C. Seventeen Key Theses

十七關要論

1. Rotate on the feet. 旋之於足

The root of your body is in your feet. When your body twists and turns, the movement starts in your feet, and goes all the way up to your fingers and your head. Your root must be stable in order to have controlled and accurate motion.

2. Move on the legs. 行之於腿

Energy is generated by the legs. When you walk, your upper body does very little, and the legs do all the work. When you push or yield, your legs move your upper half, which remains relaxed.

3. Spring on the knees. 縱之於膝

Your bent knees provide the springiness to your legs which is crucial to the generation and accumulation of *Jin*. The strength and flexibility of the sinews of the knees determines to a great extent the strength and effectiveness of the whole body.

4. Lively waist. 活潑於腰

The waist controls your energy in both offense and defense. Your waist must be flexible and relaxed in order to do this effectively.

5. Agility (Ling) passes through the back. 靈通於背

The energy that is generated by the legs and directed by the waist then passes through the body. The body, especially the back, must be relaxed in order to move freely and accurately.

6. Shen (Spirit) threads up through the head. 神貫於頂

The Taijiquan Classic by Wang, Zong-Yue states that an insubstantial energy should lead the head upward, so that it feels as if it were suspended by a thread from above. This helps the rest of the body to relax and the Spirit of Vitality to rise to the top of the head.

7. Qi should flow and move (in your entire body). 流行於氣

Cultivate your *Qi* so that it fills your whole body and circulates through all the channels. This will clear up stagnant *Qi* which can cause health problems. Doing the *Taiji* sequence stimulates and moves the *Qi*, and trains it so that it can support *Jin*.

8. Transport (Qi) to the palms. 運之於掌

To use *Taijiquan* you have to be able to use the mind to transport *Qi* instantly to any part of the body, particularly to the hands.

9. (It) passes into the fingers. 通之於指

You must be able to move *Qi* from your palms into your fingers, for that is where your will expresses itself.

10. (Qi) condenses into the marrow. 斂之於髓

After many years of practice the *Qi* will sink into the bones, making them as strong as steel.

11. Approach (the opponent's) Shen (Spirit). 達之於神

After practicing for a long time, you will be able to reach a level of enlightenment where you can sense your opponent's intentions and Spirit. Then, at your opponent's slightest move, you can move first.

12. Concentrate on the ears. 凝之於耳

In pushing hands and sparring you must pay careful attention to your opponent. You must be very sensitive to his motion and energy. This is done through the sensitivity of the skin and also by the eyes. In *Taijiquan* this acute paying attention is called "listening."

13. Breathe through the nose. 息之於鼻

Breathing, which is normally through the nose, should be regular, relaxed, and natural.

14. Exhale and inhale in the lungs. 呼吸於肺

This means your breathing should be deep, and done with the lower abdomen, so the *Qi* can sink to the *Dan Tian*. If you can breathe fully and calmly, your mind will become clear, your *Qi* will settle, and impurities will be cleansed out of your system.

15. To and fro from the mouth. 往來於口

This refers to the Hen-Ha sounds made as you draw in your opponent and expel him.

16. Let the body return to its original state. 渾靈於身

After long years of practice your body will regain the health of a little baby, and you will be able to respond to everything around you with the simplicity and naturalness of a child.

17. The entire body emits on the hair. 全身發之於毛

If your entire body is filled with *Qi* and all the small channels out to the skin (roots of the hair) are opened, then you will be more sensitive. You will be able to develop your sensing *Jins* to a very high level, and you will be able to emit *Jin* anywhere on your body.

6. The Five Mental Keys to Diligent Study

用功五誌

1. **Study wide and deep**
2. **Investigate, ask.**
3. **Ponder carefully.**
4. **Clearly discriminate.**
5. **Work perseveringly.**

博學　　　審問　　　慎思　　　明辨　　　篤行

Taijiquan has been developed and refined over many centuries. It has many facets and great depth. To truly master the art you must study the solo form including the applications for all the moves, the two-person sequence, weapons, meditation, and *Qigong*. You should push hands with as many people as possible to experience a wide range of body types and temperaments. It is desirable to study with several teachers, because each one has a different viewpoint and emphasis. You must be humble and open to learning from anyone. The more you ask and investigate, the more you will learn. You must carefully ponder everything you hear and see, discriminating good points from bad, evaluating what is true and false, and determining when something is valid or usable and when it is not. Most important of all is to persevere, for you can never approach your goal if you don't take all the steps to get there. It is desirable to have good teachers and helpful to have natural talent, but unless you are willing and able to train diligently, it is all to no avail.

7. Song of Pushing Hands

打手歌

Be conscientious about Wardoff (Peng), Rollback (Lu), Press (Ji), and Push (An). Up and down follow each other, (then) the opponent (will find it) difficult to enter.

掤攦擠按須認眞，上下相隨人難進。

Wardoff, Rollback, Press, and Push are the four basic moves of *Taiji* pushing hands. You must be serious in your study, and must practice and research these moves extensively to find out just what they are, and how and when they are used. When practicing, you and your opponent should adhere lightly to each other, following the motion back and forth, up and down. Also remember that when you attack high you are vulnerable and must cover low, and vice versa.

Similarly, when the opponent attacks high, counterattack low. If you do this, it will be difficult for the opponent to get in on you.

No matter (if) he uses enormous power to attack me, (I) use four ounces to lead (him aside), deflecting (his) one thousand pounds.

任他巨力來打我，牽動四兩撥千斤。

Taijiquan is based on the principle of not meeting force with force. When an opponent attacks with great strength, you lead his attack away from you. The key word here is "lead." You cannot push a large bull around, but if it has a ring through its sensitive nose, you can lead it this way or that with very little force. When a punch is coming at you with great force, you should adhere lightly to it, and lead it slightly off its course. If you tried to make a major change in the course of his attack, you might get bowled over by his forward momentum, and even if you succeeded, you would need a considerable force.

Guide (his power) into emptiness, then immediately attack; Adhere-Connect, Stick-Follow, do not lose him.

引進落空合即出，沾連黏隨不丟頂。

Your opponent expects his attack to meet resistance. If instead, you lead his attack past you, he will lose balance in the direction of his motion. This is the time to attack. Adhere-Connect means to attach a hand to him, and to become one with his motion, wherever he moves. Stick-Follow means to stay with him and not let him get away.

8. Song of the Real Meaning

真義歌

No shape, no shadow.
Entire body transparent and empty.
Forget your surroundings and be natural.
Like a stone chime suspended from West Mountain.
Tigers roaring, monkeys screeching.
Clear fountain, peaceful water.
Turbulent river, stormy ocean.
With your whole being, develop your life.

無形無象。	全身透空。
忘物自然。	西山懸磬。
虎吼猿鳴。	泉清水靜。
翻江鬧海。	盡性立命。

When practicing *Taijiquan* you must let go of everything. Your mind must be clear and centered. No concepts (preconceptions) should cloud your vision, no thoughts should hinder your action. The body must be relaxed and stable so that you can be light and agile. Forget your surroundings and just do what needs to be done. West Mountain is a famous mountain. "Like a stone chime suspended from West Mountain" means your mind must be clear, your head held as if suspended from above, and your body as stable and rooted as a great mountain. Sound is important in *Taijiquan* because it is linked to your *Qi* and the emission of power. Your sound must be as powerful as a tiger's roar and as penetrating as a monkey's screech. If you lift your Spirit (*Shen*) and guide your *Qi* throughout your body, your mind will be as clear and pure as a fountain full of spring water. If you practice *Taijiquan* for a long time, cultivating your *Qi*, your *Qi* will fill your body and circulate peacefully. But, like water, it can move powerfully and quickly so that nothing can stand before it.

This is not something that can be done lightly or casually, for it takes your full attention and effort. When done this way, *Taijiquan* fills your whole life, tying in to everything else you do. At this stage the separation between your life and your art disappears, and your efforts are directed at improving yourself as a whole, unified person.

9. The Secret of Withdraw and Release

撤放密訣

First Saying: Deflect

Deflect and open opponent's body and borrow opponent's Li (strength).

一曰掤，掤開彼身借彼力。

Do not meet the opponent's attack head on, or try to block it with force. Let your arm touch the opponent's arm, match his speed and direction, and deflect his attack from its original direction. If the opponent throws a right punch and you deflect it to your right, his right side will be exposed. When the opponent uses strength he will tend to be stiff. If you deflect him properly, his strength and momentum will cause him to lose balance. In this sense you are "borrowing" his strength to defeat him.

Second Saying: Lead

Lead (opponent's power) near (my) body, Jin thereby stored.

二曰引，引到身前勁始蓄。

When you neutralize an opponent's attack, draw him into you somewhat, and accumulate energy in your posture and *Qi* in your *Dan Tian* and spine. This is just like a bow accumulating energy when it is drawn, or a coil spring when it is compressed. You should also inhale in order to coordinate the motion with your *Qi*.

Third Saying: Relax

Relax and expand my Jin, without bends.

三曰鬆，鬆開我勁勿使屈。

The major difference between the *Jin* used in *Taijiquan* and the *Jin* of other styles is that *Taiji* emphasizes *Qi* support. This makes it possible to develop the *Jin* to a higher level. The first step of this development is relaxation. You must relax all of your muscles so that the *Qi* can flow wherever you want it without any hindrance. The *Qi* will then suffuse the muscles so that they function at peak efficiency.

When you counterattack you relax and emit *Jin* the way a bow relaxes from a state of tension as it shoots an arrow. Your posture should not have any kinks or awkward bends. Thus it is said: "Relax and expand my *Jin*, without bends."

When you apply force with your hand, there should be a counterforce into your rear foot to balance it. The line from the hand to the rear foot should be direct, without any "bends" (awkwardness in the posture) to disperse the energy. Thus it is said in *Taijiquan*: "*Jin* is straight and not curved."

Fourth Saying: Release

When (I) release, the waist and the feet must be timed carefully and accurately.

四曰放，放時腰腳認端的。

In order for the released *Jin* to reach its maximum level, your feet must be firmly rooted in the ground, the *Jin* must be generated from the legs, and the waist must control and direct it. Timing is critical in order to release your *Jin* effectively and efficiently. If you do not grasp the right moment to accurately express your *Jin* in attack or defense, it will be clumsy and inefficient, and you will miss the opportunity and lose the advantage. It is just like shooting at a moving target with a bow and arrow. The timing of the arrow's release and the accuracy of the aim are the keys to hitting the target.

10. Taijiquan Fundamental Key Points

太極拳基本要點

1. An insubstantial energy leads the head (upward). 虛領頂勁

The head should feel like it is suspended from above. This will raise the Spirit of Vitality and let the whole body move lightly and agilely.

2. The eye gazes with concentrated Spirit. 眼神注視

When a person has concentrated and raised his Spirit, his eyes will be bright and he will be able to pay attention to even the slightest movement of the enemy.

3. Hold the chest in, arc the back. 含胸拔背

The back between the shoulders has the feeling of being lifted, and the chest is slightly sunken. This lets the chest relax and the lungs move naturally. This is also used to neutralize the opponent's attack and to store energy within the posture.

4. Sink the shoulders, drop the elbows. 沈肩垂肘

Dropping the shoulders and elbows helps relaxation, and facilitates the transmission of energy into the hands. When the elbows and shoulders are sunken, the *Jin* can thread through from the waist to the hands so that they can function as one unit. Otherwise the *Jin* will be broken. Furthermore, sinking the elbows and shoulders will seal major cavities such as the armpit against attack. This posture also helps you to neutralize attacks because you are compact and can more easily evade or deflect an attack.

5. Settle the wrists, extend the fingers. 坐腕伸指

When the hand is extended palm downward, to "settle the wrist" means to drop the wrist slightly, so that the base of the palm is facing forward. This facilitates striking with the palm. Remember to keep the wrist relaxed. "Extend the fingers" means to let the fingers be straight, but not tensed. This should not be forced. Gradually get used to holding the fingers fairly straight so that there is no hindrance to the flow of blood and *Qi*.

6. Body central and upright. 身體中正

The body should be straight and erect, not leaning to any side.

7. Pull up the tailbone. 尾閭收住

The tailbone should be pulled up slightly to the front in order to keep the pelvis at the proper angle and the lower back straight. When the tip of the tailbone is allowed to move backward, the pelvis tilts and the lower back curves inward. This deprives the lower abdomen of its support and lets the belly bulge forward. A bent lower back also hinders the efficient transmission of energy up and down the spine. Therefore, it is very important to keep the tailbone tucked under.

8. Relax your waist and relax your thighs. 鬆腰鬆胯

The waist controls and directs the application of force. The thighs connect the waist to the knees, which are very important in all movement and in the generation of force by the legs. It is therefore important to keep the waist and thighs relaxed and movable.

9. The knees look relaxed, but are not relaxed. 膝部似鬆非鬆

In *Taijiquan*, the *Jin* is generated from the legs. In order to do this, the legs must behave like springs to release the power. Therefore, the knees must be relaxed. However, the legs are also vital in changing the steps during the fight. When this happens, they must move fast and firm. In order to move fast with a firm root, the knees must be able to change their tension skillfully. Therefore, this statement means that the knees look relaxed but can be tensed whenever necessary.

10. Soles touch the ground. (Feet flat on the ground.)
足掌貼地

The feet (or foot) must always be flat on the ground and relaxed, so that your root will be stable. Unless a specific posture calls for it, don't rest your weight on just the heels or the toes, but instead let the weight spread over the whole of the foot. Keep your attention on the center of the foot, a little bit behind the Bubbling Well point. This is where the center of gravity naturally falls.

11. Top and bottom follow each other, the entire body should be harmonious. 上下相隨，週身一致。

The entire body must move in a unified, coordinated way. Your upper body movement determines what your legs do, and your legs control your upper body. Arms and legs must move together, especially when pushing.

12. Distinguish insubstantial and substantial. 分清虛實

The body as a whole, as well as each individual part of the body, has a substantial and an insubstantial aspect. Usually only one leg and one arm should be substantial at a time. Which part of the body is substantial or insubstantial depends upon the opponent's actions. When the opponent is substantial, I become insubstantial where he contacts me and substantial somewhere else, either left or right, up or down. Also, one must clearly judge whether the opponent's attack is substantial or insubstantial. Very often an opponent can change a substantial force into insubstantial, or vice versa. Therefore, I must know my *Yin* and *Yang*, and also know my opponent's *Yin* and *Yang*. Then I know the enemy, but the enemy doesn't know me. I can control him, but I cannot be controlled.

13. Internal and external are mutually coordinated. Breathe naturally. 內外相合，呼吸自然。

Breathing, *Qi*, muscular strength and *Yi* must all act together. Breathing should be relaxed and should match your actions in a comfortable way. If the breathing is tense or jerky, then there is tension in the body, the mind is not still, and the *Qi* flow is hindered and unable to support the *Jin*.

14. Use Yi (mind), not Li (strength). 用意不用力

This means you should use skill, technique, and intelligence to defeat your opponent, and not just overwhelm him with strength. It also means that when you do a technique you should think only of what you are doing - e.g., pushing your opponent, locking an arm, etc. Do not think of *Qi*, strength, or your body, for this will split your attention and will weaken the technique. When you use *Yi* (mind) to move, *Qi* is automatically circulated, but when you use *Li* you will be more tense and *Qi* circulation will be hindered.

15. Qi circulates through the whole body; dividing, it moves up and down. 氣遍週身，分行上下。

Although *Qi* is always circulating, it is also moving simultaneously to the *Dan Tian* where it is stored, and to the spine to be used in techniques. Of these two ways, the movement down the front of the body to the storage area at the *Dan Tian* is *Yin*. The movement through the tailbone and up the spine to the hands is *Yang*. Thus it is said, *Qi* adheres closely to the bones of the spine and flows upward.

16. Where Yi (the mind) is, Qi is. 意氣相連

Qi follows the mind, so that wherever you put your attention, *Qi* accumulates. This is the reason that mental self-discipline is so important.

17. Every form of every posture follows smoothly; no forcing, no opposition, the entire body is comfortable.
式式勢順，不拗不背，週身舒適。

The entire sequence should flow smoothly from beginning to end. There should be no breaks, jerks, or sharp angles. The movements should be natural and comfortable for your body. In each posture, every part of the body contributes either directly or by counterbalancing. No part of the body should be hindering this unified flow.

18. Each form smooth. 式式均勻

Every form in the sequence should be done smoothly, with *Yi*, *Qi*, and the body all unified.

19. Postures should not be too little or too much (i.e., neither insufficient nor excessive). They (the postures) should seek to be centered and upright.
姿勢無過或不及，當求其中正。

Your body should be natural, centered, balanced, and controlled. Your arms and legs should be neither too extended nor drawn in too much. Strive to be efficient.

20. Your applications should be concealed, and not exposed. 用法含而不露。

The opponent should not be able to sense or predict your intentions. Your attack and defense should be concealed and unpredictable in order to confuse your opponent.

21. Attain stillness in motion. 動中求靜

You should maintain a meditative state while moving, then you will be calm and your mind clear.

22. Attain motion in stillness. 靜中求動

If you are in a meditative state you will move your *Qi* and body naturally and correctly without conscious effort.

23. Light, then agile; agile, then move; move, then vary.
輕則靈，靈則動，動則變。

This is *Taijiquan* in a nutshell. The first requirement is to clear the mind, relax the body, and circulate the *Qi*. Then you will be light. If you adhere to your opponent, not resisting and not letting go, then you will be agile. You can then move to attack and defend, but remember to vary your techniques so that your intentions cannot be read by your opponent.

11. Song of Application

功用歌

Light, agile, and alive, seek Dong Jin (to understand Jin); Yin and Yang cooperate mutually without the fault of stagnation; If (you) acquire (the trick), four ounces neutralizes one thousand pounds; Expand and close, stimulate the "drum," the center will be steady.

輕靈活潑求懂勁，陰陽相濟無滯病，若得四兩撥千斤，開合

鼓盪主宰定。

"Alive" here means alert and active. In practice you must pay close attention to your opponent/partner. In time you will be able to interpret his intention from the slightest of motions. Where the opponent is heavy, you are light. When one part of you is light, another part of you is heavy. You and your partner continually follow one another, never resisting, never separating. In this way the motion will continue to flow. In time you will acquire the knack of being light enough to avoid the opponent's attack, and substantial and controlled enough to deflect or attack him. Your postures alternately expand and close up with the circumstances. The drum is the abdomen in the area of the *Dan Tian*. You stimulate the *Qi* centered there with sound, attention, breathing and movement. This strengthens the *Qi* and exercises your control of it. When your attention and actions are thus centered on the *Dan Tian*, your stance will be stable and your mind calm and clear.

12. Five Key Words
五字訣

First Saying: The Xin (heart, mind) is quiet (calm).

When the heart (mind) is not quiet (calm), then (I am) not concentrated on one (thing). When I lift hands, forward and backward, left and right, (I am) totally without direction (purpose). In the beginning the movements do not follow the mind. Put the heart on recognizing and experiencing. Follow the opponent's movements, follow the curve, then expand. Don't lose (him), don't resist, don't extend or withdraw by yourself. (If the) opponent has Li (power), I also have Li, but my Li is first. (If the) opponent is without power, I also am without power, however my Yi (mind) is still first. One must be careful every movement. Wherever I am in contact, there the heart (mind) must be. One must seek information from not losing and not resisting; if I do that from now on, in one year or in half a year I will then be able to apply this with my body. All of this is using Yi (the mind), not using Jin. If I practice longer and longer, then the opponent is controlled by me, and I am not controlled by the opponent.

一曰心靜。心不靜則不專一。一舉手，前後左右，全無定向。起初舉動，未能由己，要悉心體認，隨人所動，隨屈就伸，不丟不頂，勿自伸縮。彼有力，我亦有力，我力在先。彼無力，我亦無力，我意仍在先。要刻刻留心，挨何處，心須用在何處。須向不丟不頂中討消息；從此做去，一年半載，便能施於身，此全是用意，不是用勁，久之則人為我制，我不為人制矣。

In *Taijiquan*, the mind is most important and controls movement. You cannot achieve this control by asserting your will. You must "give up yourself and follow the other." Don't resist, don't lose contact. Your power and mind are first in that you lead the opponent's attack away, rather than push it away. If you always remain lightly attached to the opponent you will gradually learn to sense his intentions. When you can follow automatically, your mind will be quiet and able to control your body and the opponent.

Second Saying: The body is agile.

If the body is stagnant, then (moving) forward and backward can't be at will. Therefore the body must be agile. When you lift your hands you must not have a clumsy appearance. When the opponent's power just touches my skin, my Yi (mind) is already deep into his bones. Two hands support, one Qi threading all through. (If) the left is heavy (attacked), then the left becomes insubstantial, (and) the right is gone (attacks). (If) the right is heavy, then the right becomes insubstantial and the left is gone. Qi is just like a cartwheel. Each part of the body must be mutually coordinated. If there is a place not mutually coordinated, then the body is dispersed and disordered, then you cannot gain power. (If you have) this fault, you must look to the waist and legs. First use your heart (mind) to master your body, following the opponent, not following your own will. Then the body will be able to follow the heart. Now you can follow your own will and also follow the opponent. If you follow your own will, then stagnation. If you follow the opponent, then you are alive. If able to follow the opponent, then the top of your hand has centimeters and inches. Weigh the opponent's Jin, big or small, then you have centimeters and millimeters with no mistakes. Measure the opponent's movement, long or short, then (you will make) no errors, even by a hairsbreadth. Forward and backward, everywhere just match (the opponent). The longer you study, then the finer your technique.

二曰身靈。身滯則進退不能自如，故要身靈。舉手不可有呆像，彼之力方礙我皮毛，我之意已入彼骨裡。兩手支撐，一氣貫穿，左重則左虛，而右已去，右重則右虛，而左已去。氣如車輪，週身俱要相隨，有不相隨處，身便散亂，便不得力，其病於腰腿求之。先以心使身，從人不從己，後身能從心，由己仍從人。從己則滯，從人則活。能從人，手上便有分寸。秤彼勁之大小，分厘不錯。權彼來之長短，毫髮無差。前進後退，處處恰合，工彌久而技彌精。

When you are light and agile and practice following for a long time, you can interpret the opponent's intentions at his lightest touch. Your two hands work together as a unit. When the opponent puts pressure on (attacks) your right side, that side becomes insubstantial (yields) and your left side has already attacked. When you can follow the opponent, then you can judge and interpret his actions and respond appropriately. The more you practice, the finer your sensitivity and control will be. It is as if your hand had a ruler or micrometer on it to measure the opponent's actions.

Third Saying: Qi condenses.

When the appearance of Qi is dispersed and diffused, then it is not conserved, and the body can easily be scattered and disordered. In order to make Qi condense into the bones your exhalation and inhalation must flow agilely (smoothly). The entire body is without gap. Inhalation is storage, and exhalation is emitting. That is because inhalation lifts up naturally (the Spirit of Vitality). It can also lift (control) the opponent. (When you) exhale, then (your Qi) can sink naturally. (You) also can release (Jin) out to the opponent. That means use Yi (your mind) to move your Qi, don't use Li (strength).

三曰氣斂。氣勢散漫，便無含蓄，身易散亂，務使氣斂入骨 ，呼吸通靈。週身罔間，吸爲蓄，呼爲發。蓋吸則自然提得 起，亦拏得人起。呼則自然沉得下，亦放人得出，此是以意 運氣，非以力運氣也。

When your *Qi* is scattered about your body in an undisciplined fashion, your body will be disorganized. You must calm the mind. When you inhale, let the *Qi* accumulate in the *Dan Tian* and spine, and raise the Spirit of Vitality. When you exhale, move the *Qi* from the spine, to the shoulders, and out to the hands. When you exhale, the *Qi* is also fully sunk to the tailbone. Breathing must be unhindered and must comfortably match your actions.

Fourth Saying: Jin is integrated.

The entire body's Jin, (when) trained, becomes one family (one unit). Distinguish clearly insubstantial and substantial. Emitting Jin must have root and origin. Jin begins at the foot's root, is controlled by the waist, expressed by the fingers, emitted by the spine and back. (You) must also lift the entire Spirit of Vitality. When the opponent's Jin is just about to be emitted, but is not yet emitted, my Jin already accepts it in (senses it). Just right, not late, not early. (It is) just like the skin (senses) fire. Like a spring bubbling up from the ground. Forward, backward, not the slightest scattering or confusion. Look for the straight in the curved. Store and then emit. (If you do this) then you will be) able to follow the (opponent's) hands and act effectively. This is borrowing the opponent's) Li to strike the opponent, and (using) four ounces to repel a thousand pounds.

四曰勁整。一身之勁，練成一家，分清虛實，發勁要有根源 ，勁起於腳根，主宰於腰，形於手指，發於脊背，又要提起 全副精神，於彼勁將出未發之際，我勁已接入彼勁。恰好不 後不先，如皮燃火，如泉湧出，前進後退，無絲毫散亂，曲 中求直，蓄而後發，方能隨手奏效，此借力打人，四兩撥千 金也。

You must learn how all parts of the body contribute to the technique, what parts are heavy or active, and what parts are light or insubstantial. *Jin* is rooted in the feet, it originates in (is generated by) the legs, is controlled by the waist, emitted by the spine, and expressed by the hands. Raising the Spirit of Vitality allows you to have a strong root and a clear mind. Timing is crucial for effective technique. You must develop the lightness and sensitivity to respond to the opponent's attack as quickly and unconsciously as the skin responds to fire. At the first touch, or even before the touch, you know his intention and are already neutralizing him. Your movement and response must be continuos and flowing like a spring bubbling up out of the ground. You are continuously moving in curves and circles. This allows you to bend like a bow or coil like a spring and accumulate energy in your posture. You also accumulate *Qi* in your spine and *Dan Tian*. When you neutralize you curve or bend, and then you attack in a straight line. If you learn these skills you will be able to defeat your opponent easily and automatically.

Fifth Saying: Spirit condenses.

All in all, (if the above four items (are) totally acquired, it comes down to condensing Shen (Spirit). When Shen condenses, then one Qi (can be) formed, like a drum. Training Qi belongs to Shen. Qi appears agitated (i.e., abundant) and smooth. The Spirit of Vitality is threaded and concentrated. Opening and closing have numbers (degrees of fineness). Insubstantial and substantial are clearly distinguished: if the left is insubstantial, then the right is substantial; if the right is insubstantial, then the left is substantial. Insubstantial doesn't mean absolutely no Li. The appearance of Qi must have agitation and smoothness; in actuality it does not happen instantly by magic). The Spirit of Vitality should be emphasized, it must be threaded and concentrated. Li is borrowed from the opponent. Qi is emitted from the spine. How can Qi come from the spine? (When) Qi sinks downward from the two shoulders, condenses into the bones of the spine, concentrates at the waist (Dan Tian), this Qi from the top to the bottom is called closing. From the waist, appearing in the bones of the spine, then spreading to the shoulders, appearing in the fingers, this Qi from the bottom to the top is called opening. Closing means to draw in, opening means to release. If able to understand opening and closing, then (you) know Yin and Yang. When you understand these steps, then (if you) practice one day, your technique is refined one day. (Then you) gradually approach (the point) where you can not but achieve what you want.

五曰神聚。上四者俱備，總歸神聚，神聚則一氣鼓鑄，練氣
歸神，氣勢騰挪，精神貫注，開合有數，虛實清楚：左虛則
右實，虛非全然無力。氣勢要有騰挪；實非全然占煞，精神
責貫注。力從人借，氣由脊發，胡能氣由脊發？氣向下沉，
由兩肩收入脊骨，注於腰間，此氣之由上而下也，謂之合。
由腰形於脊骨，布於兩膊，施於手指，此氣之由下而上也，
謂之開。合便是收，開便是放；能懂得開合，便知陰陽。到
此地步，工用一日，技精一日，漸至從心所欲，罔不如意矣
。

Just as you train your *Qi* to thread through every part of your body, so too must you train your Spirit. Your awareness must reach to every part of your body and even beyond, but yet it must also be focused or concentrated. When your Spirit is concentrated your Mind will be able to move the *Qi*. It is said "*Yi Shou Dan Tian*." This means the mind (*Yi*) is kept on the *Dan Tian*. The mind will move as you move or do techniques, but it always returns to the abdomen. As you do this you are developing and training your *Qi*, which is an important part of Spirit. As *Qi* accumulates it will fill the *Dan Tian* and the abdomen will be taut like a drum. This is not a rigid tightness. It is the firmness that comes from inflation. Like a drum, *Qi* has a vibrating and pulsating energy. The Chinese translated here as "agitated" has the sense of motion up and down like a prancing horse or a bubbling well; the word translated here as "smooth" has the sense of smooth motion back and forth. The Spirit of Vitality is an aspect of *Shen*. It must be lifted up to raise the Spirit as a whole. *Shen* does not exist in a vacuum. You must develop your techniques, and learn about *Yin* and *Yang*. Techniques do not happen by magic - they depend upon a firm grasp of principles, and *Jin* supported by *Qi*, all guided by your Spirit. You must understand closing and opening. As you neutralize an attack, you draw him into you, drawing in and borrowing his energy, as well as accumulating the energy of your own body in the *Dan Tian*. This is called closing, and is done on the inhale. *Qi* sinks from the shoulders to the *Dan Tian* down the front of the body. This is *Yin* and is used to withdraw. At the appropriate time you release the accumulated energy up the spine and out to the hands. This is called opening and is done on the exhale. *Qi* is raised from the tailbone up the spine to the shoulders and out to the fingers. This is *Yang* and is used to emit *Jin*. Again, in all of this, the mind is the master.

13. Old Taijiquan Classic of Qing Qian Long Dynasty (1736-1796 A.D.)

乾隆舊抄本歌訣

Follow the neck to thread (the Qi) to the head, the two shoulders relaxed. Condense the strong lower Qi, and support the hips. The stomach sound extends the Jin to strengthen the two fists' (Jin). Five toes grasp the ground, the top bent like a bow.

順項貫頂兩膀鬆，束烈下氣把襠撐，胃音開勁兩捶爭，五指
抓地上彎弓。

An insubstantial energy lifts the head and straightens the neck. This allows the *Qi* to flow naturally, and keeps the shoulders relaxed and sunken. The *Qi* of the lower abdomen condenses into the *Dan Tian*. The *Qi* sinks downward into the *Dan Tian* and into the feet, and at the same time there is force coming up and supporting the hips. This sinking and lifting allows the posture to be stable and flexible. The Ha sound, which comes from the "stomach" or abdomen, helps you raise the Spirit of Vitality, coordinate *Qi* and *Jin*, and extend energy out to your hands. When your feet "grasp the ground" the root should be firm and alive, but the feet should still remain relaxed. The legs should be bent like a bow. The Chinese word for toes can also mean fingers, and so an alternate meaning for this sentence can be that the hand should be shaped as if it were holding a large ball, and should be bent backward a bit.

Lift and move lightly and with agility and condense the Spirit internally. Don't be broken and then continuous, refine your one Qi. Left and right as appropriate have insubstantial and substantial places. When Yi (mind) is up, this implies down; and give up post-birth strength.

舉動輕靈神內斂，莫教斷續一氣研，左宜右有虛實處，意上
寓下後天還。

You should be light and agile and should keep your Spirit inside. If you expose your Spirit externally, people can see what you are doing and thinking. Your postures and motion should be fluid and continuous, and all should be one flow of *Qi*. The different parts of the body are substantial or insubstantial, and this changes constantly with the circumstances. To do this appropriately requires correct timing. When your attention is up, don't forget down. When the opponent attacks down, don't forget up. All of this is not done with post-birth strength (*Li*), but rather with *Qi*-supported *Jin*.

Grasp and hold the Dan Tian to train internal Gongfu. Hen, Ha, two Qis are marvelous and infinite. Move open, quiet close, bend and extend following your opponent. Slow respond (slow), fast follow (fast), the principles must be understood thoroughly.

拿住丹田練內功，哼哈二氣妙無窮，動分靜合屈伸就，緩應

急隨理貫通。

When your attention remains on your *Dan Tian* you will gradually generate internal energy. When you coordinate this with your breathing and motions, your *Gongfu* will be internal and superior to the external variety. The two sounds, Hen and Ha, help you to mobilize and express your energy. When you move, you open or extend your energy. When you close, you accumulate energy, but calmly, so the opponent doesn't notice. You bend and extend, contract and expand, yield and adhere, neutralize and attack, all depending upon your opponent. You move slow or fast, following the opponent, and always according to the *Taiji* principles.

Suddenly disappear, suddenly appear. Forward, then expand. A feather cannot be added; be perfect like the Daoist bible. Hand slow, hand fast, all not alike. Four ounces repel a thousand pounds, apply this principle and neutralize well.

忽隱忽現進則長，一羽不加至道藏，手慢手快皆非似，四兩

撥千運化良。

As you exchange substantial and insubstantial, you disappear in front of the enemy's attack and reappear elsewhere to attack him. You remain insubstantial, and when you find an opportunity you move forward and "expand," i.e., become substantial. "Forward, then expand" can also mean that when the opponent moves forward you become insubstantial in front of his attack, and attack on the other side. This is just like the *Taiji* diagram, where each side is small where the other side is large, and large where the other side is small. You must be so light, agile, and responsive that a feather cannot touch you without setting you in motion. If you can do this, your art will be as perfect as the Daoist bible. Slow or fast, the situation is always changing, but if you adhere to the principles you will be able to neutralize an attack of a thousand pounds with four ounces.

Peng (Wardoff), Lu (Rollback), Ji (Press), An (Push) are the four main directions. Cai (Pluck), Lie (Split), Zhou (Elbow), Kao (Bump) complete the four diagonal corners. Qian (Heaven), Kun (Earth), Zhen (Thunder), Dui (Lake) are the eight trigrams. Forward, backward, look to the left, look to the right, and central equilibrium are the five elements

掤攦擠按四方正，採捌肘靠斜角成，乾坤震兌乃八卦，進退

顧盼定五行。

Taijiquan is said to be comprised of thirteen postures. There are the eight basic moves and the five directions. These are coordinated with the eight trigrams (the author lists only four, assuming the reader is already quite familiar with them) and the five elements.

Qian (Heaven)	*Peng* (Wardoff)
Kun (Earth)	*Lu* (Rollback)
Kan (Water)	*Ji* (Press)
Li (Fire)	*An* (Push)
Xun (Wind)	*Cai* (Pluck)
Zhen (Thunder)	*Lie* (Split)
Dui (Lake)	*Zhou* (Elbow)
Gen (Mountain)	*Kao* (Bump)
Jin Bu (Forward)	*Jin* (Metal)
Tui Bu (Backward)	*Mu* (Wood)
Zuo Gu (Left)	*Shui* (Water)
You Pan (Right)	*Huo* (Fire)
Zhong Ding (Center)	*Tu* (Earth)

Extremely soft means hardness. That means extremely insubstantial and agile. When you transport (Qi) it is like drawing silk from a cocoon. Everywhere clear. Open and expanding, tight and compact, one right after the other, should be threaded together tightly. Wait for the opportunity, then move as a cat moves.

極柔即剛極虛靈，運若抽絲處處明，開展緊湊乃縝密，待機

而動如貓行。

In *Taiji*, you achieve hardness through softness. You remain light and agile, avoiding the opponent's attack, and waiting for the opportunity when you can mobilize all your forces and attack with certainty. Your motion is smooth, continuous and unbroken so that you can mobilize and transport your *Qi* effectively. When you are experienced at moving *Qi* throughout your body, you will be able to clearly sense where the energy is. When you are opening and closing, expanding and contracting in response to your opponent's moves, your postures should mesh together seamlessly so that there is no opportunity for him to attack. You adhere and stick, neutralize and follow, always paying careful attention. When the opportunity to attack presents itself, you attack instantly.

14. Song of Comprehension and Application

體用歌

Taijiquan, thirteen postures, it's marvelous, (because there are) two Qi's, discriminated as Yin and Yang.

太極拳，十三式，妙在二氣分陰陽。

Taijiquan, because it includes thirteen movements and directions in its fighting strategy, is also called the thirteen postures. This extraordinary training and fighting strategy is made up of two *Qi*'s - *Yin* and *Yang*. All the movements, breathing, *Qi* circulation, and techniques are based on *Yin* and *Yang* principles and derive into insubstantial and substantial fighting strategies.

Neutralization generates a thousand million (techniques), all belonging to one (principle). All belongs to one. Taijiquan has two poles, four phases, it is infinite.

化生千億歸抱一，歸抱一，太極拳兩儀四象渾無邊。

From *Yin* and *Yang* (insubstantial and substantial) fighting strategies, the principle of neutralization is generated. From the principle of neutralization, numerous techniques are created. Though the techniques are many, there is only one principle. From *Taiji*'s two poles - *Yin* and *Yang* - are generated four faces; the four faces generate eight trigrams, the eight trigrams generate sixty-four hexagrams, and the hexagrams generate everything else. The four faces are extreme *Yin*, extreme *Yang*, deficient *Yin* and deficient *Yang*. The Chinese translated here as "infinite" is literally "blurred no sides." This has the feeling of being on a foggy river where everything is indistinct and the shores cannot be seen.

If you follow the wind, how can your head be suspended? I have one guiding sentence. Today I want to tell it to the people who can comprehend. (If) the Bubbling Well (Yongquan cavity) has no root, the waist has no master, (then) you can try hard to learn until you almost die, you will still not succeed.

御風何似頂頭懸，我有一轉語，今爲知者吐。湧泉無根，腰
無主，力學垂死終無捕。

If you sway and move around like a kite in the wind, you cannot cultivate the feeling of being suspended from above. You must keep the body straight and erect, with an insubstantial energy lifting the head and giving you the feeling of being suspended from above. At the same time you must sink your *Qi* to the soles of the feet into the Bubbling Well cavities. Having a good root is absolutely essential for getting force out to the hands, or to any part of the body for any of the techniques. A good root is also necessary for effective use of the waist. If there is no root and waist control, all your practice is in vain and your techniques are useless.

When comprehension and application mutually support one another - is there any other trick to do this? (No), because marvelous Qi can approach the hands.

體用相兼豈有他，浩然氣能行乎手。

A *Taiji* practitioner must learn the principles and techniques first, and then he should ponder and comprehend the deeper meaning of the theory. Only after that can he apply all the theory and techniques. After he has gained enough experience in applying the techniques, he should go back to the theory and ponder again, and then apply it to the techniques and so on. Comprehension and application mutually support each other, and will help one become a high level *Taiji* artist. If one practices this way his *Qi* will be able to reach his hands. This will not only benefit his health, but will also be useful in martial applications.

Peng (Wardoff), Lu (Rollback), Ji (Press), An (Push), Cai (Pluck), Lie (Split), Zhou (Elbow), Kao (Bump), and Jin (Forward), Tui (Backward), Gu (Left), Pan (Right), and Ding (Center). Don't neutralize, automatically neutralize; (don't) yield, automatically yield.

掤攦擠按採挒肘，靠及進退顧盼定，不化自化走自走。

For all thirteen postures, one should follow the rule of natural response. Yielding and neutralizing should not be big, conscious moves. They should be natural and automatic. Don't try to yield. Stay calm and centered and let it happen automatically. Just stick to the enemy, follow, and automatically neutralize.

(When you) wish the foot to go forward, you must push off from the rear (foot). Your body is like moving clouds. (When you) strike with the hands, why use hands? The entire body is hands, but the hands are not your hands. However (you) must be careful to protect what should be protected at all times.

足欲向前先挫後，身似行雲打手安用手，渾身是手手非手，

但須方寸隨時守所守。

When you wish to move, push off the rear foot. Move lightly like a cloud. When you strike don't use the force of the arms. Instead use the force of the whole body, generated from the legs and controlled by the waist. It may not be necessary to use the hands at all. Instead you may use any part of the body in contact with the opponent. However, when you do this you must remember to do whatever is necessary to protect yourself.

15. Song of the Thirteen Postures

十三勢歌

All the thirteen postures (of Taijiquan) must not be treated lightly. The meaning of life originates at the waist.

十三總勢莫輕視，命意源頭在腰際。

The thirteen postures are the foundation of *Taijiquan*. The waist is important because it governs all of your movements, and because *Qi* is generated and stored in the *Dan Tian*.

(When you) vary and exchange insubstantial and substantial (you) must take care that Qi (circulates) in the entire body without the slightest stagnation.

變換虛實須留意，氣遍身軀不少滯。

When you move your body, you are changing and exchanging substantial and insubstantial and transporting *Qi* to various parts of your body. It is important that the whole body is relaxed and the mind is clear so that the *Qi* can move through the whole body without hindrance. When *Qi* moves easily there is health, when *Qi* stagnates there is illness.

Touch (find) the movement in the stillness, (although there is) stillness even in movement. Vary (your) response to the enemy and show the marvelous technique.

靜中觸動動猶靜，應敵變化示神奇。

Taiji has been called meditation in motion. While moving, the mind is still centered and quiet as in sitting meditation. At the same time, while in this meditative state one is still actively circulating *Qi*. When attacked, remain in the meditative state, calm and aware. When the principles have been learned and internalized, you can respond naturally and comfortably to the opponent's moves. *Taiji* is the art of change. As you follow the opponent's actions, your response subtly changes and varies with the situation.

Pay attention to every posture and gauge its purpose, (then you will) gain (the art) without wasting your time and energy.

勢勢存心揆用意，得來全不費功夫。

The care and seriousness you put into your study determines the degree of success you will have. Every posture has its nature and purpose, and must be researched and studied before it can be really understood.

In every movement the heart (mind) remains on the waist, the abdomen is relaxed and clear, and Qi rises up.

刻刻留心在腰間，腹內鬆淨氣騰然。

In all the postures the principle is the same: the mind must remain on the *Dan Tian* (*Yi Shou Dan Tian*). The abdomen must be relaxed and the mind calm and clear so that the *Qi* will rise up and circulate throughout the body.

The tailbone is central and upright, the Spirit is threaded through the head. The entire body is light and easy (relaxed), the top of the head is suspended.

尾閭中正神貫頂，滿身輕利頂頭懸。

The lower vertebrae must be erect and the back straight, and an insubstantial energy must lift the head upward.

Pay attention carefully in (your) research, bent-extended, open-closed follow their freedom.

仔細留心向推求，屈伸開合聽自由。

Bent-extended, open-closed are the tricks of pushing hands. Bend to neutralize the enemy's power, at the same time close to store your *Jin*, and then open and extend to emit your *Jin*. All these techniques must be natural and freely follow your opponent's intention, then you can Adhere-Connect, Stick-Follow and defeat your opponent. If you do not research these tricks with all your heart, you will not gain the key to *Taijiquan*.

To enter the door and be led along the way, one needs oral instruction; practice without ceasing, the way is through self-study.

入門引路須口授，功夫無息法自然。

To learn *Taiji* well a teacher is needed. There are so many subtleties that it is very easy to get something wrong or emphasize the wrong things. It is said "a slight error can cause a thousand mile divergence." Traditionally in the martial arts there were two kinds of students - the outer and the inner. The outer students were often accepted for their money or to test their seriousness. They were taught only the forms and a minimum of applications and principles. Once a student was judged worthy he was taken into the temple and shown the inner secrets of the style. Today it is often much easier to learn the secrets of a martial art because so much has been published. However, having a good teacher in the flesh is still almost a necessity. Once one has been shown the way, the only thing remaining is to practice unceasingly and to continually research on one's own.

If asked, what is the standard (criteria) of its (thirteen postures) application, (the answer is) Yi (mind) and Qi are the master, and the bones and muscles are the chancellor.

若問體用何爲準，意氣君來骨肉臣。

The criteria for judging whether the postures are applied correctly is: are the mind and *Qi* directing the movement? All movement is done with *Jin* supported by *Qi* and directed by *Yi* (mind). If the movement is done only with bones and muscles, it is considered *Li,* or muscular strength, and is incorrect.

Investigate in detail what the ultimate meaning is: to increase the age, extend the years, and achieve never-aging youthfulness.

詳推用意終何在，益壽延年不老春。

You must remember that the ultimate purpose of *Taiji* is to maintain a healthy body and a youthful mind.

The song, the song, one hundred and forty (words), every word is real and true, no meaning is left behind. If not approached from this (song), your time and energy are wasted in vain, and you will sigh in regret.

歌兮歌兮百四十，字字眞切意無疑。若不向此推求去，枉費

功夫貽歎息。

Whether you study the art for health or self-defense, you must follow the words of this song or your efforts will be wasted.

Appendix B
Translation and Glossary of Chinese Terms

An: 按 Push. A technique for pushing or striking the opponent. It is one of the Four Directions of the eight basic *Taiji* fighting techniques, which correspond to the Eight Trigrams (*Bagua*).

Ba Duan Jin: 八段錦 Eight Pieces of Brocade. A style of *Qigong* training, said to be created by Marshal Yue, Fei in the Song Dynasty (960-1279 A.D.). Originally called *Shi Er Duan Jin* (Twelve Pieces of Brocade), it was later shortened to eight forms.

Bagua: 八卦 The Eight Trigrams. The **Yi Jing**, a book of philosophy, lists eight basic principles, which are derived from *Yin* and *Yang*, and which in turn give rise to other variations. These eight principles are each represented by three broken and/or straight lines known as trigrams (See **Yi Jing**). In *Taijiquan* the trigrams correspond to the basic techniques *Peng, Lu, Ji, An, Cai, Lie, Zhou*, and *Kao*.

Baguazhang: 八卦掌 Eight Trigrams Palm. One of the internal Chinese martial styles, based on the *Bagua* theory. It emphasizes the application of palm techniques and circular movements. *Baguazhang* was created by Dong, Hai-Chuan in the nineteenth century.

Bai He: 白鶴 White Crane. A style of southern *Shaolin Gongfu* which imitates the fighting techniques of the crane.

Bi Qi: 閉氣 Seal the Breath. One of the four major categories of *Qin Na* techniques, it specializes in sealing (obstructing) the opponent's breath or a blood vessel, causing unconsciousness or death.

Cai: 採 Pluck. A technique for unbalancing the opponent or pulling him into an exposed position. One of the Four Corners of the eig basic *Taiji* fighting techniques.

Chang Chuan (Changquan): 長拳 Long Fist or Long Sequence. When it means Long Fist, it is a northern *Shaolin* Chinese martial style which specializes in kicking techniques. When it means Long Sequence, it refers to *Taijiquan* and implies that the *Taiji* sequence is long and flowing like a river.

Chang, San-Feng (Zhang, San-Feng): 張三豐 Said to be the creator of *Taijiquan* in the Song Dynasty (960-1279 A.D.). However, there is no certain documentary proof of this.

Chang: 長 To Grow. Another meaning is "Long."

Chen Jia Gou: 陳家溝 The name of the village of the Chen family, where *Chen* Style *Taijiquan* originated.

Chen, Chang-Xing: 陳長興　The fourteenth generation master of *Chen* Style *Taijiquan*, who taught the art to Yang, Lu-Shan.

Chen, Yan-Lin: 陳炎林　A famous Chinese *Yang* Style master. In the 1940s he wrote a book on *Taijiquan* which is still considered one of the best. Born in 1906, he is still alive and living in Shanghai, China.

Cheng, Gin-Gsao: 曾金灶　Dr. Yang, Jwing-Ming's White Crane master.

Cheng, Man-Ching: 鄭曼清　A famous *Yang* Style *Taiji* master from Taiwan, who taught in the United States during the 1960s. He taught a shortened version of the form (which is very popular here and in Taiwan) and stressed relaxation and the health aspect of *Taijiquan*.

Chin Na (Qin Na): 擒拿　Grasp and Control. An aspect of Chinese martial arts training, *Qin Na* specializes in controlling the enemy through "misplacing the joint," "dividing the muscle," "sealing the breath," and "cavity press."

Chong: 重　Layering. The same character, when pronounced as *Zhong*, means weight or heaviness.

Chuan (Quan): 拳　Fist. This term in Chinese martial arts is also used to denote a *Gongfu* style, e.g. *Shaolin Quan* or *Taijiquan*, or a sequence, for example, *Lian Bu Quan* or *Gong Li Quan*.

Da Lu: 大擾　Large Rollback. Rollback is one of the eight basic *Taiji* fighting techniques, and is a method of leading the opponent's attack past you. There are two versions - large and small Rollback. *Da Lu* also refers to a two-person pushing hands exercise which concentrates on using the four "corners" (*Cai, Lie, Zhou, Kao*), as well as the four "directions" (*Peng, Lu, Ji, An*).

Da Mo's Yi Jin Jing: 達摩易筋經　Da Mo was an Indian prince who went to China to preach Buddhism around 527 A.D. His book **Yi *Jin* Jing (*Muscle Change Classic*)** describes methods for generating and circulating *Qi* in the body to improve health. This training was later found to be useful for increasing the power of martial techniques.

Da Zhou Tian: 大周天　Grand Circulation. A *Qigong* training method in which the *Qi* is led to circulate throughout the entire body.

Dan Tian: 丹田　Field of Elixir. There are three *Dan Tians* in the body: the brain, the solar plexus area, and the lower abdomen. *Taiji* is primarily interested in the Lower *Dan Tian*. It is considered the reservoir of *Qi*, and is located approximately one and one-half inches below the navel and about a third of the way toward the spine. In acupuncture this point is known as *Qihai* (Sea of *Qi*).

Dian Xue: 點穴　Cavity Press. A high level technique in Chinese *Gongfu* in which certain acupuncture points are struck or grasped in order to injure or kill the opponent.

Du Mai: 督脈 Governing Vessel. One of the eight *Qi* vessels which, along with the twelve channels, are the major *Qi* pathways in the human body. *Du Mai* runs from the tailbone, along the spine, to the roof of the mouth.

Duan: 短 Short.

Dui: 兌 One of the Eight Trigrams (*Bagua*). Corresponds to Lake.

Femur-Futu (LI-18): 伏兔 An acupuncture cavity belonging to the Large Intestine Primary *Qi* Channel.

Fo Shou: 佛手 ,**Buddha Hand.** A *Qigong* hand form. Also the name of a Chinese martial style.

Gen: 艮 One of the eight trigrams (*Bagua*). Corresponds to Mountain.

Gong Shou: 拱手 Arc Hands. Also known as "Universal Post." It is a standing meditation form of *Qigong* training, in which *Qi* is built up in the shoulders and then circulated to the limbs and internal organs.

Gongfu (Kung Fu): 功夫 Energy and Time. Anything which takes time and energy to master is called *Gongfu*. In recent times it has come to mean Chinese martial arts.

Guoshu (Kuoshu): 國術 National Technique. The name for Chinese martial arts used by Chiang, Kai-Shek since 1926, and still used in Taiwan. Mainland China uses the term *Wushu*.

Ha: 哈 One of the two sounds used in *Taijiquan* and other Chinese martial styles. The Ha sound is positive (*Yang*) and is used to raise the Spirit of Vitality, enabling power to reach its maximum.

Hand Jueyin Pericardium Jing: 手厥陰包絡經 One of the twelve primary *Qi* channels in acupuncture.

Hand Shaoyang Triple Burner Jing: 手少陽三焦經 One of the twelve primary *Qi* channels in acupuncture.

Hand Shaoyin Heart Jing: 手少陰心經 One of the twelve primary *Qi* channels in acupuncture.

Hand Taiyang Small Intestine Jing: 手太陽小腸經 One of the twelve primary *Qi* channels in acupuncture.

Hand Taiyin Lung Jing: 手太陰肺經 One of the twelve primary *Qi* channels in acupuncture.

Hand Yangming Large Intestine Jing: 手陽明大腸經 One of the twelve primary *Qi* channels in acupuncture.

Hao Style: 郝式 A *Taijiquan* style created by Hao, Wei-Zhen who learned his *Taijiquan* from Li, Yi-Yu.

Hebei: 河北 A province in China.

Hen: 哼 One of the two sounds used in *Taijiquan*. When done on the inhale, the Hen sound is purely negative (*Yin*). It condenses the *Yi* and *Qi* into the bone marrow. When done on the exhale, Hen is negative with some positive. This allows you to attack while conserving some energy.

Henan: 河南 A province in China.

Hou Tian Fa: 後天法 Post-Heaven Techniques. A *Gongfu* style which existed hundreds of years before *Taijiquan* and was said to embody the same principles.

Hsing Yi Chuan (Xingyiquan): 形意拳 Shape Mind Fist. One of the internal Chinese martial styles. It is based on five basic motions related to the Five Elements (*Wu Xing*), as well as motions corresponding to twelve animals. It is said that this style was created by Marshal Yue, Fei during the Song Dynasty.

Hua Quan: 化拳 Neutralizing Fist. It implies a *Taijiquan* style which specialized in neutralization.

Huiyin (Co-1): 會陰 An acupuncture cavity belonging to the Conception Vessel.

Huo: 火 Fire. One of the Five Elements (*Wu Xing*).

Ji: 擠 Press or Squeeze. One of the Four Directions of the eight basic *Taiji* fighting techniques.

Jiang Fa: 蔣發 The *Taiji* master who passed the art of *Taijiquan* to the Chen family.

Jiexi (S-41): 解溪 An acupuncture cavity belonging to the Stomach Primary *Qi* Channel.

Jimen (Sp-11): 箕門 An acupuncture cavity belonging to the Spleen Primary *Qi* Channel.

Jin: 近 Near or Close.

Jin (1115-1234 A.D.): 金 A dynasty in Chinese history.

Jin: 金 Metal. One of the Five Elements (*Wu Xing*).

Jin: 勁 Power. In Chinese martial arts there are many types of *Jin*, but they all deal with the flow of energy. These range from sensing *Jins* (sensing the enemy's power), to neutralizing *Jins* (neutralizing or deflecting the enemy's power), to emitting *Jins* (emitting power in a smooth pulse). In general, the higher the level of *Jin*, the more *Qi* and the less *Li* (muscular strength) is used.

Jin Bu: 進步 Step Forward. One of the five basic strategic movements of *Taiji*.

Jin Di: 勁敵 Strong Enemy.

Jin Feng: 勁風 Strong Wind.

Jin Gang Zhi: 金剛指 Steel Finger. A special Chinese martial *Qigong* training to make the fingers as strong as steel.

Jin Gong: 勁功 A type of *Gongfu* which specializes in training *Qi* to support *Jin* so that the *Jin* can reach its maximum.

Jin Zhong Zhao: 金鐘罩 Golden Bell Cover. A *Gongfu* training which enables a person to be struck without injury.

Jing: 經 The main *Qi* (energy) channels. In the human body there are twelve pairs of these channels, which are related to the internal organs.

Jing: 精 Essence. What is left after something has been refined and purified. In Chinese medicine, *Jing* can mean semen, but it generally refers to the basic substance of the body which the *Qi* and Spirit enliven.

Jing Wu Association: 精武門 A Chinese martial arts organization, founded in 1909 by Huo, Yuan-Jia in Shanghai.

Jing-Shen: 精神 Essence of the Spirit; Spirit of Vitality. A person with a strong *Jing-Shen* is active, vigorous, and concentrated.

Jiuwei (Co-15): 鳩尾 An acupuncture cavity belonging to the Conception Vessel.

Kan: 坎 One of the eight trigrams (*Bagua*). Corresponds to Water.

Kao: 靠 Bump. A technique using the shoulder, hip, thigh, back, or any other part of the body to bump the opponent off balance. One of the Four Corners of the eight basic *Taiji* fighting techniques.

Kao, Tao: 高濤 Dr. Yang, Jwing-Ming's first *Taijiquan* master.

Kong Qi: 空氣 Air.

Kun: 昆 One of the eight trigrams (*Bagua*). Corresponds to Earth.

Li: 力 Muscular power; Strength.

Li: 離 One of the eight trigrams (*Bagua*). Corresponds to Fire.

Li Style: 李式 A style of *Taijiquan* originating from Li, Yi-Yu who learned his *Taijiquan* from Wuu, Yu-Rang.

Li, Mao-Ching: 李茂清 Dr. Yang, Jwing-Ming's Long Fist master.

Liang Dynasty: 梁代 A dynasty in Chinese history (502-557 A.D.).

Lie: 挒 Split or Rend. The use of two opposing forces to lock or unbalance the opponent. One of the Four Corners of the eight basic *Taiji* fighting techniques.

Ling: 靈 Agile.

Liu He Ba Fa: 六合八法 Six Combinations and Eight Methods. One of the internal Chinese martial styles. Said to have been created by Chen, Bo during the Song Dynasty.

Lu: 擴 Rollback. A technique for leading the opponent's attack past you. One of the Four Directions of the eight basic *Taiji* fighting techniques.

Luo: 絡 Branches. The numerous tiny *Qi* channels which extend from the major channels (*Jing*) and allow the *Qi* to reach from the skin to the marrow.

Mai: 脈 Vessels. The eight auxiliary *Qi* channels which are not associated with internal organs.

Mian Quan: 綿拳 Cotton Fist. It implies that the practice of *Taijiquan* is soft as cotton.

Ming Tai Zu (1368-1399 A.D.): 明太祖 The first emperor of China's Ming dynasty (1368-1644 A.D.).

Ming Ying Zong (1457-1465 A.D.): 明英宗 An emperor of China's Ming dynasty (1368-1644 A.D.).

Ming: 明 A dynasty in Chinese history (1368-1644 A.D.).

Mu: 木 Wood. One of the five basic elements (*Wu Xing*).

Nanking Central Guoshu Institute: 南京中央國術館 A Chinese martial arts institute, founded by the Chinese government in 1926 to promote the martial arts.

Nei Dan: 內丹 Internal Elixir. *Qigong* training in which the *Qi* is generated at the *Dan Tian*, then circulated throughout the entire body.

Nei Gong: 內功 Internal *Gongfu*. This is another name for *Qigong*.

Nei Jia: 內家 Internal Family. Refers to the internal Chinese martial styles, the most famous of which are *Taijiquan*, *Xingyi*, *Bagua*, and *Liu He Ba Fa*. The external styles are known as *Wai Jia* (External Family).

Nei Jin Li: 內勁力 Internal *Jin Li*. Same as *Nei Jin*. Called *Li* because no matter how much *Qi* you use to generate the power, you must still use the muscles to some degree. For the same reason, *Wai Jin* is also sometimes called *Wai Jin Li*.

Nei Jin: 內勁 Internal Power. The *Jin* or power in which *Qi* from the *Dan Tian* is used to support the muscles. This is characterized by relatively relaxed muscles. When the muscles predominate and local *Qi* is used to support them, it is called *Wai Jin* (External *Jin*).

Peng: 掤 Ward-off. A technique for bouncing the opponent's force back in the direction it came from. One of the Four Directions of the eight basic *Taiji* fighting techniques.

Qi Jing Ba Mai: 奇經八脈 Strange (Odd) Channels Eight Vessels. Usually referred to as the "Eight Extraordinary Vessels or simply "The Vessels." Called odd or strange because they are not well understood and some of them do not exist in pairs.

Qi (Chi): 氣 The "intrinsic energy" which circulates in all living things.

Qi Li (or Li Qi): 氣力 (力氣) *Qi*-Supported Muscular Power. When you concentrate your mind (*Yi*) and keep the muscles relaxed, the *Qi* flow will increase and invigorate the muscles.

Qian Jin Zhui: 千斤墜 Thousand Pound Sinking. A popular training in Chinese martial arts, used to develop the root and the stability of the postures. Refers to the practitioner imagining sinking into the ground as if he weighed a thousand pounds.

Qian: 乾 One of the Eight Trigrams (*Bagua*). Corresponds to Heaven.

Qigong (Chi Kung): 氣功 A type of *Gongfu* training which specializes in building up the *Qi* circulation in the body for health and/or martial purposes.

Qin Na (Chin Na): 擒拿 Grasp and Control. An aspect of Chinese martial arts training, *Qin Na* specializes in controlling the enemy through "misplacing the joint," "dividing the muscle," "sealing the breath," and "cavity press."

Qing Ling: 輕靈 Lightness and Agility. These words are often used to describe the motion of monkeys - responsive, controlled, and able to move quickly.

Qing: 輕 Lightness.

Quan (Chuan): 拳 Fist. This term in Chinese martial arts is also used to denote a *Gongfu* style, e.g. *Shaolin Quan* or *Taijiquan*, or a sequence, for example; *Lian Bu Quan*.

Quchi (LI-11): 曲池 An acupuncture cavity belonging to the Large Intestine Channel.

Ren Mai: 任脈 Conception Vessel. One of the eight auxiliary *Qi* channels (*Mai*) in the human body. It runs from the base of the body up the front and ends in the tongue.

Ruan Jin: 軟勁 Soft *Jin*. In this *Jin* the *Qi* predominates and muscle usage is reduced to the minimum.

Ruan Ying Jin: 軟硬勁 Soft Hard *Jin*. When this *Jin* is generated, the muscles are relaxed as much as possible to allow the *Qi* to flow. Just before the *Jin* reaches the target, the muscles are tightened to avoid injuring the hands, and also to focus the *Jin* on the spot being attacked.

Rugen (S-18): 乳根　An acupuncture cavity belonging to the Stomach Channel.

San Bao: 三寶　Three Treasures - *Jing* (essence), *Qi* (internal energy), and *Shen* (Spirit). The Chinese people believe that if these three things are properly cultivated and guarded, they will have a long and healthy life.

San Shi Qi Shi: 三十七勢　Thirty-Seven Postures. According to historical records, one of the predecessors of *Taijiquan*.

Shaohai (H-3): 少海　An acupuncture cavity belonging to the Heart Channel.

Shaolin: 少林　The name of a Buddihist Temple, built in 377 A.D., which later became a Chinese martial arts training center.

Shen: 神　Spirit. The consciousness within which the mind and thought function.

Shi Er Zhuang: 十二庄　Twelve Postures. A style of *Qigong* training.

Shi San Shi Lao Jia: 十三勢老架　Thirteen Posture Old Frame. The old style of thirteen postures (i.e., *Taijiquan*).

Shuang: 雙　Double or Pair.

Shuang Zhong: 雙重　Double Weighting. The fault of not distinguishing between substantial and insubstantial.

Shui: 水　Water. One of the five basic elements (*Wu Xing*).

Song Dynasty: 宋代　A dynasty in Chinese history (960-1278 A.D.).

Song Wei Zong (1101-1126 A.D.): 宋徽宗　An emperor of the Chinese Song Dynasty (960-1278 A.D.).

Sun Style: 孫式　A style of *Taijiquan* created by Sun, Lu-Tang, who learned *Taijiquan* from Hao, Wei-Zhen.

Taichong (Li-3): 太沖　An acupuncture cavity belonging to the Liver Channel.

Taiji: 太極　Grand Ultimate. The state in which opposites (known as *Yin* and *Yang*) are generated.

Taijiquan: 太極拳　Grand Ultimate Fist.

Tang Dynasty: 唐代　A dynasty in Chinese history (713-907 A.D.).

Tianzong (SI-11): 天宗　An acupuncture cavity belonging to the Small Intestine Channel.

Tiaokou (S-38): 條口　An acupuncture cavity belonging to the Stomach Channel.

Tie Bu Shan: 鐵布衫 Iron Shirt. *Gongfu* training which enables a person to endure a strike or blow without injury. Similar to Golden Bell Cover.

Tu: 土 Earth. One of the five basic elements (*Wu Xing*).

Tui Bu: 退步 Step Backward. One of the five basic strategic movements of *Taijiquan*.

Tuo Tian: 托天 Supporting the Heavens. A form of *Qigong* training used to increase the strength and endurance of the legs, and also build up *Qi* in the spine.

Wa Shou: 瓦手 Tile Hand. A typical open-hand form used in *Taijiquan*.

Wai Dan: 外丹 External Elixir. A kind of *Qigong* training in which *Qi* is generated in local areas of the body (especially the limbs) and circulated to the other parts of the body.

Wai Jin: 外勁 External Power. The type of *Jin* where the muscles predominate and only local *Qi* is used to support the muscles. See also *Nei Jin*.

Weilu: 尾閭 Tail bone. The same place is called *Changqiang* (Gv-1) in Chinese medicine.

Wu Qin Xi: 五禽戲 Five Animal Sport. A *Qigong* exercise which imitates the movements of five animals: tiger, deer, monkey, bear, and bird.

Wu Style: 吳式 A style of *Taijiquan* created by Wu, Quan-You who learned *Taijiquan* from Yang, Ban-Hou.

Wudang: 武當 A mountain located to the south of Jun Xian, in Hubei Province, China. It is believed that a number of Daoist martial arts such as *Taijiquan* and *Wudang* were created in this area.

Wuji: 無極 No Extremity. This is the state of undifferentiated emptiness before a beginning. As soon as there is a beginning or a movement, there is differentiation and opposites, and this is called *Taiji*.

Wushu: 武術 Martial Technique. In the beginning, Chinese martial arts were called *Wu Yi* (Martial Arts), and the techniques of *Wu Yi* were called *Wushu* (martial techniques). In 1926, the name was changed to *Guoshu* (*Kuoshu*) but was changed back to *Wushu* in 1949 in China. It is still called *Guoshu* (*Kuoshu*) in Taiwan.

Wuu Style: 武式 A style of *Taijiquan* created by Wuu, Yu-Rang who learned new style *Taijiquan* from Chen, Qing-Ping and old style *Taijiquan* from Yang, Lu-Chan.

Xiao Jiu Tian: 小九天 Small Nine Heaven. According to the historical records, one of the predecessors of *Taijiquan*.

Xiao Lu: 小攦 Small Rollback.

Xiao Zhou Tian: 小周天 Small Circulation. *Nei Dan Qigong* training in which *Qi* is generated at the *Dan Tian*, and then moved in a circle through the Conception and Governing Vessels.

Xiaohai (SI-8): 小海 An acupuncture cavity belonging to the Small Intestine Channel.

Xiayin: 下陰 Lower *Yin*. It means the groin area.

Xin: 心 Heart. In Chinese it often means "mind." It refers to an intention, idea or thought which has not been expressed.

Xin-Yi: 心意 Heart-Mind. *Xin* has the sense of "mind," and *Yi* has the sense of "intention." When used together they refer to the desire to do something specific.

Xing Jin: 形勁 Shape *Jin*. Manifested power that can be seen physically.

Xingyiquan (Hsing Yi Chuan): 形意拳 Shape Mind Fist. One of the internal Chinese martial styles. It is based on five basic motions related to the Five Elements (*Wu Xing*), as well as motions corresponding to twelve animals. It is said that this style was created by Marshal Yue, Fei during the Song Dynasty.

Xuehai (Sp-10): 血海 An acupuncture cavity belonging to the Spleen Channel.

Xun: 巽 One of the eight trigrams (*Bagua*). Corresponds to Wind.

Yang: 陽 The positive pole of *Taiji* (Grand Ultimate), the other pole being *Yin* (Negative). The Chinese believe that everything follows from the interaction of *Yin* and *Yang*.

Yang Quan: 楊拳 *Yang* Fist. It means the style originating from the Yang family.

Yang, Cheng-Fu: 楊澄甫 A famous *Taijiquan* master (1883-1935 A.D.).

Yang, Jian-Hou (1842-1917 A.D.): 楊健侯 A famous *Taijiquan* master and the father of Yang, Cheng-Fu.

Yang, Jwing-Ming: 楊俊敏 Author of this book.

Yang, Lu-Chan (1799-1872 A.D.): 楊露禪 The first generation master of *Yang* Style *Taijiquan*. He learned his *Taijiquan* from Chen, Chang-Xing.

Yi: 意 Mind. It is commonly expressed as *Xin-Yi*. *Xin* is an idea and *Yi* is the expression of this idea. Therefore, *Yi* by itself can be translated as "Mind."

Yi Jing: 易經 ***The Book of Changes***. One of the most ancient philosophic writings in existence, this classic has influenced Chinese culture and tradition for thousands of years. See also *Bagua*.

Yi Zhi Chan: 一指禪 One Finger Contemplation. A *Qigong* training method.

Yin: 陰 The negative pole of *Taiji* (Grand Ultimate). See also *Yang*.

Ying Jin: 硬勁 Hard *Jin*. A type of *Jin* in which the muscles predominate in the expression of power. In this *Jin* the muscles are relatively stiff and supported by local *Qi*.

Yingchuang (S-16): 膺窗 An acupuncture cavity belonging to the Stomach Channel.

Yongquan (K-1): 湧泉 An acupuncture cavity belonging to the Kidney Channel.

You Pan: 右盼 Look to the Right. One of the five basic *Taiji* strategic movements.

Yuan: 元 A dynasty in Chinese history (1206-1368 A.D.).

Yuan: 遠 Far or Long Distance.

Zhang, San-Feng (Chang, San-Feng): 張三豐 Said to be the creator of *Taijiquan* in the Song Dynasty (960-1279 A.D.). However, there is no certain documentary proof of this.

Zhangmen (Li-13): 章門 An acupuncture cavity belonging to the Liver Channel.

Zhao Bao Style: 趙堡派 A style of *Taijiquan* created by Chen, Qing-Ping who learned *Taijiquan* from Chen, You-Ben.

Zhen: 震 One of the eight trigrams (*Bagua*). Corresponds to Thunder.

Zhong Ding: 中定 Central Equilibrium. One of the five basic strategic movements.

Zhong: 重 Weight or Heaviness. The same Chinese character, when pronounced as *Chong*, means "layering."

Zhongdu (Li-6): 中都 An acupuncture cavity belonging to the Liver Channel.

Zhongwan (Co-12): 中脘 An acupuncture cavity belonging to the Conception Vessel.

Zhou: 肘 Elbow. The technique of striking or neutralizing with the elbow. One of the Four Corners of the eight basic *Taiji* fighting techniques.

Zhuan Xin: 專心 Concentrated Mind.

Zuo Gu: 左顧 Beware of the Left. One of the five fundamental strategic movements which correspond to the Five Elements.

Index

Books & Videos from YMAA

YMAA Publication Center Books

YMAA Publication Center Videotapes

YMAA Publication Center 楊氏東方文化出版中心

4354 Washington Street • Boston, MA 02131
1-800-669-8892 • ymaa@aol.com • www.ymaa.com